My
Pages®, Numbers®, and Keynote®

Brad Miser

que®

800 East 96th Street,
Indianapolis, Indiana 46240 USA

ii

My Pages®, Numbers®, and Keynote®

Copyright © 2015 by Pearson Education, Inc.

ISBN-13: 978-0-7897-5267-3
ISBN-10: 0-7897-5267-0

Library of Congress Control Number: 2015932631

Printed in the United States of America

First Printing: April 2015

Trademarks

All terms mentioned in this book that are known to be trademarks or service marks have been appropriately capitalized. Que Publishing cannot attest to the accuracy of this information. Use of a term in this book should not be regarded as affecting the validity of any trademark or service mark.

Pages, Numbers, Keynote, and Mac are registered trademarks of Apple, Inc.

Warning and Disclaimer

Every effort has been made to make this book as complete and as accurate as possible, but no warranty or fitness is implied. The information provided is on an "as is" basis. The author and the publisher shall have neither liability nor responsibility to any person or entity with respect to any loss or damages arising from the information contained in this book.

Special Sales

For information about buying this title in bulk quantities, or for special sales opportunities (which may include electronic versions; custom cover designs; and content particular to your business, training goals, marketing focus, or branding interests), please contact our corporate sales department at corpsales@pearsoned.com or (800) 382-3419.

For government sales inquiries, please contact governmentsales@pearsoned.com.

For questions about sales outside the U.S., please contact international@pearsoned.com.

Editor-in-Chief
Greg Wiegand

Senior Acquisitions Editor
Laura Norman

Development Editor
Lora Baughey

Managing Editor
Sandra Schroeder

Senior Project Editor
Tonya Simpson

Copy Editor
Karen Gill

Senior Indexer
Cheryl Lenser

Proofreader
The Wordsmithery LLC

Technical Editor
Paul A. Sihvonen-Binder

Editorial Assistant
Kristen Watterson

Cover Designer
Mark Shirar

Compositor
Trina Wurst

Contents at a Glance

Table of Contents

About the Author

Brad Miser has written extensively about technology, with his favorite topic being the amazing Apple hardware and software that helps us to be so creative and productive, including Macs, iPhones, iPads, iCloud, and the iWork apps. In addition to *My Pages, Numbers, and Keynote*, Brad has written many other books, including *My iPhone*, Eighth Edition, and *My iPhone for Seniors*. He has been an author, development editor, or technical editor for more than 100 titles. He has also created videos and other content on a variety of topics.

Brad is or has been a sales support specialist, the director of product and customer services, and the manager of education and support services for several software development companies. Previously, he was the lead proposal specialist for an aircraft engine manufacturer, a development editor for a computer book publisher, and a civilian aviation test officer/engineer for the U.S. Army. Brad holds a bachelor of science degree in mechanical engineering from California Polytechnic State University at San Luis Obispo and has received advanced education in maintainability engineering, business, and other topics.

In addition to his passion for silicon-based technology, Brad is active in building and flying radio-controlled aircraft.

Originally from California, Brad now lives in Brownsburg, Indiana, with his wife Amy. Their proudest accomplishment and greatest joy in life was raising their three daughters, Jill, Emily, and Grace.

Brad would love to hear about your experiences with this book—the good, the bad, and the ugly. You can write to him at bradmiser@icloud.com.

Dedication

To those who have given the last full measure of devotion so that the rest of us can be free.

Acknowledgments

To the following people on the *My Pages, Numbers, and Keynote* project team, my sincere appreciation for your hard work on this book:

Laura Norman, my acquisitions editor, provided me with the opportunity to write this book and advised me along the way. Laura is an incredible professional and person; I've been blessed to be able to work with her on many projects over a long period.

Lora Baughey and Todd Brakke, my development editors, reviewed the book as it was being written and provided valuable feedback to make sure it stayed on track and provided content that would help people use Pages, Numbers, and Keynote more effectively.

Paul Sihvonen-Binder, my technical editor, carefully reviewed the content in this book and made numerous suggestions to correct my mistakes and add valuable information to it.

Karen Gill, my copy editor, transformed my bumbling, stumbling text into something that actually makes sense and follows the complex rules of proper writing, which, believe me, is no small feat!

Tonya Simpson, my project editor, skillfully managed the hundreds of files and production process that it took to make this book.

Mark Shirar took care of the cover design for the book.

Que's production and sales team printed the book and got it into your hands.

We Want to Hear from You!

As the reader of this book, *you* are our most important critic and commentator. We value your opinion and want to know what we're doing right, what we could do better, what areas you'd like to see us publish in, and any other words of wisdom you're willing to pass our way.

We welcome your comments. You can email or write to let us know what you did or didn't like about this book—as well as what we can do to make our books better.

Please note that we cannot help you with technical problems related to the topic of this book.

When you write, please be sure to include this book's title and author as well as your name and email address. We will carefully review your comments and share them with the author and editors who worked on the book.

Email: feedback@quepublishing.com

Mail: Que Publishing
            ATTN: Reader Feedback
            800 East 96th Street
            Indianapolis, IN 46240 USA

Reader Services

Visit our website and register this book at quepublishing.com/register for convenient access to any updates, downloads, or errata that might be available for this book.

Introducing Pages, Numbers, and Keynote

Originally a suite of software called iWork, Pages, Numbers, and Keynote are Apple's office/business productivity software applications. These apps are roughly the equivalent of Microsoft Office's Word, Excel, and PowerPoint in purpose, but they are implemented quite differently due to Apple's different approach to design and functionality.

Pages is the word processing and page layout application. You can use it to easily create a range of documents from basic letters to elaborate brochures and proposals. Pages makes it easier to produce polished documents because Apple provides a variety of templates that you can start with; of course, your own creativity is never limited because you can make any changes to documents you wish, even if you start with a template document.

Numbers is the spreadsheet application. You can use it to organize, analyze, and present data in tables that can include automatic calculations and formulas. From basic budgets to complex business analysis, Numbers can crunch the numbers for you. It also has nice charting tools that you can use to present your data graphically.

Keynote is the presentation application. You can create presentations that include slides you design and format in just about any way you can imagine. To keep things interesting for the audience and to make the information more meaningful at the same time, you can animate your presentations to make your information come alive.

Because they were originally part of a suite, each of the apps offers a similar set of tools. This is great because once you learn how to do something in one app, you automatically know how to do it in the others. For example, you can format text using the same tools in Pages, Numbers, and Keynote. This consistent interface makes the software much easier to learn and use than applications that don't have this common approach to the user interface.

Of course, because each app has its own purposes, there are some tools in each one that are unique to it. For example, Keynote is the only app that offers animation tools because animation really doesn't apply to text documents or spreadsheets.

Another great thing about these apps is that they are designed to work together. This makes it easy to share content among the various types of documents you create. Suppose you want to include a bar chart showing information in a Pages document. You can create that chart in Numbers and then copy and paste it into the Pages document.

Speaking of sharing, even more good news is that in addition to the Mac versions of these apps, there are versions for iPhones and iPads, too. And with an iCloud account, there are also online versions of the apps that you can use on any computer with a web browser and Internet connection. So not only can you share content across the apps, you can share content in the apps on the different devices you use.

As you work through this book, you'll find out how useful and easy to use these great apps are.

Using This Book

This book has been designed to help you learn how to use each app quickly and easily. As you can tell, the book relies heavily on pictures to show you how the software works. It is also task focused so that you can quickly learn the specific steps to follow to do all the cool things that Pages, Numbers, and Keynote enable you to do. You can flip to a task that you want to learn and follow the steps to learn how to complete it. The figures show you exactly where you perform each step on the screen.

The book begins and ends with information that is applicable to all three apps starting with Chapter 1, "Working with iWork Documents," and finishing with Chapter 17, "Publishing and Sharing Pages, Numbers, and Keynote Documents." Between those chapters, there are groups of chapters devoted to each app.

Chapter 2, "Working with Text in Pages Documents," through Chapter 6, "Collaborating with Others on Pages Documents," teach you how to use Pages to create great text documents. In Chapter 7, "Developing Numbers Spreadsheets," through Chapter 10, "Finishing and Collaborating on Numbers Spreadsheets," you learn about Numbers. Last but not least, you learn about Keynote in Chapter 11, "Developing Keynote Presentations," through Chapter 16, "Presenting Keynote Presentations"; those chapters show you all you need to create amazing presentations.

Because there is so much commonality between the apps, instead of repeating a topic for each app, you see references back to where a topic is covered in detail. For example, you learn how to format text in Pages in Chapter 2. Because you use the same tools to format text in Numbers and Keynote, you won't find the details repeated for those apps, but you can easily use the reference to quickly jump back to the detailed information.

I recommend you start with Chapter 1 because it applies to all three apps. From there, choose the first chapter that covers the app that you want to start with (such as Chapter 7 if you want to use Numbers) and let your interests guide you through the rest of the book. As you move through each chapter, your skills quickly grow and you'll be able to use these apps to create amazing documents, spreadsheets, and presentations.

You can choose to store
your iWork documents
on a local drive, too

An iCloud Drive makes it easy
to work with iWork documents
from any device

Pages, Numbers, and
Keynote use the same
Open and Save dialogs

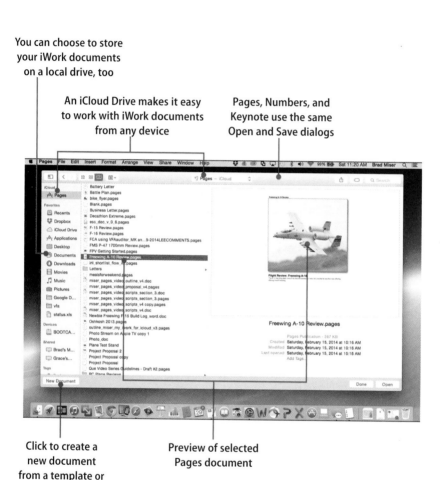

Click to create a
new document
from a template or
from scratch

Preview of selected
Pages document

In this chapter, you learn how to create new documents, save new or updated documents, and open existing documents in the three iWork apps. Topics include the following:

→ Use iCloud with iWork Documents
→ Create New iWork Documents
→ Save New iWork Documents
→ Open Existing iWork Documents
→ Share iWork Documents with Other Apps

Working with iWork Documents

Of course, the reason you use the Pages, Numbers, and Keynote apps is to create and work with word processing, spreadsheet, and presentation documents, respectively. While these apps work with very different types of content, they use the same interface to enable you to create, open, and save your documents. In this chapter, you learn how to accomplish each of these tasks.

As you are working with documents, an important point to consider is where you save those documents. There are two basic options: local or online (more commonly known as the Internet "cloud").

Saving documents locally means saving them on the disk drive in your computer. There are a couple of advantages in doing this. One is that accessing your documents is fast. The other is that you can access your documents without an Internet connection. This location also has a couple of downsides, and they are big ones. First, documents you save locally are accessible only from the device on which you saved them, so you can't work with your documents on multiple devices very easily. Second, documents you save only on your computer's disk are vulnerable; if something happens to the disk, you may lose your documents.

Saving documents online (in the cloud) offers a number of benefits. First, you can easily access your documents from multiple devices. For example, you might start a document on your work computer and then continue working on it from home on an iPad. This can be a seamless process so that ultimately it doesn't matter which device you happen to be using at any particular time because all your devices access the same documents and, as importantly, the same versions of those documents. Second, when you store documents online, they are protected because the online locations have sophisticated backup processes in place so that there is virtually no chance that you will ever lose a document.

Because storing your documents on the cloud makes accessing them from multiple devices easy, the cloud is used in tasks that deal with creating, saving, or opening documents. (Sidebars later in this chapter explain saving documents on your Mac, which isn't any harder.)

>>>Go Further

ONLINE OPTIONS

The iCloud "cloud" is the primary online option covered in this book because iCloud is integrated into Apple devices—namely, Macintosh computers, iPads, and iPhones. And although it is not integrated into the Windows operating system as it is in OS X and iOS, you can access the iCloud cloud almost as easily on Windows computers. This means using iCloud to store your Pages, Numbers, and Keynote documents is virtually seamless on any of these devices.

There are other cloud services that you can use. Of these, perhaps the most widely used is Dropbox. Dropbox enables you to store documents on the cloud and access them from a variety of devices. Dropbox and similar services work pretty much like iCloud does by providing online storage space on which you store your documents so that you can access them from any device configured for your account. (However, these services aren't as well integrated into OS X and iOS as iCloud is.)

Use iCloud with iWork Documents

Because iCloud is integrated into OS X (your Mac's operating system software) and iOS (the system software that runs iPads, iPhones, and iPod touches), your iCloud Drive is a great way to store documents for the iWork apps. Your iCloud Drive enables you to access the same documents from multiple devices and keeps your documents backed up. Because it is integrated into Apple operating systems, it works for you automatically once you have it configured on each device. In this section, you see an explanation of how iCloud can be used for your documents and how to set up and use your iCloud Drive on a Mac.

Understand How the iCloud Drive Works with iWork App Documents

An iCloud Drive is your personal storage space on the Internet that you access through your iCloud account. An overview of how it works is shown in the following figure:

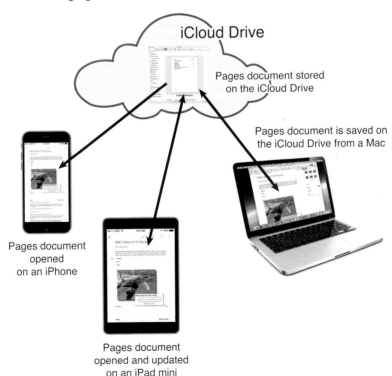

iCloud Drive

Pages document stored on the iCloud Drive

Pages document is saved on the iCloud Drive from a Mac

Pages document opened on an iPhone

Pages document opened and updated on an iPad mini

When you save a document to your iCloud Drive, it is stored in your online storage space on the cloud. As you make changes to the document and save it, and as the app saves changes automatically, the updates you make are also copied to the cloud so that the version on the cloud stays current with the version you have open and are working on.

When you open that document on a different device, such as an iPad, the current version of the document is downloaded from the iCloud Drive and opens on the device you are using. As you make changes from that device, those changes are also copied back onto the iCloud Drive. When you open the document on yet a different device, such as an iPhone, you see the current version including the most recent changes you made.

You don't have to worry about synchronizing changes to a document and its versions, even when you work with that document on multiple devices. The iCloud Drive manages all that for you. For example, if you make changes to the same document at the same time on different devices, you're prompted about which version you want to keep or if you want to keep both versions. (If you keep both, you rename one of the copies so that they become separate and distinct documents.)

iCloud Account

In this book, I've assumed you already have an iCloud account. If you don't, you can get one for free. To do so on your Mac, open the iCloud pane of the System Preferences app and click iCloud. Click Create Apple ID; the Create an Apple ID dialog opens. Follow the onscreen instructions to create your account.

You can also create an iCloud account from an iPad or iPhone by opening the Settings app, tapping iCloud, and then tapping Create a New Apple ID. Follow the onscreen instructions, and in just a few minutes, you'll have a new iCloud account.

Configure Your Mac to Use Your iCloud Drive

To use your iCloud Drive on your Mac, you need to sign into your iCloud account and enable iCloud Drive as follows:

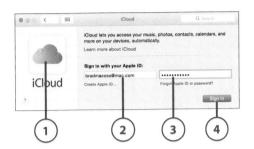

1. Open the System Preferences app and click the iCloud icon to open the iCloud pane. If you see your iCloud account information, you are already signed into your account and can skip to step 13. If you see the Sign In button and Your Apple ID fields, continue with these steps.

2. Type your Apple ID.

3. Type your password.

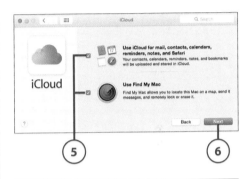

4. Click Sign In. You start the sign-in process and are prompted to enable specific functions.

5. Leave the two check boxes checked.

6. Click Next.

7. Click Allow to enable the Find My Mac service.

8. If prompted to set up your iCloud Keychain, enter your Apple ID password; if you aren't prompted to do this, skip to step 12.

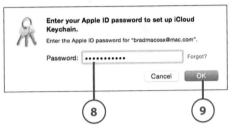

9. Click OK.

10. Click Request Approval to approve access to your Keychain on a different device. (If you have your security code, you can click Use Code and then enter your code instead.)

11. Click OK. (On one of your other devices, you need to approve the request for the Keychain to be enabled.) You move to the iCloud pane and see your account information.

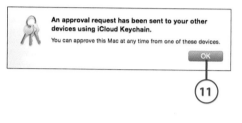

12. Ensure the iCloud Drive check box is checked. You see an explanation of the iCloud Drive features you will or will not be able to use based on the computer you are using.

13. Click Options for the iCloud Drive.

14. Ensure the check boxes for Pages, Numbers, and Keynote are checked. These check boxes enable the apps to use your iCloud Drive.

15. Click Done. You're ready to use your iCloud Drive to store and manage your iWork documents.

Configuring iCloud on an iPad or iPhone

To configure your iCloud account on an iPad or iPhone, open the Settings app and tap iCloud. On the iCloud screen, enter your Apple ID and password, and then tap Sign In. You're prompted to enable some of the iCloud features, such as Find My iPhone. When that process is done, you see the iCloud screen with the controls you use to configure your iCloud account. Ensure that the iCloud Drive shows On as its status. If it doesn't, tap iCloud Drive and set the iCloud Drive switch to on (green) so that your iPad or iPhone can work with documents stored on your iCloud Drive, too.

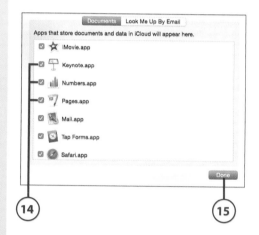

Access Your iCloud Drive from the Mac Desktop

In later tasks, you learn how you can use your iCloud Drive from within the iWork apps. You can also access it directly from the Mac desktop as you do other drives that are accessible to your Mac.

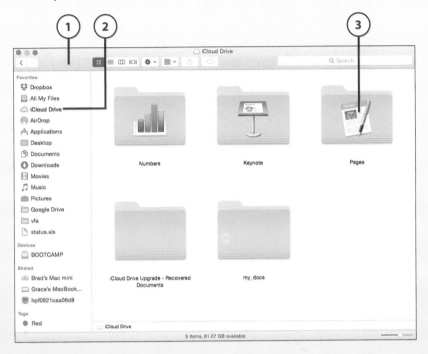

1. Open a Finder window.

2. Click iCloud Drive on the Sidebar. You see a folder for each of the iWork apps.

3. To work with an iWork app's document, open its folder.

But Wait; That's Not All

You can use the iCloud Drive just like the drive installed in your computer; for example, you can create new folders to store any documents you want to keep in the cloud. This works in the same way as any other storage location available on your computer, such as its primary drive.

4. Double-click a document to open it. It opens in the associated app, just like documents stored on your computer.

>>>Go Further

WORKING WITH YOUR IWORK DOCUMENTS FROM A WINDOWS PC

You can work with your iWork documents using a Windows PC in a couple of ways, but the best way is through your iCloud website because you can then use the online versions of the Pages, Numbers, and Keynote apps. (There aren't Windows versions of these apps.) To do this, open a web browser, such as Google Chrome, and move to icloud.com. Use your Apple ID and password to sign into your account. On the Home page, click the app you want to use, such as Pages. The Document Manager window opens, and you can open the Pages documents stored on your iCloud Drive or create new documents. Using the online versions of Pages, Numbers, and Keynote is similar to using the Mac desktop versions that are described in this book.

Create New iWork Documents

You can create new iWork documents in two primary ways. One is to start with a template, whereas the other is to start "from scratch."

The iWork templates are professionally designed documents that make it easier and faster to create great-looking documents because they include text and graphics placeholders that you can replace with your own content. You get to take advantage of the design work that has been done for you, allowing you to focus more on content and less on formatting and other design tasks.

If you don't want to start with a template, you can create a blank document and do your own formatting and document design.

Create New iWork Documents Using Templates

To create a new document based on a template, perform the following steps:

1. Open the app in which you want to create a new document; these steps show Pages, but creating a document using a template works similarly in the other two apps. The Open dialog appears.

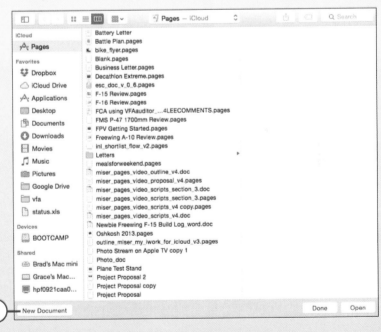

2. Click New Document. The Choose a Template dialog appears. In the left pane, you see the categories of templates available, which are based on the type of content to be included in the document. In the right pane, you see the templates in the category selected in the left pane. By default, All is selected, which shows all the templates available in the app.

3.   If you can't see all the templates in the window, scroll up and down to browse all of them.

4.   Click the category of templates of interest to you. The templates in that category appear in the right pane.

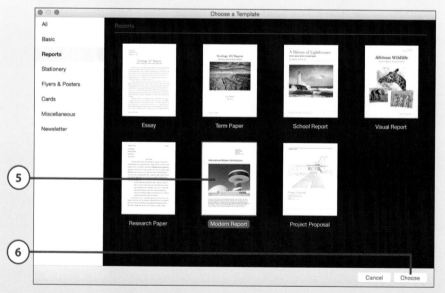

5.   Click the template you want to use.

6.   Click Choose. A new document is created based on the template you selected.

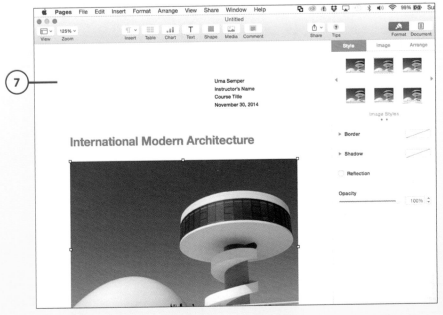

7. Create your document by replacing the placeholder content and saving it. (You learn how to save documents in the next task, and you learn how to work with content and format documents in later chapters.)

Create New iWork Documents from Scratch

In some cases, you might want to have total control over a document by starting with a "clean slate." You can do this by using one of the appropriately named Blank templates, as this example showing the Numbers app demonstrates.

1. Perform steps 1 through 4 in the previous task.

2. Select the Blank template you want to use. (Sometimes there are multiple versions of the Blank template in different orientations.)

3. Click Choose. A new, empty document is created.

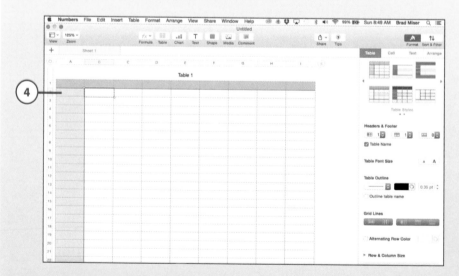

4. Create your document by adding content and saving it. (You learn how to save documents in the next task, and you learn how to work with content and format documents in later chapters.)

Save New iWork Documents

Saving documents in the iWork apps is similar to saving documents in other apps. However, you should ensure that you save documents on your iCloud Drive so you can take advantage of its capabilities.

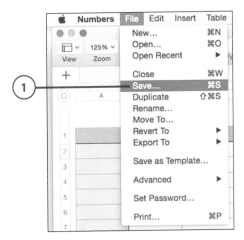

1. If you are working with a new, untitled document, open the File menu and choose Save. The Save dialog appears with the current name of the document "Untitled" selected so it is ready to be replaced.

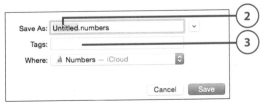

2. Type the name of the new document.

3. Click in the Tags field and the available tags appear, or if you don't want to apply tags to the document, skip to step 6. (Tags help you find and organize files more easily; for example, on the Mac desktop, you can search for files based on tags. To configure the tags available to you, open the Finder Preferences dialog and click the Tags tab.)

Show and Tell

To see all the tags available, click Show All at the bottom of the tags list, which isn't shown in the figure because it has already been clicked.

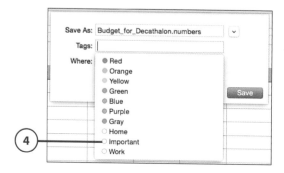

4.   Click the first tag you want to apply to the document.

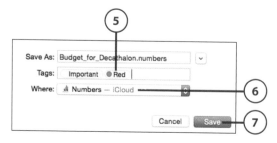

5.   Apply other tags to the document. The more tags you apply to a document, the more specific you can make your searches to find it.

6.   Ensure the appropriate iCloud Drive folder is shown on the Where menu; for example, when you save a Numbers document, this should be the Numbers folder. If the correct folder isn't shown, open the Where menu and choose the folder in which you want to store the document. (You can click the downward-facing arrow next to the Save As box to expand the dialog and see all its options.)

7.   Click Save. The document is saved with the name you entered, with the tags you added, and in the selected location.

New filename

8.   Continue working with the document.

>>>Go Further

SAVING EXISTING DOCUMENTS

You can save existing documents in a number of ways:

- To save an existing document under its current name, choose File and then choose Save or press ⌘+S. It's a good idea to frequently save your documents as you work on them. When there are unsaved changes in a document, "- Edited" appears at the end of the document's name at the top of the screen.

- To create a copy of the document and save it, choose File and then choose Duplicate. A copy of the document is created, and its name at the top of the document window is highlighted. Type a name for the duplicate document and press the Enter key. The document is saved in the same location as the original and has the same tags applied.

- To save an existing document under a new name or to change its location or tags, open the File menu, hold down the Option key, and choose Save As. The Save dialog opens, and you can rename the document, set its tags, and choose a location in which to save just as you do when you save a new document.

Open Existing iWork Documents

There are two primary ways to open existing iWork documents: from the app's Open dialog or from the Mac desktop. Rarely, when you open a document, you see an out-of-sync message; you need to understand what this means and how to deal with it.

Open Existing iWork Documents from the Open Dialog

As its name implies, you can open documents using the Open dialog.

1. When you first open an iWork app, the Open dialog appears automatically; if the app is already running, choose File, Open. By default, the save location is the one in which the document is currently saved. The iCloud Drive folder appropriate to the app you are using is selected automatically, such as the Keynote folder when you are using Keynote, and you see the documents located there.

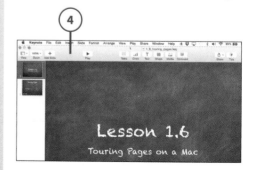

More Than iCloud Drive

While the appropriate iCloud Drive folder is selected, you can use the Open dialog to move to any location accessible to choose a document stored there to open. For example, you can select the Documents folder to open a document stored in the Documents folder on your Mac.

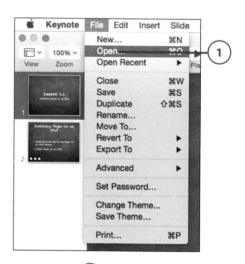

2. Navigate to and select the document you want to open.

3. Click Open. The document opens.

4. Work with the document you opened.

Open Faster

You can quickly open documents with which you've recently worked by choosing File, Open Recent, and then choosing the file you want to open on the list that appears.

Open Existing iWork Documents from the Mac Desktop

Earlier, you learned that you can access your iCloud Drive just like other drives available on your Mac. You can use this to open documents from your Mac's desktop.

1. On the Sidebar, select iCloud Drive.

2. Open the folder containing the type of documents you want to work with.

3. Double-click the document that you want to open. It opens in the appropriate app, and you can work on it.

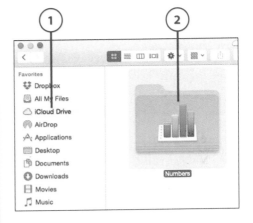

The First Time

If you have a lot of documents stored on your iCloud Drive when you first enable it on a device, it can take a while for all the documents to be downloaded to the device so you can work with them. In the Open dialog on a Mac, you see the progress of the files as they download. On an iOS device, you see the Updating status message at the top of the screen. You must wait for a document to be downloaded to be able to open it. After all the iCloud Drive documents have been downloaded once, you won't have to wait again.

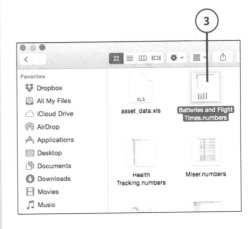

Manage Out-of-Sync Documents

Occasionally, documents stored on your iCloud Drive can become out-of-sync. This can happen when you make changes to the same document on two devices simultaneously. When the changes in these documents are saved back to the cloud, iCloud doesn't know which version to keep, so it keeps all of them. The next time you open the document, you're prompted to manage the out-of-sync documents as follows:

1. Review the versions of the documents that are available.

2. To keep only one of the documents, check its check box and perform step 3. To keep more than one version, skip to step 4.

3. Click Keep One. The version you selected is saved and opens so you can work with it. Any other versions of the document are deleted, so make sure you've selected the version you want to keep in step 2 before performing this step. Skip the rest of these steps.

4. Check the check box next to each version you want to keep.

5. Click the Keep button; the name of this button reflects the number of versions you are keeping. For example, when you select two documents, this button is called Keep Both. Each version you selected to keep opens.

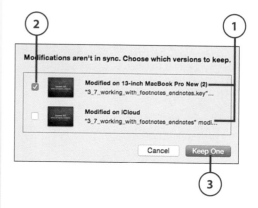

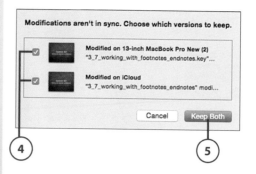

One version retains the original name, and a sequential number is appended to the names of the other versions (for example, 2 for the second version).

6. Move into a document with "-Edited" in its name. This indicates a version of the document that is not currently saved. These versions have a sequential number appended to their titles as well.

7. Click on the document's name. The Save dialog appears.

8. Update the version's name. Rename the document so the version will be meaningful to you by its name.

9. Add tags or change the save location as needed.

10. Press the Enter key. The document is renamed.

11. Save the new document.

12. Repeat steps 6 through 11 until you have renamed and saved each version of the document that you want to keep. Each one becomes a separate document that iCloud manages independently of the other versions.

Two versions of the document that were kept

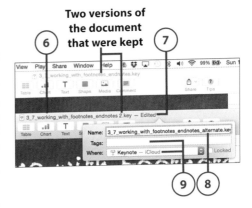

Share iWork Documents with Other Apps

Although it's obvious that you can work with documents you have created with the iWork apps in those apps, it might not be so obvious that you can also work with documents created in other apps. Perhaps the most useful of these are documents created in the Microsoft Office equivalent of the iWork apps—namely Word, Excel, and PowerPoint. You can open and work with these types of documents using the iWork apps, which is handy if you don't have copies of the Office apps available to you. Because Word, Excel, and PowerPoint are the most widely used apps for their corresponding types of documents, this enables you to be compatible with just about everyone with whom you might want to share documents. You can open Word documents in Pages, Excel documents in Numbers, and PowerPoint documents in Keynote.

You can also export your iWork apps in formats that are compatible with other apps, so sharing documents can go in both directions.

Use an iWork App to Open a Document Created in a Different App

Microsoft Word is by far the most widely used app for creating text and word processing documents, so it serves as a good example of how you can open documents created in other apps using an iWork app, in this case, Pages. You can open Excel and PowerPoint files in Numbers and Keynote, respectively, using similar steps.

1. Open a Finder window and select the Word document you want to open in Pages.

2. Choose File, Open With.

3. Select the Pages app on the list of apps that appears. The document opens in the Pages app.

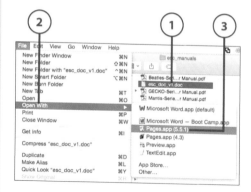

4. Use Pages to work with the Word document.

5. Choose File, Save.

6. Use the resulting Save dialog to name the document, apply tags, and save it. From that point on, it becomes a native iWork app document.

Nobody's Perfect

When you open a file from a different app in an iWork app, you may see warning dialogs about things associated with the file that aren't compatible with the iWork app. These messages can include things like missing fonts or even features that aren't supported by the iWork app. The warning dialogs are sometimes informational, meaning there's nothing you can do to fix the issue, while in other situations, they provide controls you can use to correct the issue. The same is true when you save iWork documents in other formats. The apps corresponding to those formats may or may not be able to use all the elements that are in the iWork version.

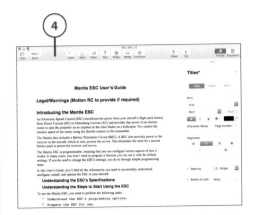

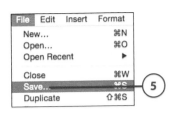

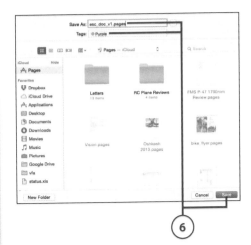

Save an iWork Document in a Format Compatible with Other Apps

In some situations, you might want to save an iWork app document in a different format. For example, you might want to save a Pages document in the Microsoft Word format so that you can share it with someone who uses Word instead of Pages. You can use similar steps to save documents in the other iWorks apps in formats that are compatible with their Microsoft Office counterparts.

1. With the iWork document you want to convert to a different format open, choose File, Export To.

2. Choose the format to which you want to export the document—Word in this case.

3. Click Next.

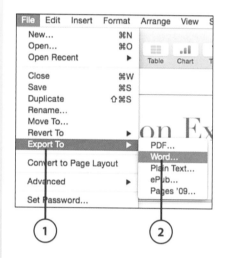

4. Rename the file as needed. (Don't change the filename extension "docx," or the file might not be correctly recognized as a Word file.)

5. Apply tags if required.

6. Choose a location in which to save the document; because you are creating a Word file, it's better not to save it to the Pages folder on your iCloud Drive. You can save it to a different folder on your iCloud Drive or on another drive entirely.

7. Click Export. The file is converted from the Pages format to the Word format and saved with the name and tags you gave it in the location you selected. The document is now ready for you to share with people who use Microsoft Word.

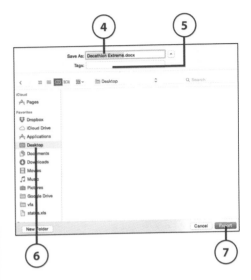

Enter text in your document by typing, dictating, or copying and pasting it

Use the Ruler to position your text

Use styles to quickly and consistently format text

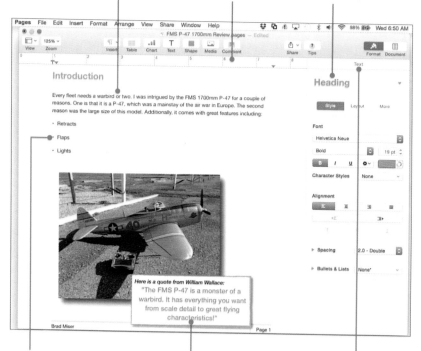

Introduction

Every fleet needs a warbird or two. I was intrigued by the FMS 1700mm P-47 for a couple of reasons. One is that it is a P-47, which was a mainstay of the air war in Europe. The second reason was the large size of this model. Additionally, it comes with great features including:

· Retracts

· Flaps

· Lights

Here is a quote from William Wallace:
"The FMS P-47 is a monster of a warbird. It has everything you want from scale detail to great flying characteristics!"

Brad Miser

Page 1

Heading

Style   Layout   More

Font
Helvetica Neue
Bold   19 pt
B I U ☼
Character Styles   None

Alignment

▶ Spacing   2.0 - Double

▶ Bullets & Lists   None

Use the text formatting tools in Pages to design the text in your documents

Use text boxes to emphasize important information for the reader

Use the Inspector to format text and other objects in your Pages documents

In this chapter, you learn how to add and format text and text boxes in your Pages documents. Topics include the following:

→ Add Text to Pages Documents
→ Meet the Inspector
→ Format Text in Pages Documents
→ Work with Text Boxes in Pages

Working with Text in Pages Documents

Text is a major part of most Pages documents. In Pages, there are two kinds of text you can use. Body text is the primary content in your document and includes text in headings, paragraphs, and captions for figures; body text flows from the beginning of the document to its end. Text boxes are independent elements you can add to documents to emphasize key points or improve a document's visual appeal; text boxes don't fit into the flow of the body text, and you can place them anywhere you'd like.

In this chapter, you learn how to add and format both types of text in your Pages documents. You should develop your own process for these two text tasks. Adding all the text to a document and then formatting it later might be more efficient for you, or you may want to format text as you add it to a document.

What's in a Name?

For the remainder of this chapter, the term *text* refers to body text, whereas the term *text boxes* continues to refer to, well, text boxes.

Add Text to Pages Documents

There are several ways to add text to your Pages documents. The most obvious is to type text into a document, and it is likely you'll do most of your text creation in this way. You can also use OS X's dictation feature to speak text into Pages documents; how well this works depends on a number of factors, such as the ambient noise in your location and the quality of your word enunciation. There is also the old reliable copy and paste method that enables you to easily reuse text that exists in another document in your Pages documents.

You'll probably use most or all of these methods as you add text to your documents at different times. You learn the ins and outs of each of these methods in the following tasks.

Adding Text with Style

In the "Format Text in Pages Documents" section that's coming up, you learn how to use the Styles feature of Pages to quickly, easily, and consistently format the text in your documents. You can apply styles before or after you add text to a document, or you might prefer a combination of both techniques. Often, it's a good idea to apply styles as you input text because it simplifies formatting your document later. For example, before you type a heading, choose the appropriate heading style, or before you type text in a paragraph, choose the paragraph text style. You can then format these elements throughout the document just by changing the format of the styles. For clarity, adding and formatting text are explained as two different tasks, but in practice, you'll probably do both simultaneously.

Input Text Manually in Pages Documents

Typing text directly into Pages documents is likely the most common way you'll add text content to your documents.

1. Place the cursor where you want to start entering text.

2. If you use styles to format text, choose the style appropriate for the type of text you are going to type. (See "Format Text in Pages Documents" later in this chapter.)

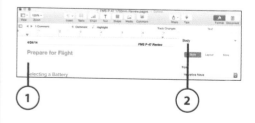

3. Type the text.

4. When you reach the end of a paragraph, press the Enter key.

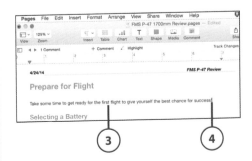

Prepare Your Mac to Take Dictation

Using OS X's dictation feature, you can speak text into a Pages document. First, make sure your Mac is set up for dictation using the following steps:

1. Ensure your Mac has a microphone available. If you use an iMac or MacBook Pro, the microphone is built in. If you use a Mac mini or Mac Pro, your Mac needs to be connected to a display that has a microphone (such as the Apple displays) or to a USB or other type of external microphone.

2. Open the Sound pane of the System Preferences app.

3. Click the Input tab.

4. Click the microphone you want to use.

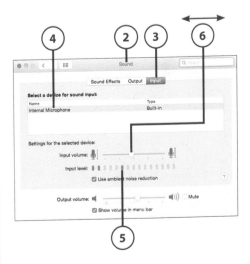

5. Speak in a normal voice, and watch the volume indicator to see the volume level as you speak. The gray bar that stays solid indicates the maximum volume being received. You want this to be somewhere between ½ and ¾ of the full range to ensure good reception of your voice.

6. Drag the slider to the right to increase the volume level or to the left to decrease it.

7. Repeat steps 5 and 6 until the maximum volume level is between ½ and ¾ of the full range.

8. Ensure the Use ambient noise reduction check box is checked. This helps minimize your Mac picking up extraneous noises as you dictate to it.

9. Open the Dictation & Speech pane of the System Preferences app.

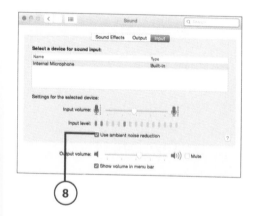

Pick a Mic, Any Mic

On the Dictation & Speech pane of the System Preferences app, you can choose the microphone you are using by clicking the label under the microphone icon and choosing the microphone you want to use. The amount that the icon "fills in" shows the relative volume level being received by the Mac through the selected microphone. You need to use the Sound pane to change this volume level.

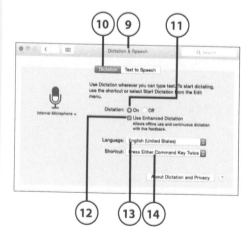

10. Click the Dictation tab.

11. Click the Dictation On radio button if it isn't selected already.

12. If your Mac has plenty of disk space and you want to be able to dictate when your Mac isn't connected to the Internet, check the Use Enhanced Dictation check box. The required software is downloaded and installed on your Mac. This process can take several minutes, but you don't need to wait for it to finish.

13. Choose the language in which you want to speak on the Language menu.

14. On the Shortcut menu, choose the keys you want to be able to press to put your Mac into "listening" mode so you can dictate. The options are

None, if you don't want to use a keyboard shortcut; various presses of the ⌘ or fn keys; or Customize, which enables you to create a custom keyboard shortcut. Your Mac is ready to take dictation.

Dictate Text into Pages Documents

With your Mac ready to take dictation, add text to a Pages document by speaking it using these steps:

1. Place the cursor where you want to start entering text.

2. If you use styles to format text, choose the style appropriate for the type of text you are going to type. (See "Format Text in Pages Documents" later in this chapter.)

3. Activate the dictation mode using the option you selected in step 14 of the previous task. When your Mac is ready to take dictation, the microphone icon appears on the screen. The amount of the icon that is dark indicates the relative volume level at which the Mac is "hearing" sound.

4. Speak the text you want to enter into the document.

5. When you're done entering text, click Done. Pages exits Dictation mode, and the microphone disappears.

6. Review and edit the text you dictated. Dictation works remarkably well, but it isn't perfect. (Then again, neither is most people's typing!)

Your Mac is ready to take dictation

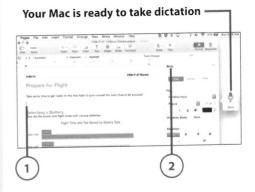

1   **2**

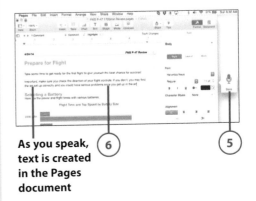

As you speak,   **6**   **5**
text is created
in the Pages
document

Other Ways to Add Text to Pages Documents

You can also copy text from different documents and paste it into your Pages documents, such as other word processing documents, or you can copy and paste text from just about any place where you see text.

In the previous chapter, you learned how to open documents of other types with Pages. This enables you to add text from Microsoft Word and other apps into your Pages documents. This can be useful if you are starting with or taking large amounts of text from an existing document in a different format. Open that document in Pages and save it as a new document, or open it and copy and paste its content into your current Pages document.

Meet the Inspector

Click to show the Inspector

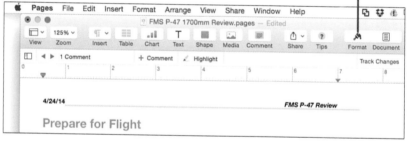

When you format objects in Pages and the other iWork apps, you use the Inspector, which appears on the right side of the app window. You can show or hide the Inspector as needed by clicking the Format button on the toolbar. The Format button toggles the Inspector, meaning that the button shows the Inspector if it is hidden or hides it if it is shown.

When the Inspector is open, you see a variety of tools you can use to format the object you are currently working with. In other words, the tools you see on the Inspector are contextual. For example, when you are working with text, you see the Text formatting tools, as shown on the top left in the figure on the following page. The Inspector shown in the figure on the right on the top of the following page shows the formatting tools for a chart that is selected in the document.

Throughout the rest of this chapter, you'll be using the Inspector with text. In later chapters, you'll learn to use it with other objects, such as tables and charts, in Pages documents, and with text and other objects in the Numbers and Keynote apps.

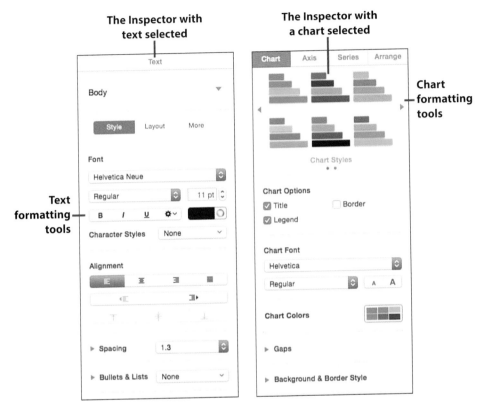

The Inspector with text selected

The Inspector with a chart selected

Chart formatting tools

Text formatting tools

Format Text in Pages Documents

Applying formatting to the text in your documents is important for several reasons. The format of text impacts how easy a document is to read; a poorly formatted document makes it more difficult for the reader to absorb the information you are trying to communicate, whereas a document formatted well makes it easier for the reader to receive your messages. You can also use the format of text in your documents to improve the visual appeal of your documents and to express your creativity and personal style. The format of the text in a document also helps communicate the purpose and tone of the document. For example, the format of text in a formal business proposal should be all business, whereas the format for the text in a story you are telling might be casual or whimsical.

There are many text formatting options you can use, including type and size of font, spacing between paragraphs, paragraph alignment, color, bold, italics, and lists (bulleted or numbered). You can apply these options manually or through styles.

Formatting text manually is straightforward, as you see in the following task. Select the text you want to format, and then apply the formatting you want by configuring the options on the Format pane of the Inspector. The selected text is formatted with the options you choose.

Formatting text manually is easy to do, but it is also time consuming because you have to select each instance of text that you want to format and click at least once for each formatting option you want to apply. It is also difficult to consistently format a document when you style text manually because you have to remember the options you chose for each element that should look the same.

A *style* is a collection of formatting options, such as bold and italics applied to 28 point Helvetica font. You can format text by selecting the text you want to format and then applying the style you want to use; the selected text is formatted with all the options in the style with one click. You can apply styles to an entire paragraph or to individual words or characters.

Using styles to format text offers many benefits. It is much faster than formatting text manually because you can apply many options with a single click. Styles also make it much easier to format your documents consistently because all the elements formatted with the same style look the same. And it is much, much easier to change the look of your documents because you can reformat text by simply changing the formatting options in the style. For example, if you decide you want all the paragraph text in your document to use the Georgia font instead of Helvetica, you simply change the definition of the style, and all the text using that style is reformatted automatically.

The templates that come with Pages include multiple styles that you can use. You can create your own styles in your documents and change existing styles, too.

The text formatting tools available to you on the Style tab of the Text Inspector are explained in Table 2.1. You use these tools when you are formatting text manually and when you are defining the options for styles.

Table 2.1 Formatting Tools on the Style Tab of the Text Inspector

Icon	Description
Helvetica Neue	Choose the font family you want to use.
Regular	Choose the version of the font, such as bold italic or black. Different font families offer different versions on this menu. The "basic" version of a font family is Regular, which all offer.
11 pt	Choose or enter the font size. The size applied to the current text is shown.
B	Make the text bold.
I	Put the text in italics.
U	Underline the text. (Generally, you should avoid underlining text because underlining typically indicates a link to a website. Instead, use bold or italics to emphasize text.)
⚙︎	Click to see the Advanced Options menu. (See the Go Further "Advanced Text Formatting" later in this chapter for more information.)
▬	Choose the color of the text from a default menu of colors.
◯	Open the Color Picker to choose or create a color for text.
Character Styles None	Apply a character style.
☰	Align the text to the left margin.
☰	Align the text to the center of the margins.
☰	Align the text to the right margin.
☰	Align the text to both margins.
⬅☰	Indent the text to the right.
☰➡	Indent the text to the left.
↑ ↓ ↓	Align text in table cells (covered in Chapter 3, "Working with Tables in Pages Documents").
Spacing 1.3	Choose the space between lines in a paragraph.
▶	Click the triangle to expand the Spacing controls to set the space before and after paragraphs (shown in the next task).
▶ Bullets & Lists None	Create bulleted or numbered lists (explained in "Format Text as Lists in Pages Documents" later in this chapter).

Use the Ruler to precisely align your text and to configure tab stops

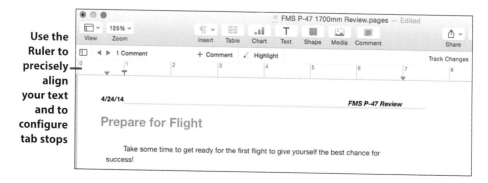

Another useful tool for formatting text is the Ruler, which appears at the top of the window. Like the Inspector, it can be displayed or hidden. (Choose View, Show/Hide Ruler.) As you learn in the task "Use the Ruler to Format Text in Pages Documents" later in this chapter, the Ruler is useful in aligning paragraphs on the page because you use it to set the margins for paragraphs and to configure tab stops. The Ruler has the icons shown in Table 2.2.

Table 2.2   Icons on the Ruler

Icon	Description
▼	Left paragraph margin
⊤	First line indentation
▶	Left-aligned tab stop
◀	Right-aligned tab stop
●	Decimal-aligned tab stop
◆	Center-aligned tab stop
▼	Right paragraph margin

Manually Format Text in Pages Documents

To manually format text, perform the following steps:

1. Select the text you want to format.

2. Click the Format button to show in the Inspector if it is hidden.

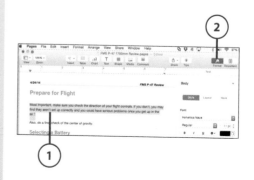

Leave the Inspector Shown

Rather than showing and hiding the Inspector each time you format something, it's usually better to just leave it shown so you can jump into it faster and more easily.

3. Click the Style tab.

4. Use the tools in the Font area to format the text's font. (Refer to Table 2.1 for the options available.) Some of these tools are menus on which you make a selection (such as to choose the font family you want to apply), whereas others are buttons (for example, Bold). You can apply multiple options at the same time (such as bold and italic). When you apply an option, the corresponding button is highlighted. As you make changes using these tools, you see the results on the selected text immediately.

I See Colors, Beautiful Colors

There are two options for applying color to text. You can use the color menu to choose a standard color to apply. Or you can click the Color Picker button to open OS X's Color Picker. The Color Picker enables you to choose from different color sets and create your own custom colors.

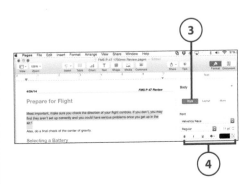

5. Use the tools in the Alignment section to change how the text aligns with the page. For example, click the Align Left button to align the text with the left margin of the document. (Note that these options apply to the entire paragraphs in which text is selected or in which the cursor is currently located.) Click the Indent Right button to move the paragraph to the right; if text is already indented to the right, you can click the Indent Left button to move it to the left.

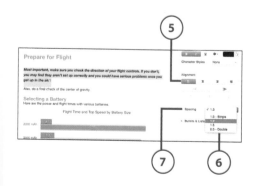

6. Use the Spacing menu to change the amount of space between lines in the paragraph.

7. Click the disclosure triangle next to Spacing to reveal more tools.

8. Open the menu to more precisely select the spacing option you want to use. Lines sets the distance between the top of the letters and the bottom of the letters on the line above them at the same distance; the amount of space changes with font size. At Least sets a minimum space between the lines. Exactly creates a fixed amount of space between the lines. Between sets the amount of space between the lines instead of the height of the lines.

9. Use the size tool to configure the spacing option you selected in step 8. You can enter values directly into the box or click the up arrow to increase the amount or the down arrow to decrease it.

10. Use the Before Paragraph tool to set the amount of space before the paragraph. You can enter an amount directly in the box or click the arrows to change it.

11. Use the After Paragraph tool to set the space after the paragraph.

12. Select the next text you want to format, and repeat these steps to format it.

Use Paragraph Styles to Format Text in Pages Documents

Styles make it simple to format text because you can apply many options with just a couple of clicks. Additionally, using styles results in more consistent formatting.

1. Click in the paragraph you want to format. (Paragraph styles format all the text in a paragraph.) You can apply a style to multiple paragraphs at the same time by dragging through the paragraphs you want to format.

2. Click the Style menu at the top of the Inspector; the style currently applied is shown in the menu, such as Body.

3. Click the style you want to apply to the paragraph. The paragraph's text is immediately reformatted according to the options in the selected style.

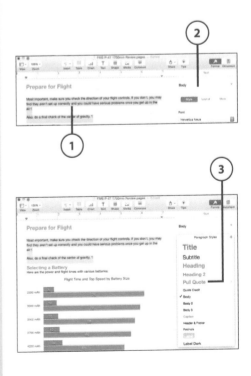

What's in a Name?

Styles are typically named according to the element for which they are intended. For example, the Heading style is used for section headings, whereas the Body style is used for text in the main paragraphs of the document. (Some style names don't correspond to the elements on which they are used so directly.) The specific style name doesn't really matter so much as long as you consistently apply the same style to the same type of object. For example, make sure all the paragraphs of body text have the same style applied. This makes your formatting more consistent and easier to change.

Formatting of applied style   **Style applied to text**

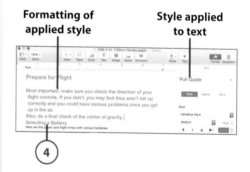

4. Apply styles to other paragraphs to reformat them.

Use Character Styles to Format Text in Pages Documents

Character styles are similar to paragraph styles; the difference is that character styles apply only to the characters you select.

1. Select the text to which you want to apply a character style.

2. Click the Character Styles menu.

3. Click the style you want to apply. The selected text is reformatted accordingly. The paragraph style name reflects the character style, and an asterisk is appended to its name. This indicates that the paragraph style has been overridden for this text.

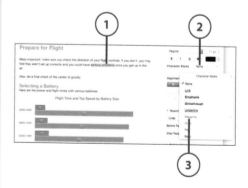

4. Use character styles to reformat other text.

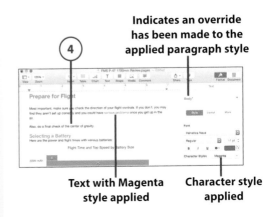

Indicates an override has been made to the applied paragraph style

Text with Magenta style applied

Character style applied

Override the Override

If you reapply a paragraph style to a paragraph in which you've applied a character style, the character style is overridden so that the entire paragraph receives the paragraph style. You should try to avoid applying character styles until you're sure the appropriate paragraph styles have been applied.

Update Existing Styles in Pages Documents

As mentioned earlier, one of the great benefits of using styles is that you can quickly and easily reformat a document by changing the options included in a style. Suppose the Body style in a document uses an 11-point font, but you decide you want to use 12 point. If you simply update the format options in the style, all the text using the Body style is reformatted automatically.

1. Select text to which the style you want to update is applied.

2. Use the formatting tools on the Inspector to make changes to the text in the paragraph, such as to increase its font's point size or change its spacing. As soon as you make a change, you see that an asterisk is appended to the style's name, and the Update button appears.

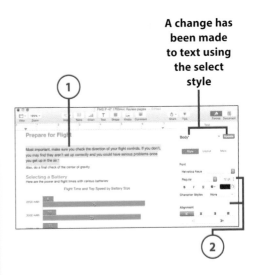

A change has been made to text using the select style

3. When you have made all the formatting changes you want to make, click Update. All the text with the style applied is reformatted according to the changes you made. The asterisk disappears, and any new text you apply the style to is formatted according to its updated options.

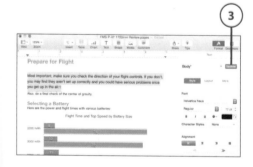

Create New Styles in Pages Documents

When you use a Pages template, it includes many styles that you can use. However, you aren't limited to those styles because you can create new styles to use in a document.

1. Move into a paragraph with the style that is most similar to the style you want to create.

2. Open the Style menu and click the Add button (+). A new style is added to the list, and its name is ready to be edited.

3. Type the name of the style you are creating.

4. Press the Enter key. The new style is created and applied to the paragraph in which the cursor is located.

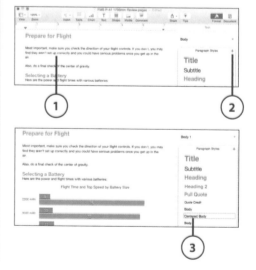

It Works for Character Styles, Too

You can update character styles similarly to the way you update paragraph styles. Select text with a character style applied, and change its format using the tools on the Inspector. Like paragraph styles, when you make a change, the character style's name is marked with an asterisk. When you've made all the changes you want, open the Character Styles menu and click the Update button. The character style is updated with the change you made, and any text with that style applied is reformatted accordingly.

5. Click back in the paragraph where you were in step 1.

6. Use the formatting tools to change the format of the text to be what you want included in the style.

7. Click Update. The new style is saved with the formatting options you configured, and you can apply it to text just like default styles.

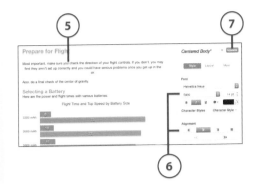

You Can Create New Character Styles, Too

You can create new character styles in a similar way to what you did for paragraph styles. Select and format some text. Then open the Character Styles menu and click Add (+). Name the new style and press the Enter key. The new character style is created, and you can use it just like the other character styles you see.

>>>Go Further

MORE STYLE TRICKS

When you click the right-facing arrow along the right side of the style menu items, you see a submenu with the following commands. (These are enabled only when appropriate.)

- **Redefine from Selection.** This does the same thing as clicking the Update button.

- **Clear Override.** This removes any changes to the formatting you made and returns the text to the format options of the style as it currently is saved.

- **Rename Style.** Use this to change a style's name.

- **Delete Style.** You can use this to remove styles you no longer want to use. You're prompted to choose the style that should be applied to any text that currently has the applied style you are deleting. Choose the new style, and click OK.

- **Shortcut.** Choose a keyboard shortcut you can press to apply the style so that you don't have to choose an option on the menu. Assigning a shortcut to the styles you use most frequently enables you to just press the shortcut's keys to apply a style, which is quick. When you apply a shortcut to a style, it appears next to the style's name on the menu.

Format Text as Lists in Pages Documents

Bulleted and numbered lists are useful ways to communicate certain kinds of information. You can use text formatting tools in Pages to create both types of lists.

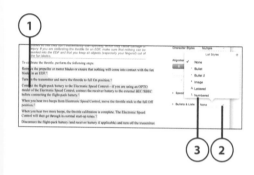

1. Select the text you want to format as a list.

2. Open the Bullets & Lists menu.

3. Click the list style you want to apply to the selected list. For example, click Numbered to create a numbered list. The text you selected is formatted into a list based on your selection.

List Styles Are, Eh, Styles

List styles are just like the other text styles in many ways. For example, you can change the formatting associated with text styled with a list style by making the changes to the text's style and then updating it. When you choose a list style, its name appears in the Style menu at the top of the Inspector, albeit in an abbreviated way (for example, Numbered appears as NL on the Style menu).

---

4. If you are satisfied with the list as it is, skip the rest of these steps, or to do additional formatting, continue with them.

5. Click the Disclosure triangle next to the Bullets & Lists text. The section expands, and you see additional formatting controls for the type of list you are working with. This example shows the options for a numbered list; you will see different options for a bulleted list.

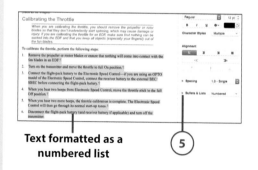

Text formatted as a numbered list

Expand the List

You can add to a list by moving to the end of the last item in the list and pressing the Return key. A new paragraph is created and continues in the style of the list. You can start a new list by choosing a list style and typing the first item on the list; each subsequent paragraph continues the list until you choose a different style (such as choosing a body style to stop the list and return to "regular" text).

6. Use the additional controls to further format the list. For example, when you are working with a numbered list, you can use the Continue from previous option to have the numbering in the current list continue from the previous list or use the Start from tool to set the first number in the list. Other controls enable you to change the format of the numbers, change their size, and so on.

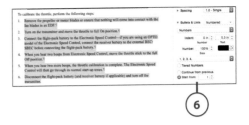

6

Numbered Versus Bulleted Lists

You should only use a numbered list when the order of the items in the list matters. The most common situation in which you use a numbered list is for step-by-step instructions (such as tasks in a book), where the reader should follow the sequence of the steps as they are written. If the order of the items in the list doesn't matter, use a bulleted list. One way to think about it is that you should use numbered lists when you are providing instructions and bulleted lists when you are providing information.

Use the Ruler to Format Text in Pages Documents

You can use the Ruler to position text on a page with respect to the document's margins and to set tab stops.

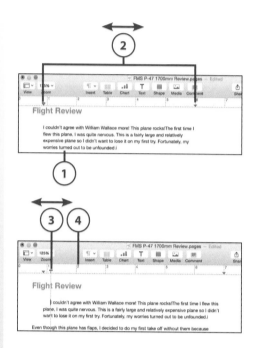

1. Click in the paragraph for which to configure the Ruler. You see the current Ruler settings, which are, by default, the left and right paragraph margins. (If the Ruler isn't shown, choose View, Show Ruler.) Refer to Table 2.2 for an explanation of the icons you see on the Ruler.

2. Drag the paragraph margins to set the width of the paragraph. As you drag the margin markers, the paragraph is resized accordingly.

3. To indent the first line of a paragraph, click on the top of the left margin marker and drag. The marker separates into two parts. The horizontal line marks the start of the first line in the paragraph, and the triangle indicates the left margin for the rest of the paragraph. As you drag, the first line of text moves, and a yellow vertical line appears to enable you to place the start of the line precisely. When it is in position, release the mouse button or trackpad. The first line indent marker is placed at that spot.

4. To set a tab stop, click on the Ruler where you want the tab stop to be. The tab marker appears on the Ruler.

5. Drag the tab stop to the left or right.

6. To change the type of tab stop, hold the control key down and click on the tab stop marker. A menu appears.

7. Click the type of tab stop you want to set. The text is moved according to the tab stop you selected. For example, if you choose Center tab, the text starts at the centerline between the paragraph margins.

8. Continue setting tabs; you can have multiple tab stops in the same paragraph.

9. To remove a tab stop, drag it off the Ruler. When it moves off the Ruler, it disappears and no longer applies to the current paragraph.

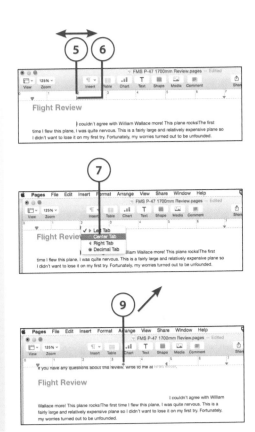

The Ruler and Styles

Ruler settings are part of the formatting options saved in styles. If you want to reuse the Ruler settings, update the text's style once you configure the Ruler settings you want to reuse. The Ruler settings are applied to any existing text using that style, and any new text you format in that style also receives those Ruler settings.

>>>*Go Further*

ADVANCED TEXT FORMATTING

When you click the gear icon next to the Underline button in the Text Inspector, you see Advanced Options for formatting text. You probably won't use these often, but it is good to know they are available if you need to access them. A number of these options are related to more precise spacing of text and include Character Spacing, Baseline Shift, and Baseline. The Capitalization menu enables you to format the case of text, such as All Caps, Small Caps, or Title Case; these can be useful to change the case of existing text. The Ligatures menu can be used to join characters. The Character Fill Color menu and Color Picker enable you to fill characters with color. The Outline, Strikethrough, and Shadow check boxes enable you to apply those formatting options to text. (These work just like the Bold, Italics, and Underline buttons.)

Work with Text Boxes in Pages Documents

Text boxes are useful to emphasize certain points in your documents. For example, you might want to use a text box to highlight a quote from a customer in a proposal document or highlight some facts about the topic about which you are writing. Text boxes are not part of the document's text flow but exist as separate objects, much like the images in a document.

After you add a text box to a document, you fill the box with text. You can use the text formatting tools you learned about in the previous tasks to format the text within the box. You can also style the box itself, such as by choosing a border or adding a drop shadow. You use the Arrange tools to determine how the text box interacts with the surrounding text, for example, to have it float with the text so it remains in context or to fix its location on the page.

As with body text, you use the Inspector to format, style, and arrange text boxes.

Add Text Boxes to Pages Documents

To add a text box to a document, perform the following steps:

1. Position the cursor roughly where you want the text box to appear; this doesn't need to be precise, because you can reposition the text box at any time.

2. Click the Text button. A new empty text box appears.

3. Add text to the text box; this works just like adding text to the body of the document. You're ready to format the text and the text box.

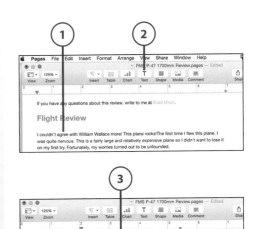

Format the Text in Text Boxes in Pages Documents

You can format the text within text boxes just like text in other locations.

1. Select text in the text box that you want to format. (In some cases, it's better to style the text box first, as explained in the following task, because those styles change the text style, too.)

2. Format the text manually or by using styles.

3. Continue formatting the text in the box until you've formatted all of it.

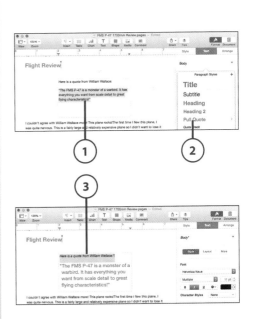

Style Text Boxes in Pages Documents

You can also style the text box in which the text is contained, as follows:

1. Select the text box you want to style.

2. Click the Style tab on the Inspector.

3. Browse through the available styles at the top of the Inspector by clicking the left and right arrows.

4. Click the style you want to apply to the text box. The text box is restyled accordingly. Note: if you've formatted the text in the box as described in the previous task, that formatting is overwritten when you apply a style to the text box.

5. To format the box's fill, click the disclosure triangle next to Fill.

6. Choose the type of fill you want to use on the menu.

7. Use the controls that appear based on the type of fill you selected to configure the fill, such as setting the color for the Color Fill option.

8. To format the box's border, click the disclosure triangle next to Border.

9. Choose the type of border you want to apply on the menu.

10. Use the resulting controls to configure the border, such as to set its width and size.

11. To format the box's drop shadow, click the disclosure triangle next to Shadow.

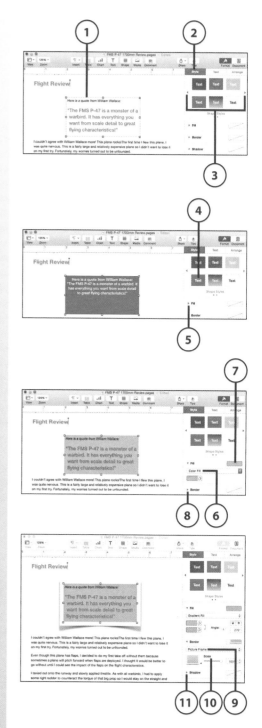

12. Choose the type of drop shadow you want to apply on the menu.

13. Configure the drop shadow you selected using the tools that appear.

14. To apply a reflection, check the Reflection check box and use the slider or box to set the percentage of reflection for the text box. As with the other changes, the results on the screen appear immediately so you can see how each change affects the text box.

15. Use the Opacity tool to set the level of opacity of the text box.

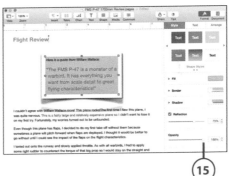

>>>Go Further

SAVE YOUR TEXT BOX DESIGNS

If you want to be able to reuse a text box design, select the design you want to save, move to the Style tab in the Text Box Inspector, and click the right-facing arrow at the top of the Inspector until you see an empty box with a "+." Click that box. The design of the text box you selected is saved. You can apply your custom design to any text box by selecting the text box and clicking your custom design on the Style tab.

Arrange Text Boxes in Pages Documents

The positioning of text boxes on a page is important because it impacts how a page looks and how the text box interacts with surrounding text or images.

1. Select the text box.

2. Click the Arrange tab.

3. If you want the text box to remain on the page as content is added above it, click Stay on Page, or if you want the text box to flow with the text it is near, click Move with Text.

4. Use the Text Wrap menu to determine how the text box interacts with the text surrounding it. For example, if you choose Around, the surrounding text flows around each side of the text box; in contrast, if you choose Above and Below, text flows above and below the box, but not on its sides.

5. Use the other options on the menu to place the text box on the page more precisely, control the amount of space between the box and surrounding text, and so on. You learn more about these options in later chapters.

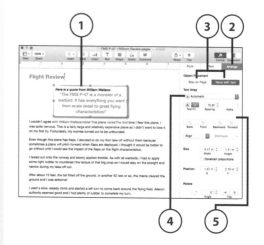

6. To change the location of the text box on the page, drag it to where you want it to be. As you drag, you see the location of the box in the pop-up window.

7. To resize a text box, select it and then drag one of its selection handles.

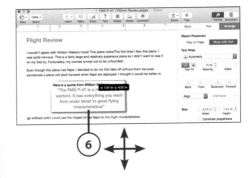

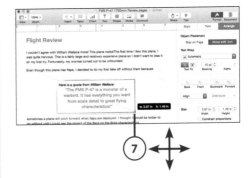

Use tables to effectively communicate facts in Pages documents

Pages provides lots of tools you can use to design the way tables look

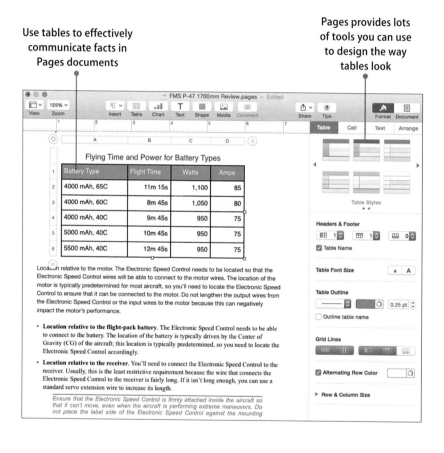

In this chapter, you learn how to add tables to and format tables in your Pages documents. Topics include the following:

→ Add Tables to Page Documents
→ Select Tables, Cells, Rows, or Columns in Pages Documents
→ Format Tables in Pages Documents
→ Add Tables and Charts Created in Numbers to Pages Documents

Working with Tables in Pages Documents

Tables are an excellent way to communicate certain types of information, especially numeric data. They're also handy whenever there are multiple, related items, such as the power output of a motor with different input voltages. Pages offers great tools you can use to add and format tables in your Pages documents. When a table involves calculations or formulas, it can be better to create the table in Numbers and then add it your Pages document; that topic is covered in this chapter, too.

Add Tables to Pages Documents

You can easily add tables to Pages documents and then add content to those tables. When you add a table, you first choose the design for the table and then insert it into the document. After that, you add content to the table.

Insert Tables into Pages Documents

To add a table to a Pages document, do the following:

1. Place the cursor where you want the table to be located.

2. Click the Table button on the toolbar. The Table palette appears.

3. Click the left and right arrows to browse the available table designs. These include different color schemes, footer rows, and other options. You can always restyle a table later, so you don't have to concern yourself overly much with picking a specific style.

4. Click the table you want to insert into the document. The table is added at the cursor location. It is selected automatically so that you see the table tools in the Inspector. You're ready to add content to the table.

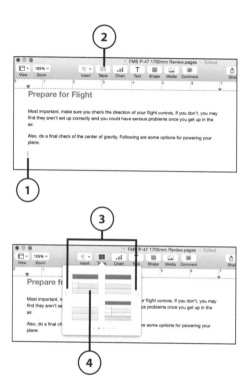

When a table is selected, you see the column (letters) and row (numbers) labels

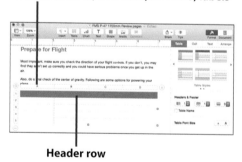

Header row

Add Content to Cells in Tables in Pages Documents

Adding content to a table is straightforward, as you can see in the following steps:

1. If the table isn't selected already, click it. (If you see the column and row labels, the table is selected.)

2. Click on the cell to which you want to add content. The cell becomes selected, which is indicated by the selection handles and border.

3. Type the content of the cell into the row.

4. Press the Tab key to move to the next cell.

5. Type the content of that cell.

6. Press the Tab key to move to the next cell. When you reach the last cell in a row, the cursor moves into the first cell of the next row automatically. (If there aren't enough columns in the table, see "Add Columns or Rows to Tables in Pages Documents.")

7. Repeat steps 5 and 6 until you've added content to all the cells in the table.

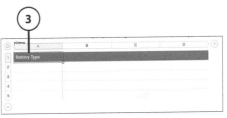

—Selected cell

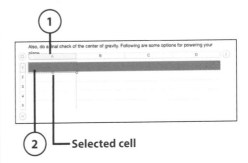

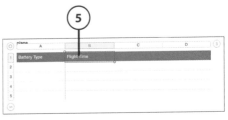

Automatic Expansion

If you reach the end of the table and press the Tab key again, a new row is added so that you can add as much information to the table as you want regardless of how many rows were included in the table initially.

Select Tables, Cells, Rows, or Columns in Pages Documents

When you work with tables, it's important to know how to select the entire table or the parts of a table with which you want to work.

Row (numbers) and column (letters) labels appear when a table is selected

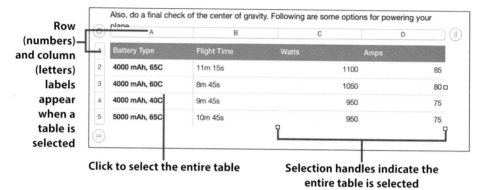

Click to select the entire table   **Selection handles indicate the entire table is selected**

When you want to work with a table as an entity, such as when you want to move it, you need to select the table with which you want to work. To select a table, click it. When the table is selected, you see selection handles, row and column labels, and buttons in various locations.

Click a column's label to select the column

This column is selected

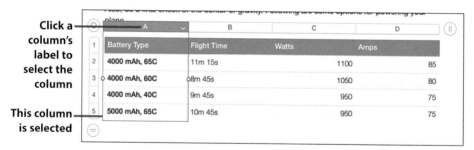

To select an entire column, click its label (letter). The column label is highlighted, and you see a box around the column. You can then take action on the column, such as resizing it.

Click a row's label to select the row

This row is selected

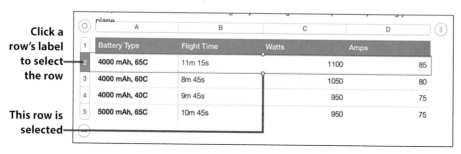

Similar to columns, to select a row, clicks its label (number). The row's label is highlighted, and it is surrounded in a box with selection handles. This indicates that you can take action on the entire row.

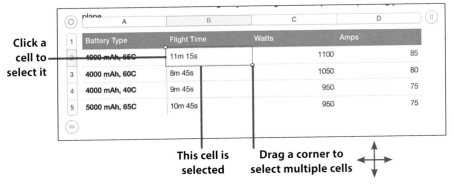

Click a cell to select it

This cell is selected   **Drag a corner to select multiple cells**

To select a cell, click it. It is highlighted in the selection box, and you can see the corresponding column and row labels highlighted that indicate the cell's position, such as B2. You can now take action on that cell.

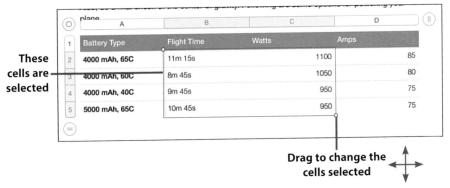

These cells are selected

Drag to change the cells selected

To select a range of cells, select the first cell in the range and drag the selection handle in the lower-right corner of the cell until the box encompasses all the cells you want to select. As when you select a single cell, the corresponding column and row labels are highlighted to show which cells are selected, such as B2 through C5.

Format Tables in Pages Documents

You can format tables in your Pages documents to make the information they contain easier to understand for the reader and to make your documents more visually appealing. Some of the formatting you do with tables is accomplished by acting directly on the table, such as adding rows or columns, and you can use the Inspector to configure other formatting options, such as borders and fill.

When a table is selected, the Inspector has four tabs: Table, Cell, Text, and Arrange. The tools on the Table and Cell tabs are explained in Tables 3.1 and 3.2.

Table 3.1 Formatting Tools on the Style Tab of the Table Inspector

Icon	Description
	The table style buttons apply a template to the table with which you are working. These templates include colors, headers and footers, borders, and other options. Typically, selecting a table style should be the first step when you are formatting a table because doing so overwrites format options currently applied to the table. Additionally, these types have predefined options that go well together; you can use them to make your tables look nice with minimal effort.
⊞ 1	This changes the number of header columns in a table. Header columns identify the content in each row. Most tables have a single header column, but you can add more if needed. Header columns have different formatting options applied in most table styles.
⊞ 1	This changes the number of header rows in a table. Header rows contain the column headings for the table, which identify the contents of the column. Like header columns, most tables have a single header row, but you can add more as needed. Header rows also have unique formatting options in most styles.
⊞ 0	This adds or changes the number of footer rows. A footer row appears at the bottom of a table and is most often used to summarize the contents of the rows above it. For example, if a column contains numbers, the footer row can contain the sum of the numbers in the rows above it. It's usually a good idea to apply formatting to footer rows to make it clear that they are different from the other rows in the table.
Table Name	The table name identifies a table. Each table must have a unique name, which you can show or hide using this check box. The default table name is Table X, where X is a sequential number. Table names are useful to give the reader an idea about what content is included in the table and to use as a reference in the text. (An example might be, "See Table 5 for an explanation of flight times with various battery sizes.")
A A	These buttons decrease or increase the font size used for all the text in the table.
Table Outline None	Use this menu to apply an outline to a table. You can choose different line styles, colors, and other options for the lines that border the outside of the table.

| | These buttons show or hide the grid lines for the rows or columns in the body of the table (excluding the header rows and columns and footers). When a button is highlighted, the corresponding grid lines are shown. |

These buttons show or hide the grid lines for the header columns, header rows, or footers.

☑ Alternating Row Color — Use the check box and color tool to determine if alternating rows in the table have different colors, and if they do, what colors are used.

▶ Row & Column Size — Click the disclosure triangle to reveal options for setting row and column size. In most cases, you can do this just as easily by dragging their borders, as you learn in "Resize Table Rows and Columns in Pages Documents" later in this chapter. To more precisely size rows or columns, expand this area and enter the sizes or use the Fit button to set the size based on cell content.

Table 3.2   Formatting Tools on the Cell Tab of the Table Inspector

Icon	Description
Data Format / Automatic	Use the menu to apply a format to the content of cells. For example, choose Currency when cells contain values related to currency. When you select an option, you can make additional choices to further refine the formation you selected, such as the number of decimal places shown.
▼ Fill	Use the Fill tools to fill cells with colors or patterns. When you click the disclosure triangle, you see a menu that enables you to choose from a number of options, such as Color Fill and Gradient Fill. When you make a selection, additional tools appear that enable you to configure the option you selected.
Border	These enable you to apply borders to the cells in the table. You can choose which sides of the cells contain borders and then configure the lines by choosing widths, patterns, and colors.
Conditional Highlighting...	This enables you to create conditional formatting for cells, such as filling a cell with red when it contains a negative number. Click the Conditional Highlighting button, and then use the resulting tools to configure the conditions and highlighting you want to use.

The Text tab contains the same tools you use to format text, which you learned about in the previous chapter.

As with other objects, when you select a table, you can use the Arrange tab to determine if the table stays on the current page or flows with the surrounding text and how the table interacts with that surrounding text.

Add Columns or Rows to Tables in Pages Documents

Earlier, you saw how Pages automatically adds rows to tables as you enter content in cells. You can manually add columns and rows to tables at any time.

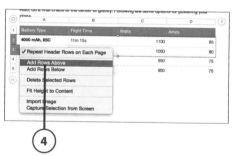

1. Select the table to which you want to add a row or column.

2. To add a single row or column, click its label, or to add multiple rows or columns, hold down the ⌘ and click the surrounding rows or columns until you've selected the number of rows or columns you want to add. (For example, to add two rows, select two rows.) When you make a selection, an arrow appears where your selection ends.

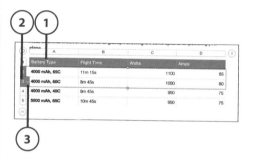

3. Click the arrow. A contextual menu (meaning that the commands on the menu depend on what you have selected) appears.

4. Choose the Add command, such as Add Rows Above or Add Rows Below.

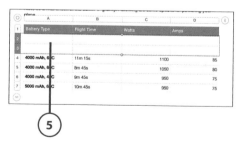

5. Add content to the new rows or columns.

Another Way to Add Columns or Rows

To add columns to a table, click the button containing two parallel vertical lines to the right of the last column label, and on the resulting menu, enter the total number of columns you want in the table, or use the up or down arrows to add or remove columns. (You can't remove columns that contain data.) You can add rows in a similar way by clicking the button containing two parallel horizontal lines just below the last row label and then configuring the number of rows in the table. (You can't remove rows that contain information.) When you add columns or rows in this way, they are added to the end of the table.

Configure Table Names in Pages Documents

As mentioned earlier, table names are useful to help the reader identify the content in the table and for you to use to reference the table in the text. You can hide or show a table's name, and you can add to or change the default table name that Pages creates for you.

1. Select the table.

2. Click the Table tab of the Inspector.

3. Check the Table Name check box. The table name appears at the top of the table. The default name is Table X, where X is a sequential number.

4. To replace the table name, triple-click it, or to append a title onto the default name, double-click after the default name.

5. Edit the default name so the table name is what you want it to be.

6. If you use the Table Outline feature and want the table name to have an outline, too, check the Outline table name check box.

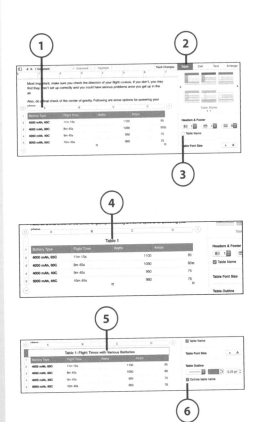

It's Not All Good

Unfortunately, the sequential number that Pages adds to a table number doesn't update based on the table's position; it is based only on the order in which you create the tables in a document. For example, the first table you create is named Table 1. If you create another table below it, that is named Table 2, as you might expect. However, if you create another new table above Table 1, it is named Table 3. It would be nice if the tables renumbered based on their position, but once created, the number included in a table name is static. Therefore, you can rename tables as you wish. As you add tables above existing tables, you need to update the table numbers so they accurately reflect the table's position in the document.

>>>Go Further
MORE ON CONTEXTUAL MENUS

As you saw when you added rows or columns to a table, the contextual menu contains lots of commands, some of which are very useful. Examples of these include the following:

- Delete selected rows or columns.
- Repeat header rows on each page.
- Sort a table.
- Add header columns or rows.
- Fit size to content.

As you work with different table objects, open their contextual menus by performing a secondary click (for example, click the right mouse button or hold down the control key while you click on something) to see the commands there so you can decide which will be useful for you.

Resize Table Rows and Columns in Pages Documents

As you work with tables, you'll likely want to resize columns and rows. Here's how:

1. Select the table whose columns or rows you want to resize.

2. Select the columns or rows you want to resize.

3. Move the pointer to an edge of the columns or rows you have selected so that it becomes a vertical line with arrows projecting from it. This indicates that you can drag the border to resize the columns or rows.

4. Drag the border to the left or right to resize a column or up or down to resize a row. As you drag, the current dimension (width or height) is shown.

5. When the column or row is the size you want it to be, release the border.

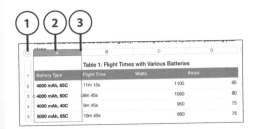

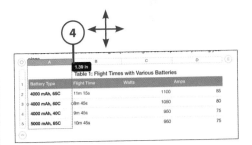

Resizing Made Even Easier

To quickly resize a column or row based on the content in its cells, select the rows or columns you want to resize. Open the contextual menu and choose the related Fit command (such as Fit Width to Content if you are resizing a column). The size of the selected columns or rows is adjusted until they fit the content they include.

Change the Style of Tables in Pages Documents

You can apply a style to a table when you add it to a document, or you can restyle a table later.

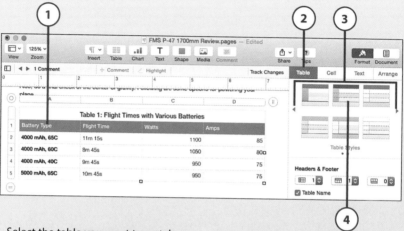

1. Select the table you want to restyle.

2. Click the Table tab of the Inspector.

3. Click the right- and left-facing arrows to browse the available styles.

4. Click the style you want to apply. The table is reformatted according to the style you selected.

>>>Go Further

ROLL YOUR OWN TABLE STYLES

The table styles are only a starting point for you. You can design and reformat tables as much as you want to fully customize them. If you create a custom table style that you want to be able to reuse easily, you can add it to the styles on the Table tab. First, create the table style you want using the tools in the Inspector. Second, open the Table tab and browse the styles until you see one that contains the add (+) button. Click that style, and your custom style (which includes all the settings you have configured) is saved in that space. You can apply custom styles that you save just like the default styles in Pages.

Customize a Table's Design

You can use the commands on the Table tab to design many aspects of a table's appearance:

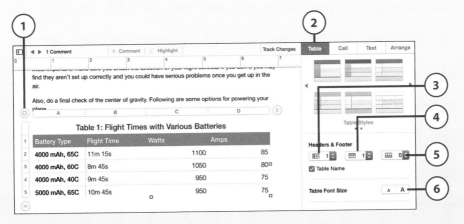

1. Select the table you want to design.

2. Open the Table tab of the Inspector.

3. Use the column header menu to choose the number of column headers in the table.

4. Use the row header menu to choose the number of row headers in the table.

5. Use the footer menu to add footer rows to the table.

6. Click the Table Font Size buttons to increase or decrease the size of all the text in the table. (To change the font of specific text, you use the Cell tab, as explained in a later task.)

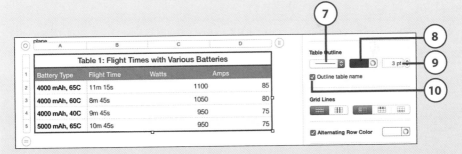

7. To add an outline to the table, choose the outline style you want to use on the Table Outline menu.

8. Use the Color tool to choose a color for the outline.

9. Use the Size tool to set the width of the outline.

10. To apply the outline to the table name (if shown), check the Outline table name check box.

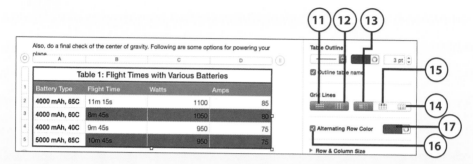

11. Enable grid lines between the rows by clicking the Row Grid Line button. (When the grid lines are enabled, the corresponding button is highlighted.)

12. Enable grid lines between the columns by clicking the Column Grid Line button.

13. To add grid lines between the header columns and body cells, click the Header Columns Grid Line button.

14. To add grid lines between the header rows and body cells, click the Header Rows Grid Line button.

15. Enable grid lines between the footer rows and body cells by clicking the Column Grid Line button.

16. To use colors on alternating rows, check the Alternating Row Color check box and perform the next step; if you don't want to use color in this way, skip this and the next step.

17. Use the Color tool to configure the color used on alternate rows.

Format the Cells in Tables in Pages Documents

You can apply formatting options to the cells in a table as follows:

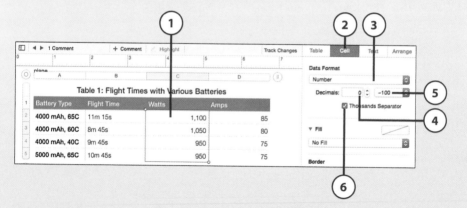

1. Select the cells in the table that you want to format.

2. Click the Cell tab.

3. Choose the format for the data in the selected cells on the Data Format menu. There are a number of options, such as Number, Currency, and Percentage. When you make a selection, the data in the selected cells is formatted accordingly, and you see controls appropriate for the format you selected. This example shows the Number format, but you follow similar steps to configure any format you choose.

4. Choose the number of decimals to be shown.

5. Configure how negative numbers should be formatted, such as using a "-" or being shown in red.

6. Check the Thousands Separator check box to place a comma at the thousands position in a number.

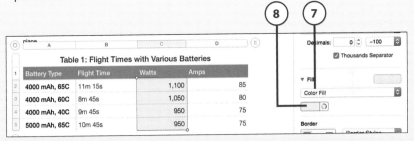

7. To fill the cells, choose an option on the Fill menu. Options include Color Fill and Gradient Fill, among others. When you make a selection, controls for configuring the option you selected appear. This example shows the Color Fill option, but you can configure the other options using similar steps.

8. Use the Color tool to configure the fill color. (Some options have more controls, such as the Gradient Fill that enables you to choose two colors for the gradient along with its direction.)

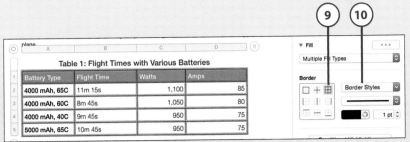

9. Click the locations where you want borders to be used.

10. Choose the style of the border lines. These include various widths and colors and the Default Style, which sets the borders as they are defined in the style applied to the table.

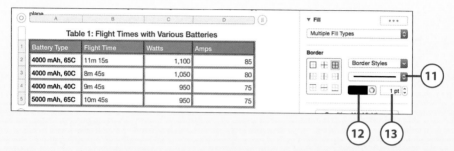

11.   Choose the pattern of the border line, which is solid, dashed, dotted, or no border.

12.   Use the Color tool to choose the color of the border lines.

13.   Use the Size tool to set the thickness of the border lines.

Custom Data Formats

If you choose Create Custom Format, you can create your own data formats and save them for easy reuse. Any formats you create appear on the Data Format menu, just like the default formats.

Format the Text in Tables in Pages Documents

Using the controls on the Table tab, such as selecting a style and changing the font size, you can do some basic design of the text in tables. Using the Text tab, you can control all aspects of text in a table:

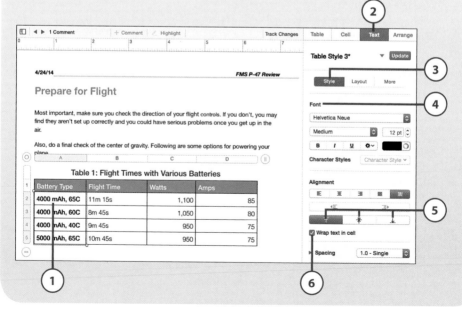

1. Select the cells containing the text you want to format.

2. Click the Text tab.

3. Click the Style tab.

4. Use the tools you see to format the text. These are the same as the text tools you learned about in Chapter 2, "Working with Text in Pages Documents." For example, you can apply styles to text, change the font, and apply bold or italic.

5. Use the three alignment buttons to configure how text aligns vertically within cells (these buttons are inactive for text outside of tables); the options are (from left to right): align with the top of the cell, align with the center of the cell, and align with bottom of the cell.

6. Check the Wrap text in cell check box if you want text to wrap around when it expands beyond the width of the cell.

Position Tables in Pages Documents

Like other objects in Pages documents, you can position tables on pages as part of your document design. This works similarly to positioning text boxes, which you learned about in Chapter 2.

1. Drag a table by its handle to move it around the page.

2. Click the Arrange tab.

3. Use the controls on the Arrange tab to determine how the table interacts with the text on the page. These work just as they do for text boxes. (See Chapter 2 for details.) For example, click Stay on Page to lock the table on the current page or Move with Text to have the table stay in relative proximity to the surrounding text. Or use the Text Wrap menu to determine how text flows around a table.

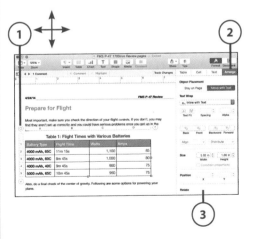

Add Tables and Charts Created in Numbers to Pages Documents

As you learn in Chapters 7 through 10, Numbers is a great app to use when dealing with numeric information—especially anything that requires calculations. Also, Numbers is great for creating charts to present numeric information visually. For tables that are mostly text or include very simple numeric information, creating a table directly in Pages is probably easier and better. However, for more complex or complicated numeric information, it is better to create a table or chart in Numbers and add it to your Pages document.

First, use Numbers to create the table or chart you want to include in your Pages document. (Refer to Chapters 7 through 10.) When the table is done, use the following steps to copy that table into a Pages document.

1. In Numbers, select the table you want to add to a Pages document. (Selecting tables in Numbers is just like selecting tables in Pages.)

2. Choose Edit, Copy.

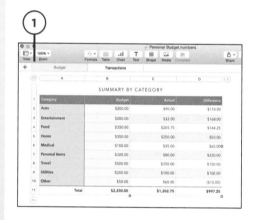

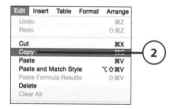

3. Move into the Pages document to which you want to add the table from Numbers.

4. Place the cursor where you want the table from Numbers to be placed.

5. Choose Edit, Paste. The table from Numbers is copied into the Pages document.

6. Edit and format the table using the tools in Pages that you learned about in earlier tasks.

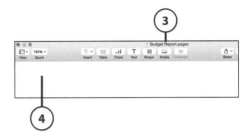

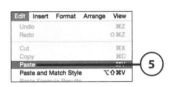

Table created in Numbers

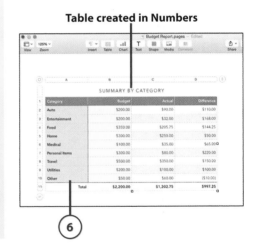

The Calculations Remain the Same

Calculations that were created in Numbers are transferred into the table in Pages. When you change the data in the table in Pages, the results of the calculations are updated just as they are in Numbers.

Use photos and other images to make your Pages documents more interesting and effective

The Inspector offers lots of tools you can use to improve the design of the graphics in your documents

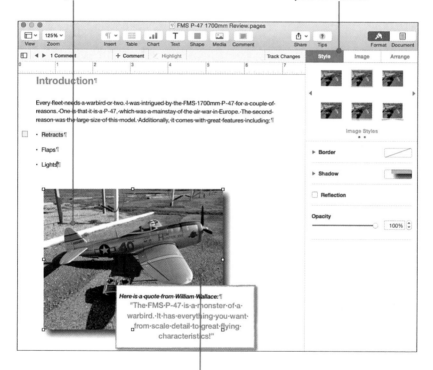

You can easily add any photos in your iPhoto or Aperture libraries to Pages documents

In this chapter, you learn how to include photos and other graphics in your Pages documents. Topics include the following:

→ Insert Photos and Other Graphics into Pages Documents

→ Design the Photos and Other Images in Pages Documents

Working with Photos, Graphics, and Other Objects in Pages Documents

One age-old and extremely overused cliché states, "A picture is worth a thousand words." This cliché is used so often because the idea that it expresses—that images communicate effectively—happens to be true. What the cliché doesn't say is that pictures alone don't usually tell a complete story. The most effective communication typically includes both words and images. As you've seen in previous chapters, Pages enables you to do a lot with text and tables. In this chapter, you learn how to use the app's great graphics tools to include visual elements, such as photos, to enhance both the effectiveness and the visual appeal of your Pages documents.

Insert Photos and Other Graphics into Pages Documents

You can use many different types of graphics in your documents, including photos stored in your iPhoto or Aperture library, photos you've stored in other places on your Mac, images you've created and stored on your computer, and images you've downloaded. (Make sure you don't violate any copyright or other use restrictions if you are going to use a downloaded image in a document.)

There are a number of ways you can add photos and other images to your Pages documents, including these:

- Replace an image placeholder with a photo from iPhoto.

- Add an image from the Media Browser.

- Drag an image from your desktop into a document.

Each of these options is explained in the following tasks.

But Wait; There's More

You can also insert audio and video into Pages documents. Although this isn't useful for documents you deliver in hard copy format, it can be very useful when you are delivering electronic documents, such as ones in the PDF format. For example, when you are explaining the steps in a process, you can insert a video showing those steps into the document. Someone reading the PDF can view the video and read the surrounding text. Although this chapter is focused on static images, you can use similar steps to place audio or movie files into your documents. When you use audio or movie files in Pages documents, you should test your final documents, such as the PDF version, to make sure that content plays correctly before you distribute them. If possible, also test the document on a different type of device you expect your readers to use, such as an iPad or a Windows PC.

Replace an Image Placeholder with a Photo from iPhoto

Many of the Pages document templates include image placeholders that you can replace with your own images.

1. Click the icon located in the lower-right corner of the image placeholder. The Media Browser appears.

2. Click the Photos tab. You see the photos stored in your iPhoto Photo Library. Along the left side of the browser, you see the sources of photos, which are the same as they are in iPhoto.

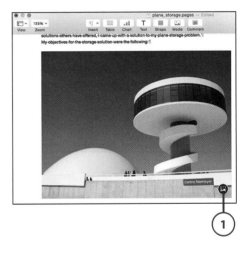

Use Aperture?

If you use Aperture, the Media Browser shows the photos in your Aperture library. However, if you upgraded from iPhoto to Aperture as I did, Aperture actually uses your iPhoto Library, and the Media Browser is currently labeled iPhoto. This doesn't matter so much because the browser looks at the current photo library no matter which of the two apps you use.

3. Select the source of photos you want to browse. The photos in that source appear.

4. Browse the photos in the selected source.

5. Click the photo with which you want to replace the image placeholder. The photo replaces the placeholder. (Note that the image placeholder icon disappears.)

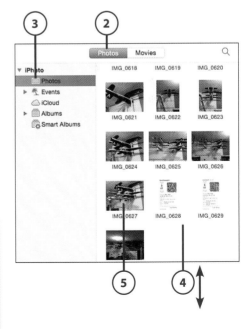

Searchin' for Photos in All the Right Places

You can search for photos to insert by clicking the magnifying glass icon in the upper-right corner of the Media Browser. Enter your search term in the resulting Search bar. The photos you see in the browser are reduced to include only those that relate to the term you entered.

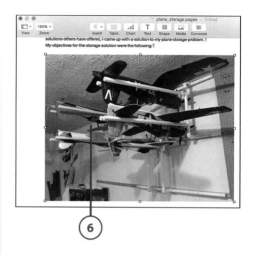

6. Use the tools in Pages to design the photo (explained in "Design Photos and Other Images in Pages Documents" later in this chapter).

Use the Media Browser to Insert Photos into Pages Documents

You can use the Media Browser to add a photo to any location in a document.

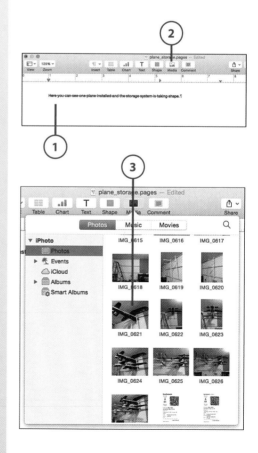

1. Position the cursor in the approximate location where you want the photo. (You can easily reposition it later.)

2. Click the Media button on the toolbar. The Media Browser appears.

3. Use steps 2 through 5 in the previous task to select the photo you want to insert into the document.

4. Use the tools in Pages to design the photo (explained in "Design Photos and Other Images in Pages Documents" later in this chapter).

>>>*Go Further*

ADD SHAPES TO PAGES DOCUMENTS

You can add various kinds of shapes to your Pages documents, such as lines, curves, circles, squares, and stars. You can add shapes from the templates available in Pages and then customize them for your specific use. For example, you can change the fill color, resize them, and so on. Working with shapes is quite similar to other objects you've learned about. Click the Shape button on the Pages toolbar. Then browse the available shapes to find the one closest to the shape you want to add to your document. Click that shape, and it is added at the current location of the cursor. You can then resize the shape, position it on the page, and use the shape tools in the Inspector to format it.

Drag Photos and Other Graphics from the Mac Desktop into Pages Documents

The Media Browser can access only photos and graphics stored in iPhoto or Aperture. You can place any image stored on your Mac into a Pages document by dragging it from the desktop into the document.

1. Position the cursor in the approximate location where you want the photo. (You can easily reposition it later.)

2. Open a Finder window, and navigate to the location of the photo you want to place in the document.

3. Drag the document from the Finder window onto the Pages document. The photo is copied into the document.

4. Use the tools in Pages to design the photo (explained in "Design Photos and Other Images in Pages Documents" later in this chapter).

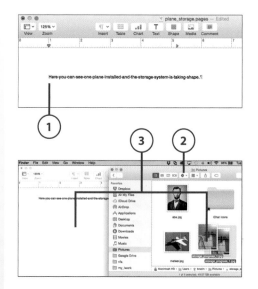

Is Dragging a Drag?

For yet another option, you can add a photo by choosing Insert, Other. Use the resulting dialog to move to and select the image file you want to insert, select it, and click Open. The image you selected is placed at the current cursor location. This option can be easier than dragging because you don't need to deal with positioning the Finder window so that you can see it and your Pages document at the same time.

Hold Slip

Oxford

Fri Jan 29 2016

My Pages, Numbers, and Keynote / Brad Wiser.

ITEM: 31842029877717

Hold note:

ELLIOTT, DOUGLAS R.

JR

Don't Have the Image Yet?

In some cases, you may know you want to use an image in a document, but you might not have the final version of that image ready. In this case, you can create an image placeholder to create a space for an image and replace the placeholder with the final image when it is ready. To create a placeholder, add an image to the document and size it as you will want the final image to be sized. Select the image and choose Format, Advanced, Define as Media Placeholder. The image becomes a placeholder and is marked with the placeholder icon in the lower-right corner. You can then replace it with the final image, as described in the task "Replace an Image Placeholder with a Photo from iPhoto," earlier in the chapter.

Design Photos and Other Images in Pages Documents

You can design the photos and other images in your Pages documents in a number of ways, including the following:

- **Resize photos or images.** You can change the size of images to make them fit the page or size them appropriately for their level of detail or importance to the content. You can also change the proportion of images, but this can have unintended consequences. So be careful about changing the size of images out of their original proportions, or you may end up with squished or stretched versions.

- **Rotate photos or images.** You can change the orientation of images or flip them horizontally or vertically.

- **Style photos or images.** You can use the Inspector to change the appearance of photos and images by adding borders, using drop shadows, applying a reflection, and changing their opacity. These tools enable you to make images more visually appealing and increase their impact; they also enable you to express your creativity. Like styling other elements, such as text and tables, you can use the built-in styles in Pages or create and save your own styles.

- **Mask photos or images.** Masking is useful to remove parts of images that you don't want to appear in a document. Masking is similar to cropping except that when you mask an image, you don't actually change the image; rather, you choose the part of the image you want to be shown, and the rest is covered over so that it can't be seen. Masking is nice because it is easy to adjust the mask or simply remove it to display the full image again. (This is in contrast to cropping, in which part of the image is actually removed and is no longer available.)

- **Remove background from photos or images.** Sometimes an image has something in the background that is distracting. You can use the tools in Pages to remove the background from images so that the primary subject becomes more prominent.

- **Adjust photos or images.** Although Pages isn't a photo-editing app, it does have some basic tools you can use to improve the quality of images in your documents. These include adjusting the exposure, contrast, saturation, and other aspects of photos. You can also use the Enhance tool in Pages to have the app make semi-automatic adjustments to a photo. It's often a good idea to start with the Enhance tool, and if you don't like the changes it makes, you can easily undo them and adjust the photo manually.

- **Position photos or images manually.** You usually want photos and images to be in the area of text to which they relate. Like other objects in Pages, you can manually position photos on a page.

- **Use the Arrange tab to place photos or images.** The Inspector's Arrange tab provides tools you use to determine how photos and images interact with surrounding text. You can configure photos and images to remain on a page or float with the surrounding text. You can also layer images, rotate them, and more.

Refer to the following tasks for the details to accomplish each of these design activities.

Shorthand

Because photos are the most likely types of images you add to Pages documents, all the examples you see in this chapter use photos. Up to now, I've referred to photos and images just to make it clear that you can use the same information to add images, such as drawings, to Pages documents, too. From now to the end of the chapter, I'll be referring only to photos, but most of the rest of the information in this chapter applies to other kinds of images as well.

Resize Photos in Pages Documents

You can easily resize images in documents as follows:

1. Select the image you want to resize.

2. Drag a selection handle located on the photo's corners to make the photo larger or smaller. As you drag, a line appears across the diagonal of the image, and its current dimensions appear next to the selection handle you grabbed.

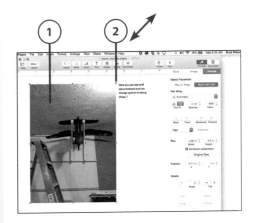

Resizing Other Kinds of Graphics

Pages assumes you want to maintain the proportion of photos you add to documents. This is not true for other kinds of graphics you may use. To ensure you maintain the proportions of any graphic, hold down the Shift key and drag a corner of the image. Its proportions are maintained as you resize it. If you don't hold down the Shift key, the proportions may not be maintained depending on the type of graphic you are working with.

3. When the photo is the size you want it to be, release the selection handle.

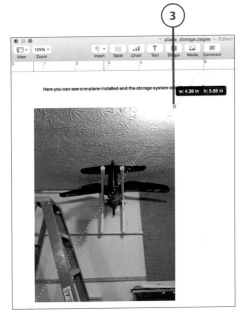

Be Precise

For more precision in resizing images, select the image you want to resize and click the Arrange tab in the Inspector. Use the Size tools to resize the image. You can enter or choose the Width and Height dimensions. Check the Constrain proportions check box to keep the image at its current proportion when you change dimensions. Click Original Size to return the image to the size it was when you placed it into the document.

Rotate Photos in Pages Documents

You can change the orientation of images or photos in your documents by performing the following steps:

1. Select the image you want to rotate.

2. Click the Arrange tab of the Inspector.

3. In the Angle box, enter the angle with which you want to rotate the image; for example, to rotate it clockwise by 90 degrees, enter -90.

4. Press Enter. The image is rotated by the amount you input.

5. To rotate a photo, drag the Rotate wheel clockwise or counterclockwise. As you drag, the image rotates, and you see the current angle in the Angle box.

6. To flip an image horizontally, click the horizontal arrow.

7. To flip an image vertically, click the vertical arrow.

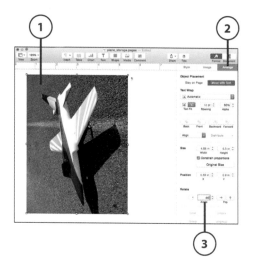

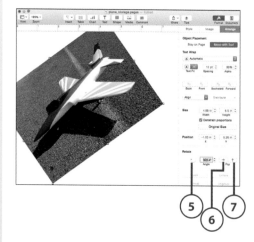

Style Photos in Pages Documents

Use the style tools to add visual interest to photos and other images in Pages documents.

1. Select the image you want to style.

2. Click the Style tab in the Inspector.

3. Click the left- or right-facing arrows to browse the available styles.

4. Click a style you want to apply to the photo. The photo is restyled accordingly. If you are happy with the photo, you can skip the rest of these steps.

5. To manually apply a border, click the disclosure triangle next to Border.

6. Choose the type of border you want to apply. The options are Line, Picture Frame, and No Border.

7. Configure the options for the type you selected; when you choose Picture Frame, click the frame menu.

8. Click the style of frame you want to apply.

9. Drag the Scale slider to the left to reduce the thickness of the border or to the right to increase it; or use the scale box to enter or choose a scale.

10. To apply a shadow to the image, click the disclosure triangle next to Shadow.

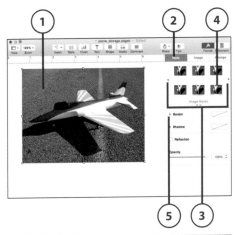

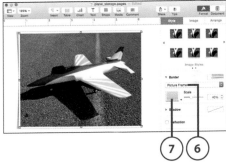

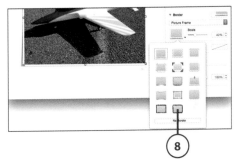

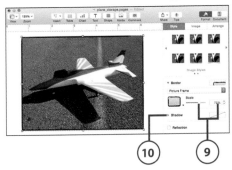

11. On the Shadow menu, choose the type of shadow you want to apply. The options are None, Drop Shadow, Contact Shadow, and Curved Shadow. These steps show the Curved Shadow option, but using the others is similar.

12. Drag the Inward slider to the left or right to determine if the shadow curves toward the image or away from it and what the amount of curvature should be.

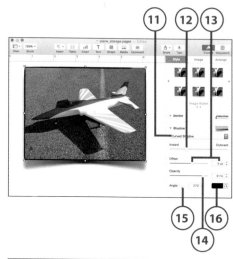

13. Use the Offset slider or box to change the size of the shadow relative to the bottom (using a positive offset) or the top of the photo (using a negative offset).

14. Use the Opacity slider or box to make the shadow more opaque or more transparent.

15. Use the Angle wheel or box to change the angle of the shadow.

16. Use the Color tool to change the shadow's color.

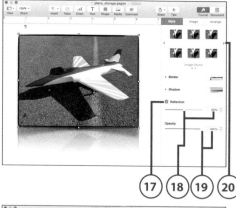

17. To apply a reflection to the image, check the Reflection check box.

18. Use the Reflection slider or box to set the amount of reflection.

19. Use the Opacity slider or box to make the photo more opaque or more transparent.

20. If you want to be able to reuse the styles you have applied, click the right-facing arrow at the top of the Style tab until you see an empty style with the add (+) icon.

21. Click the empty style to save your current style settings.

22. To apply your custom style, select the image to which you want to apply it, and click the style you saved.

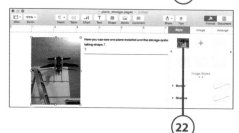

Delete Custom Styles

To delete styles you've saved, perform a secondary click on them and choose Delete Style. The saved style is removed.

Mask Photos in Pages Documents

To hide parts of photos you don't want to appear in a document, you can mask them.

1. Select the image you want to mask.

2. Click the Image tab of the Inspector.

3. Click Edit Mask. The mask tool appears.

4. Drag the slider to the left to increase, or to the right to decrease, the size of the photo within the frame. The parts of the image that won't be displayed are grayed out.

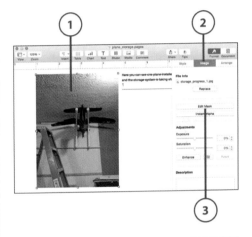

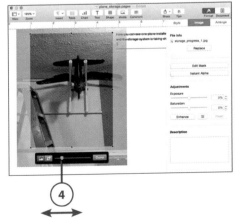

5. Drag the selection handles on the mask box to change the proportions of the box.

6. Drag the image around inside the box to change the part of the image that is displayed.

7. When you're done making changes, click Done. The photo is masked.

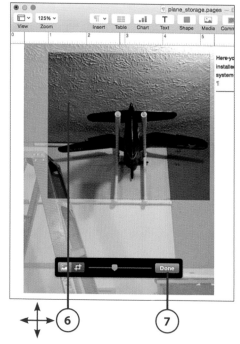

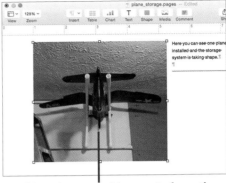

Masking photos enables you to focus them to show the important parts

Remove Background from Photos in Pages Documents

To remove background elements, or any color for that matter, from photos, use the Instant Alpha tool.

1. Select the photo you want to change.

2. Click the Image tab.

3. Click Instant Alpha.

4. Drag over areas of color that you want to remove from the photo. As colors are selected, the corresponding parts of the photo that will be hidden are highlighted in blue. (To remove a single color, just click on it instead of dragging around.)

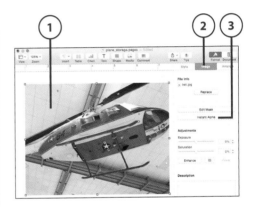

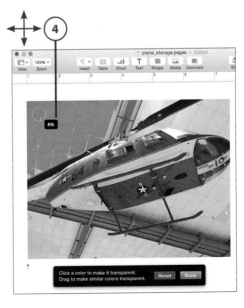

5. Continue selecting colors to remove.

6. When the image appears as you want it to be in the document, click Done.

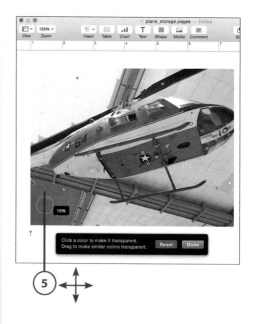

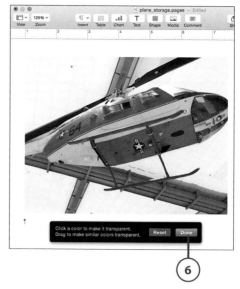

Adjust Photos in Pages Documents

Although Pages isn't a photo editing app, you can do some basic photo editing as follows:

1. Select the photo you want to adjust.

2. Click the Image tab.

3. Click Enhance to have Pages adjust the photo for you. If you like the results, you're done. If not, continue to make manual adjustments.

4. Use the Exposure slider and box to change the photo's exposure.

5. Use the Saturation slider and box to change the saturation of the colors in the photo.

6. For even more options, click the Adjust Image button. The Adjust Image palette appears.

7. Use the tools on the Adjust Image palette to make more adjustments to the image.

8. Close the palette when you're done adjusting the image.

I Take It Back!

Most of the photo tools in Pages offer a reset option that you can use to undo whatever changes you have made. For example, if you end up not liking a photo better after you have adjusted it, click Reset.

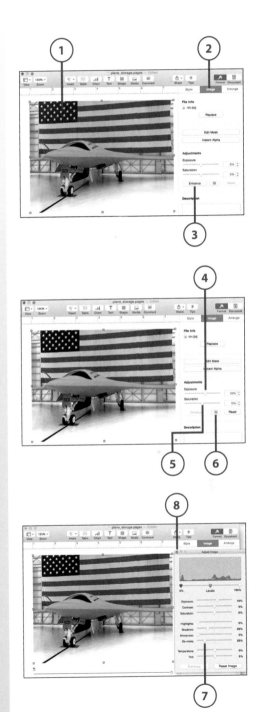

Position Photos Manually in Pages Documents

You can easily change the position of photos and other images in your Pages documents by dragging them.

1. Select the photo you want to move.

2. Drag the photo around the document. As you move it, its current location appears in the black pop-up box. Yellow alignment lines appear to show when the photo is lined up with something. For example, when you see a yellow line down the center of the photo, that means its centerline is aligned with the centerline of the document. Alignment lines can appear on each side or the top or bottom, too. Text around the photo flows according to its arrange settings (covered in the next task).

3. When the photo is where you want it, release it.

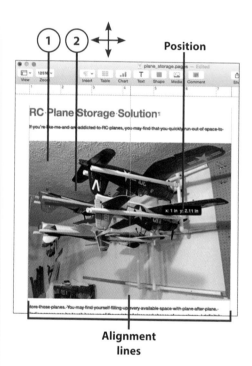

Distribute Graphics

When you have multiple graphics, you can distribute them evenly across the page. Just select the graphics you want to distribute. On the Arrange tab of the Inspector, open the Distribute menu and choose how you want the images distributed. For example, choose Horizontally to have the graphics distributed evenly across the width of the page.

Position Photos Using the Arrange Tab in Pages Documents

Configuring a photo's Arrange settings, determine how it interacts with the text and other objects on the page on which it appears.

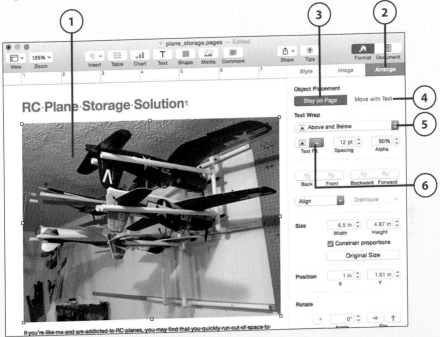

1. Select the photo you want to configure.

2. Click the Arrange tab.

3. If you want the photo to remain on the current page when text is added above it, click Stay on Page.

4. If you want the photo to float so that it remains in the context of the text around it when you add text or other content before it, click Move with Text.

5. On the Text Wrap menu, choose how you want the photo to interact with the text around it. Choose Automatic to have Pages flow the text automatically. Choose Around to have the text flow around the top, bottom, and sides of the image. Or choose Above and Below to have text flow along the top and bottom of the image but not along its sides.

6. Use the Text Fit buttons to determine how closely text follows the borders of the image. Click the button on the left to have the text conform to the rectangular boundary of the image. Click the button on the right to have the text flow to the shape of the image. This setting is most useful for shapes and other graphics that aren't rectangular.

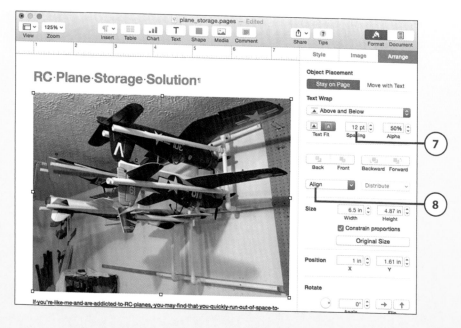

7. Use the Spacing box to set the amount of space between the photo and the surrounding text.

8. Use the Align menu to align the photo left to right or top to bottom.

Lock It

To prevent a photo's position from changing, you can lock it. Select the photo, click the Arrange tab, and click Lock.

>>>*Go Further*

LAYER GRAPHICS

You can layer photos or other graphics on top of each other. For example, you might want to include a smaller photo on top of a larger one, with the smaller one showing a close-up detail that is important. To do this layering, place the first graphic in your document. Then place the second one. Drag the second one on top of the first one. You can repeat this as many times as you'd like. To change the order of the stack, use the Back, Front, Backward, and Forward buttons on the Inspector.

Finish your Pages documents by adding elements such as a table of contents

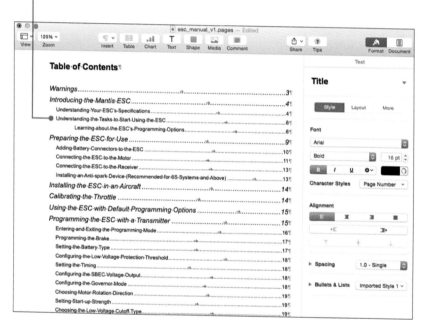

Table of Contents¶

In this chapter, you learn how to complete your Pages documents by adding a table of contents, checking the spelling, and polishing up its design. Topics include the following:

→ Work with the Table of Contents in a Pages Document
→ Work with Headers and Footers in a Pages Document
→ Complete a Pages Document

Finishing Pages Documents

In the previous chapters, you learned how to add different types of content to your Pages documents, including text, tables, and graphics. You also learned how to format that content. In this chapter, you learn how to finish your documents by adding a table of contents, headers, and footers. You also learn how to include cross-references so you can refer readers to specific information within the document. In addition, you learn how to use the spell checking tools in Pages and how to find and replace content. This chapter ends with some additional document design tasks, such as working with margins, page breaks, sections, and your document's final design. When you've completed the tasks in this chapter, your document should be ready for others to review.

Work with the Table of Contents in a Pages Document

A table of contents provides readers with a guide to the content in a document. Not all documents require a table of contents; for example, letters don't include a table of contents, and neither do brochures, resumes, and other short, fairly simple documents. You should include a table of contents when a document has multiple sections that are separated by headings. A table of contents includes a listing of the sections in a document; most of the time, a table of contents also includes page numbers so readers can quickly move to sections of interest. In some cases, you might want to leave out page numbers, in which case the table of contents is an outline of the document.

Adding a table of contents to a document involves two tasks.

First, insert the table of contents into the document. When you do this, you choose the entries for the table of contents by selecting the section headings in the document based on their styles. For example, if a document has a style called Heading 1 that you apply to first-level headings, you can include text formatted in the Heading 1 style in the table of contents. You can also include Heading 2 text and any other elements that you want to appear in the table of contents. (The elements with styles that you don't select won't appear in the table of contents.) This enables you to take the table of contents down to as "low" a level in the document as you want the reader to be able to quickly locate.

Second, format the table of contents. After you have inserted a table of contents, you can format its text to design the way it looks.

You don't need to manually update the table of contents in Pages. Whenever you add new text and style it using a style that is included in the table of contents, a reference to that text is added to the table of contents automatically. For example, suppose you have included text styled with the Heading 2 style in the table of contents. If you add a new paragraph styled with Heading 2, a reference to that new text is added to the table of contents automatically.

You can change a table of contents by defining the styles it contains, adding or removing page numbers, and reformatting it.

Insert a Table of Contents in a Pages Document

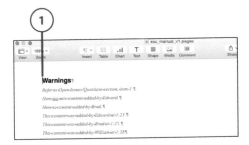

To add a table of contents to a document, perform the following steps:

1. Place the cursor where you want the table of contents to start. Typically, this is between a cover page and other front matter and the start of the document's content in the first section.

2. Add a title for the table of contents.

3. Format the title you added. You should use a style for the title that isn't used for any text you want to include in the table of contents. You usually don't want to include the table of contents itself in the table of contents, so its title needs to have a style you can exclude.

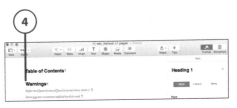

4. Place the cursor to where you want the table of contents to start, which should be on the next line after the title you created in step 2.

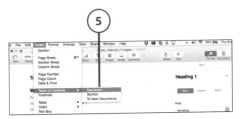

5. Choose Insert, Table of Contents, Document. Pages starts to build the table of contents and presents the Table of Contents pane in the Sidebar.

It's Not All Good

If you forget to add a title to the table of contents (as shown in step 2) before you generate it, it can be difficult to add one later because an automatic page break addition prevents you from inserting anything right before the table of contents. To add a title after the table of contents has been generated, delete the current table of contents and generate a new one.

6. Check the check box for the styles you want to be included in the table of contents. For example, if you check the check box for the Heading 1 style, any text using that style appears in the table of contents.

7. Uncheck the check box for any styles you don't want to be included in the table of contents. For example, you usually don't want to include body text in the table of contents. You're ready to format the table of contents.

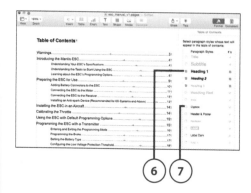

>>>Go Further

ADVANCED TABLE OF CONTENTS

The previous task shows you how easy it is to create a basic table of contents. Following are a couple more pointers to help you get even more out of your table of contents:

- When you insert a table of contents, you see there are three options. Document creates a table of contents for the entire document. Section creates a table of contents for the current section. (You learn about using sections in "Add and Format Sections in a Pages Document" later in this chapter.) To Next Occurrence creates a table of contents between where the cursor is now and the next table of contents in the document.

  The Section option is useful when a document includes multiple sections that are long and you want the reader to have a "mini" table of contents for each section. It can also be useful if the sections in your document are somewhat independent.

  You can change the portion of the document to which an existing table of contents applies using the Range menu at the bottom of the Table of Contents tab. It has the same three options (except Document is called Entire Document) as when you create a table of contents.

- You can insert multiple table of contents into the same document. This is useful when you want to create lists of different objects in a document. For example, you might want to have a list of tables or figures in a document along with its table of contents. You can create such a list by generating a table of contents and including only the style associated with table titles or figure captions.

Format a Table of Contents in a Pages Document

When you add a table of contents, Pages applies default formatting to it. You can reformat a table of contents as follows:

1. Click an element (or level) in the table of contents that you want to format. All the entries associated with that style are selected automatically.

2. Click the Text tab.

3. Use the text formatting tools to change the format of the elements you selected in step 1. (These tools were covered in Chapter 2, "Working with Text in Pages Documents.")

4. Select the next level in the outline.

5. Format that level's text.

6. Repeat steps 4 and 5 until you've formatted all the levels in the table of contents.

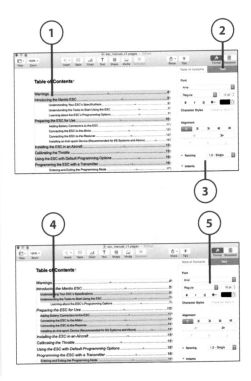

It's Not All Good

Unfortunately, Pages doesn't enable you to use styles to format the text in a table of contents. You must select and then manually format the text in your table of contents, which takes more time than using styles. At least when you click a level in a table of contents, everything at that level is selected, which is sort of like using styles. Still, it would be better if you could apply styles to the various levels in a table of contents to format it; hopefully, this will be added in a future version of Pages.

Page Numbers Are More Than They Appear to Be

Page numbers in a table of contents are actually links. When you move the cursor over a page number, you see the cursor change to the hand icon. When you click the icon, you jump to the location of that entry in the document. This is especially useful when you distribute documents in electronic format, such as PDF, because readers can simply click on the sections that they want to read.

Change a Table of Contents in a Pages Document

You can change the existing table of contents as follows:

1. Click in the table of contents you want to change.

2. Click the Table of Contents tab.

3. Uncheck the check boxes for any styles you want to remove from the table of contents. Headings in those styles are removed from the table of contents.

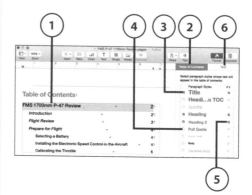

Grayed-Out Styles

When a style on the Table of Contents tab is grayed out, that means that even though the style exists in the document, it is not currently applied to any text and can't be included in the table of contents.

4. Check the check boxes for any styles you want to add to the table of contents. Headings in those styles are added to the table of contents.

5. Uncheck the #s check box to remove the page numbers for a style. The page numbers for those styles are hidden.

6. Click the Text tab and use the steps in "Format a Table of Contents in a Pages Document" to change the text formatting.

Delete a Table of Contents

To delete a table of contents from a document, click it so it becomes selected. Then press the Delete key. The table of contents is deleted. However, the page break that Pages automatically inserted before the table of contents isn't deleted, leaving an empty page in the document. To remove that page break, select it and press Delete. (You learn more about working with page breaks later in this chapter.)

Work with Headers and Footers in a Pages Document

Headers and footers appear on each page of the document. Typically, they include content such as the document name, page number, date, and other information to help the reader identify the document. You can also include graphics in headers and footers, such as a company logo.

Headers and footers usually appear on each page of the document, but in many cases, you want to hide the header and footer on the first page of the document. (A common example of this is when using a cover page.)

You can also use different headers and footers in various sections of the document. For example, if you are using numbered sections, you might want to include the section number in the page number, such as Page 1-2. To do this, you create a section in Pages for each section of the document and then configure the header and footer for each section. Sections are explained in "Add and Format Sections in a Pages Document" later in this chapter.

Pages provides three boxes (left, center, and right) at the top of the page for your header content and three at the bottom (also left, center, and right) of the page for the footer content. If you leave these boxes empty, nothing appears in those spaces in the document. Whatever content you place in the boxes appears in the appropriate locations on the page. As content expands beyond the original size of the boxes, the boxes expand to accommodate the content; other boxes shrink accordingly.

It's Not All Good

It's fairly common to use a line to separate headers and footers from the content of documents. Unfortunately, Pages currently doesn't provide an easy way to do this. The task "Add a Border to Headers and Footers in a Pages Document" later in this chapter shows you a workaround, which isn't ideal, but it works. Hopefully, an easier fix will be added to a future version of Pages.

Invisibles and Layout

Pages uses the term Invisibles and Layout for markers on the page that indicate boundaries, paragraph breaks, and other elements of a document. You can show the Invisibles and Layout, as you learn in "Configure View Options for a Pages Document," later in this chapter. It's a good idea to jump ahead to that section and show both of these before creating headers and footers. It is much easier to work with headers and footers when Invisibles and Layout are shown as they are in the figures in this task.

Add Headers and Footers in a Pages Document

To add headers and footers to a Pages document, perform the following steps:

1. Click in the box on the top left of the page. If you haven't added a page number yet, you see the Insert Page Number prompt. Ignore this for now because the page number typically appears on the right side of the page.

2. Type what you want to appear on the left side of header. This can be any text you want, such as the document or section title.

3. Use the text formatting tools to format the text in the header. Pages provides a standard Header & Footer style you can use, or you can manually apply formatting just like text in other areas of a document.

Header boxes

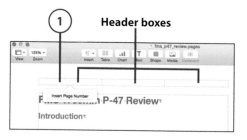

4. Click in the next section of the header where you want to place content.

5. Click the Insert button on the toolbar.

6. Click what you want to insert, such as Date & Time.

7. Click on the date and time you inserted.

8. Click the format for the date and time you want to use.

9. To set the date and time to the current date and time, click Set to Today; then skip to step 13.

10. To set a specific date and time, click the Calendar button.

11. Use the calendar, calendar box, and time box to configure the date and time you want to associate with the document.

12. To update all dates and times in the document with what you are configuring, click Update All.

13. Move up the page so you can see the footer boxes.

14. Click in the first footer box.

15. Choose Insert, Choose.

Adding Shapes

You can add shapes to headers and footers by placing your cursor in the box where you want to place a shape and clicking the Shape tool on the toolbar.

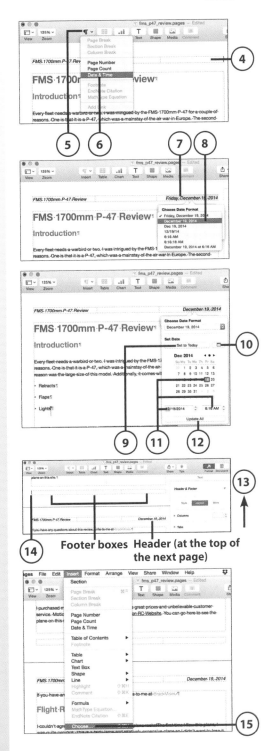

Footer boxes   Header (at the top of the next page)

16. Move to and select the file you want to insert.

17. Click Insert. The file is placed at the current location in the Pages document.

18. Use Pages tools to resize and format the graphic. (See Chapter 4, "Working with Photos, Graphics, and Other Objects in Pages Documents.")

19. Click in the next footer field where you want to place content.

20. Click Insert Page Number.

21. Click the page number format you want to use.

22. Format the headers and footers until they look the way you want them to.

23. Click Document.

24. Click Section.

25. To hide the headers and footers on the first page, check the Hide on first page of section check box.

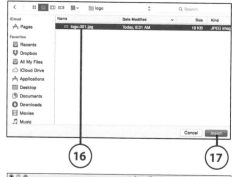

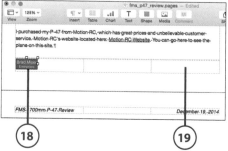

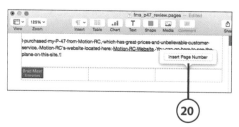

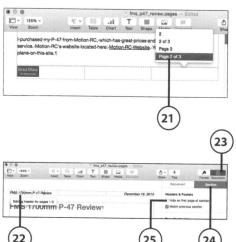

Add a Border to Headers and Footers in a Pages Document

Adding a border to headers and footers is harder than it should be, but the following steps get it done:

1. Click the header box on the left. When you click in a header or footer box that has content, you see a pop-up message that indicates you are editing that header or footer box.

2. Click the Format button on the toolbar.

3. Click the Layout tab.

4. Click the disclosure triangle for Borders & Rules.

5. Choose the style of the line you want to use for the border, such as a solid line or a dotted line.

6. Use the Color tool to pick the border's color.

7. Use the weight box to enter or choose the thickness of the line.

8. Click the position for the border; on the header, you might want to place the border at the bottom so it is between the header and body while placing it on top in the footer.

9. Use the Offset box to enter or choose the separation between the border and the header. You see the border line in the header, but it is only as long as the text in the border box.

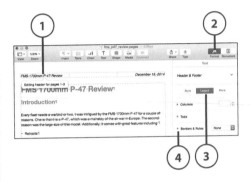

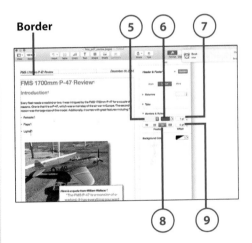

Border

10. Place the cursor at the end of the text in the header box.

11. Press the Space key until the border stretches across the header. The markers indicating spaces appear to cover content in the other boxes, but they don't impact the content in the other boxes. You can add content to or edit the content in those boxes regardless of the spaces generated in one of the other boxes.

12. Move the left box in the footer.

13. Use steps 5 through 9 to configure the border you want for the footer.

14. Enter spaces after the content currently in the left box until the border stretches across the page.

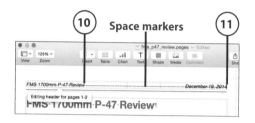

Space markers

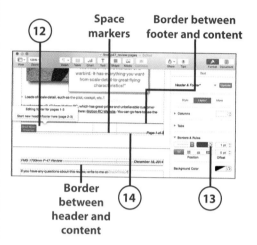

Space markers

Border between footer and content

Border between header and content

>>>Go Further
FOOTNOTES AND ENDNOTES

Footnotes and endnotes are useful to provide additional information or cite references. Footnotes appear in the footer of the page on which they are inserted, whereas endnotes appear at the end of a document or the end of a section. Place the cursor where you want to insert a footnote. Click the Insert button (which is located to the left of the Table button on the toolbar) and choose Footnote. (You have to insert a footnote the first time you do this.) The footnote section appears at the bottom of the page. Enter the footnote's text. If you want to use endnotes rather than footnotes, click in a footnote. Click the Footnotes tab in the Inspector. On the Type menu, choose Document Endnotes or Section Endnotes. (Note that you can only use one type of these notes in the same document.) You can use the other tools on the Footnotes tab to set the number formatting, determine whether numbering is continuous, and so on. You can style the text in footnotes or endnotes as you can other text.

Complete a Pages Document

When your document's content is largely complete, it's time to finish it up by doing some or all of the following tasks:

- **Configure view options.** View options in Pages make the document easier to format and edit. You saw one example of these in the previous tasks. The view options include Layout, which shows borders around various elements on a page; Invisibles, which are markers for paragraph breaks, spaces, and other objects you don't see in a final document but that do impact its appearance; Guides, which show alignment lines as you move objects around a page; and Zoom, which controls the level of magnification at which you are viewing a page.

- **Check spelling.** Pages uses OS X spell-checking tools so you can correct spelling as you go or all at once.

- **Find and replace content.** Performing a find and replace makes it easy to make changes consistently in documents.

- **Set dimensions.** You can configure the dimensions of pages, headers, footers, and so on.

- **Add page breaks.** You can manually force where pages stop and start. For example, you might want to have a page break before the major heading sections in a document.

- **Use sections.** Sections can be used to break a document into different parts. You can then configure each part, such as using different headers and footers, using distinct page numbers, and so on. If your document has chapters or major subsections, you might want to place each in its own section so that you can use distinct headers, footers, and page numbers to designate those major subsections.

- **Update a document's design.** You can use the tools you've learned about in previous chapters to design each page of your document by resizing objects, moving them, changing the relationship between body text and figures, updating text styles, and much more.

For organizational purposes, I've listed these tasks separately after a document's content is done; however, you'll probably do some of these as you work with a document's content. For example, it can be useful to show invisibles while you are entering content, correct the spelling as you go, and so on.

Configure View Options for a Pages Document

Pages offers a number of view options you may find useful:

1. Choose Pages, Preferences.

2. Click Rulers.

3. To change the color of the alignment guides that appear when you are moving objects, such as pictures, on a page, click the Color button next to Alignment Guides and choose the color you want to use.

4. To show the center guide, check the Show guides at object center check box.

5. To show the edge guides, check the Show guides at object edges check box.

6. Close the Preferences dialog.

7. Open the View menu and choose Show Layout. The layout lines appear.

8. Open the View menu and choose Show Invisibles. The invisible markers appear.

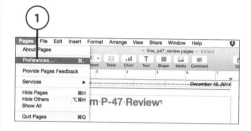

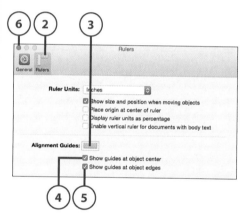

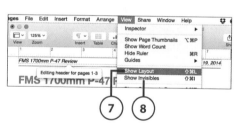

Mysteriously Disappearing Borders

At the time I wrote this, when the Invisibles view setting was changed, parts of the border on headers or footers created using the work-around in the earlier task disap-peared. To restore them, simply click in the associated header or footer.

9. To change the level of zoom you are using, open the Zoom button on the toolbar and choose a percentage to increase or decrease the level of zoom to that percentage, Fit Width to set the zoom so that the width of the page you are viewing matches the width of the Pages window, or Fit Page to set the zoom level so that you can see the entire page in the Pages window.

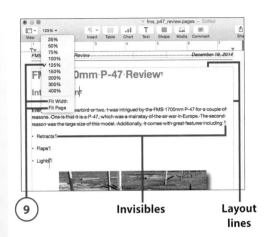

Invisibles   **Layout lines**

Correct Spelling in a Pages Document

You can configure how Pages checks the spelling in a document to easily correct spelling as you type or at any other time.

1. Choose Edit, Spelling and Grammar.

2. Set Check Spelling While Typing to on (so it is marked with a check mark) to have Pages highlight misspelled words as you type so that you can correct spelling as you go.

3. Set Check Grammar With Spelling to on (marked with a check mark) if you want Pages to check grammar when it checks spelling.

4. Set Correct Spelling Automatically to have Pages automatically change the spelling of words it thinks are incorrect.

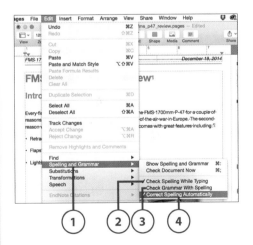

5. To open the Spelling and Grammar tool, choose Show Spelling and Grammar. The Spelling and Grammar tool opens, and you can use it to correct spelling. The rest of these steps are with this closed as many people find it more efficient to check spelling as they type.

6. To manually check spelling (and grammar if you enabled that option), select Check Document Now. You return to the document, and the first potential misspelled word is highlighted.

7. Perform a secondary click on any words with a red underline, which indicates that Pages thinks the word is misspelled. The Spelling menu appears.

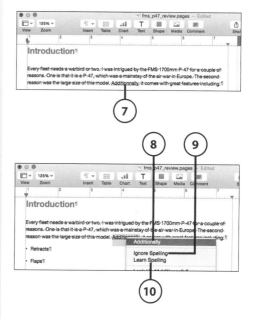

8. If one of the suggested words is the correct spelling, click it to replace the misspelled word.

9. To ignore the word's spelling, click Ignore Spelling.

10. To add the word to the dictionary so it isn't flagged as a misspelled word anymore, click Learn Spelling.

Find and Replace Content in a Pages Document

The Find and Replace tool is useful for replacing words or phrases throughout a document.

1. Click the View button on the toolbar and choose Show Find & Replace.

2. Click the Gear button and choose Find & Replace.

3. Enter the term you want to find. Pages highlights the term throughout the document. The selected occurrence is highlighted in yellow.

4. Enter the term you want to replace the term with. You can replace the entire term, add to it, and so on.

5. Click Replace All to replace all occurrences of the term; if you do this, skip to step 10.

6. Click Replace & Find to replace the currently selected instance (the one in yellow) and move to the next occurrence. (You see other occurrences of the search term in gray boxes.)

7. Click Replace to replace the current instance but not move to the next one.

8. Click the left and right arrows to move back to the previous or next, respectively, instance of the term without taking any action on the current one.

9. Repeat steps 6 through 8 until you've replaced all the occurrences of the term that you want to replace.

10. Close the Find & Replace tool.

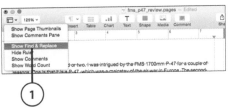

Current search term   Other search term found

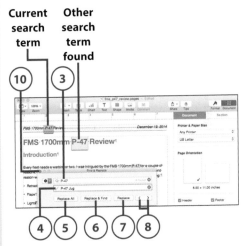

Set Size, Orientation, and Margins for a Pages Document

To configure size parameters for a document, do the following:

1. Click the Document button on the toolbar to open the Document Inspector.

2. Click the Document tab.

3. Use the controls on the Printer & Paper Size menus to select the settings you want to use when you print the document.

4. Click the Portrait Orientation button to orient the document in the portrait format or the Landscape Orientation button to change it to that orientation.

5. To use a header, check the Header check box.

6. If you enable the header, use the Size box to set its size. You may need to make it larger to display more content or smaller if you are displaying less.

7. Do the same for the footer.

8. Use the Document Margins size boxes to set the size of the margins at the top, right, bottom, and left sides of the document.

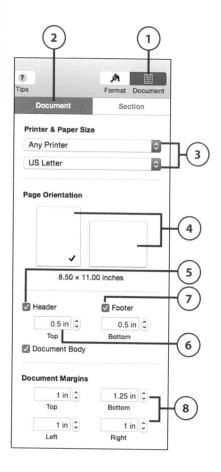

Add Page Breaks to a Pages Document

It can be useful to force pages to end at specific places, such as at the end of a major section of content.

1. Place the cursor where you want the current page to end.

2. Click the Insert button on the toolbar and choose Page Break. The page break is created, which you see if Invisibles are displayed.

3. To remove a page break, select it and press the Delete key.

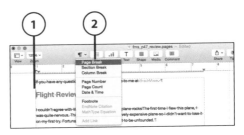

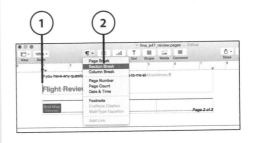

Page break

Add and Format Sections in a Pages Document

Sections are useful to break a document into major segments, based on the type of content or using different elements, such as page numbers. When you create a document, it has only one section. You can add sections and update section formats using the following steps:

1. Place the cursor where you want a new section to start.

2. Click the Insert button on the toolbar and choose Section Break. The page break is created, which you see if Invisibles are displayed. A new section is created; if Invisibles are displayed, you see the new section marker on the screen right before the location you selected in step 1.

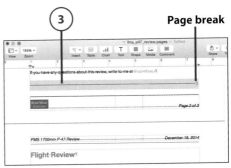

3. Click the Document button on the toolbar.

4. Click the Section button. You see the Section Inspector.

5. If you want to hide the header and footer on the first page of the section, check the Hide on first page of section check box. (You can use this to hide the header and footer even if the document has only one section.)

6. If you want to use the same header and footer as the previous section does, check the Match previous section check box and skip to step 8; if you want to create a unique header or footer for the section, uncheck the Match previous section check box.

7. Edit the header and footer for the section as needed.

8. Choose the format for page numbers in the section. (Use this to set the page number for the entire document if there is only one section.)

9. To continue the page numbers from the previous section, click the Continue from previous section radio button; to start page numbers with a different number, such as 1, click the Start at radio button and enter the starting number in the box.

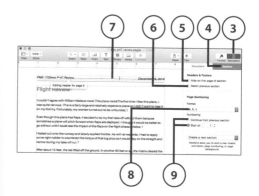

Palettes

As you've seen, many of the tools you use while designing documents are available in the Inspector. You can also have some of these on separate palettes. This is useful because you can have multiple palettes open at the same time so that you don't spend so much time navigating around the Inspector. To open these palettes, use the View menu to choose Show Arrange tools, Show Colors, or Show Adjust Colors. Each toolset you choose appears as an independent palette.

>>>Go Further

DESIGNING DOCUMENTS

A major part of finishing documents is doing the final design. For example, you can move or resize figures, redefine text styles, add page breaks, and many other tweaks to make the final document just right. You use the Inspector to perform many of these tasks, as you learned in previous chapters. For others, such as resizing or moving objects, you can simply drag the object to move it or use its Resize handles to change its size. Remember that the settings on the Arrange tab of the Inspector control many aspects of how objects are arranged on the page, such as how they interact with surrounding text. It's good practice to get all the content into a document and do a rough design without fussing over details too much. Once the document is complete from the content perspective, you can then tweak the design based on its final content. Content and design definitely impact each other, so it's somewhat of a balancing act to get a document "just right." This can also be quite an enjoyable process as you apply your creativity to create your own "brand" of documents.

Use the Pages collaboration features, such as change tracking, to work with others on your documents

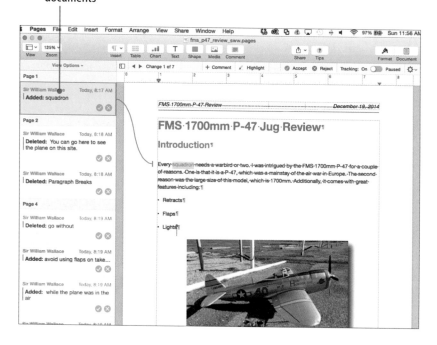

In this chapter, you learn how to collaborate with others on Pages documents. Topics include the following:

→ Work with Comments in Pages Documents
→ Work with Track Changes in Pages Documents
→ Collaborate on Pages Documents Via iCloud Sharing

Collaborating with Others on Pages Documents

Developing Pages documents is sometimes a group effort. Most of the time a group effort involves a primary author (or authors) with other people participating as reviewers. The authors are responsible for developing the content and design of the document while the reviewers provide feedback. Ideally, reviewers are similar to the people for whom a document is intended, so their feedback helps you better craft a document for your target audience.

Pages provides three types of tools that facilitate collaboration:

- **Comments.** Comments are feedback that reviewers provide without making changes to a document's content. Comments might point out mistakes, suggest improvements in or reorganization of existing content, point you to related sources of information, or even recommend new content to be included.

- **Changes.** Sometimes reviewers make changes directly in a document in addition to commenting about it. You can review these changes and decide to accept or reject them. Changes you accept become part of the document, and changes you reject are removed.

- **Real-time iCloud collaboration.** You can share Pages documents with others via iCloud so that you can work on them together in real time in true collaboration as opposed to sending documents to reviewers, having them review the documents on their own, and then returning the documents to you.

Work with Comments in Pages Documents

The comment tools in Pages track who makes comments and enable you to read and then delete (presumably after you've made any corresponding changes in the document) them. Hopefully, the comments others make help you improve your documents.

Before making comments in Pages documents, you should ensure you are properly identified as an author so that any comments you make are automatically tagged with your name and associated color.

Set Author Name, Text Size, and Color for Comments in Pages Documents

To set up an author in Pages, perform the following steps:

1. Choose Pages, Preferences.

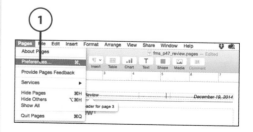

2. Click the General tab.

3. Enter your name in the Author box.

4. On the Text Size menu, select the size you want to use for comments and change tracking.

5. Close the Preferences window.

6. Choose View, Comments & Changes, Author Color, and then choose the color you want to use for your comments and changes.

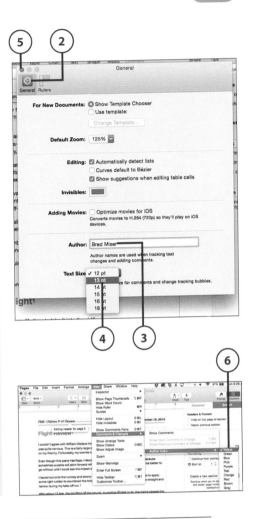

And Comments for All

You should ask anyone who makes comments in your documents to make sure he sets his name and color so you can easily identify who has made comments in your document. The same tools described in these tasks, such as viewing comments, work for comments you and others make in a document.

Add Comments to Pages Documents

To add comments to a Pages document, do the following:

1. Select the content about which you want to make a comment. You can select words, phrases, paragraphs, and more. This is important because selecting the appropriate content provides context for people who read your comments.

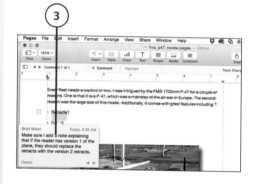

2. Click the Comment button on the toolbar. The Comments box appears.

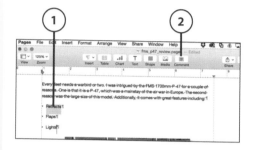

3. Type your comment. It is automatically tagged with your name, the color you selected, and the date and time.

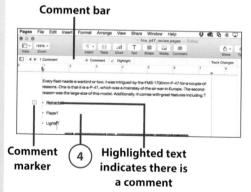

4. Click outside the Comments box to close it. The object associated with the comment is highlighted with your color, and the comment marker appears. (You can show or hide these as you see in the next task.) The Comment bar also appears at the top of the screen.

Comment bar

Comment marker

Highlighted text indicates there is a comment

Address Comments Individually That You or Others Make in Your Pages Documents

You can work with comments inline with your document as follows:

1. Open the document containing comments. You see highlights and comment markers where comments have been made.

2. Click the comment marker for the comment you want to read. The Comment box appears. At its top, you see the name of the person who made the comment along with the time and date when the comment was added. The color of the box is the author color for the person making the comment.

3. Read the comment.

4. To remove the comment, click Delete. The comment is deleted, and you can move to and select the next comment to read it.

5. To move to the next comment without deleting the current one, click the right-facing arrow.

6. Repeat steps 3 through 5 until you've addressed all the comments in the document.

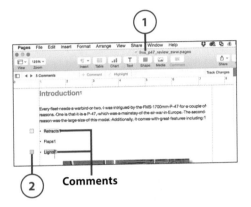

Comments

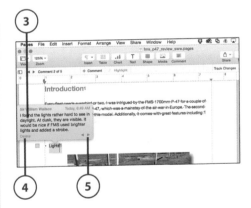

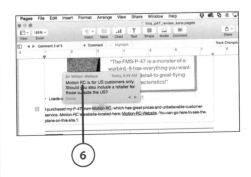

Use the Comments Pane to Address Comments in Pages Documents

The Comments pane is useful for reviewing multiple comments:

1. Choose View, Show Comments Pane. (If you see Hide Comments pane instead, the pane is already visible.)

2. Browse up and down the comments to review them.

3. Click a comment to view its location in the document. The document shifts so you can see where the comment is located, and a line connects the comment to the comment marker.

4. To delete a comment, point to it and click Delete.

5. Click View Options.

6. Choose Sort by Page to show comments sorted by the page on which they appear.

7. Choose Sort by Date to show comments sorted by the date and time on which they were made.

8. Choose Filter by Author and then select the author whose comments you want to see. Only those comments appear in the Comments pane.

9. Choose Hide Comments to hide comments and close the Comments pane. (Repeat step 1 to open it again.)

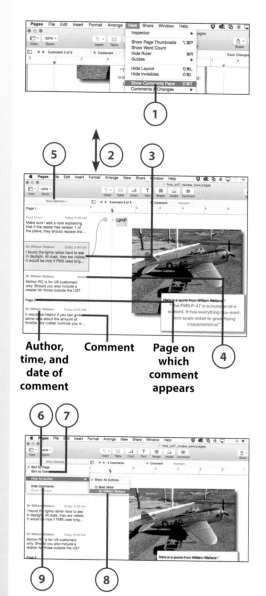

Author, time, and date of comment

Comment

Page on which comment appears

10. Click Show All to see all the comments in the Comments pane again.

11. Click the Show/Hide Comments pane button to hide the Comments pane.

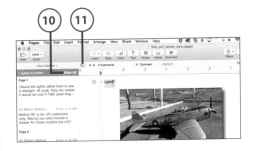

Use the Comments Bar, Luke

The Comments bar appears just below the toolbar when comments are shown. You can click the Show/Hide Comments pane button to open or close the Comments pane. Click the left- or right-facing arrows to move to the previous or next comment, respectively, in the document. You also see the number of comments next to these arrows. Select content in the document and click + Comment to add a comment. To show or hide comments and the Comments bar, choose View, Comments & Changes, Show/Hide Comments.

Work with Track Changes in Pages Documents

As you collaborate with others, they can make changes in your document. Pages can track these changes for you. It also provides tools you can use to review and accept or reject changes that others make. To get started, enable track changes in a document and then send it to the people who will be reviewing it. When it comes back to you, you can review and address the changes the reviewers made.

Enable Track Changes in Pages Documents

To enable changes to be tracked in a Pages document, do the following:

1. Choose Edit, Track Changes. Change tracking is turned on and the Comments bar appears, which now displays the track changes tools, too.

2. Save the document by pressing ⌘-S.

3. Send the document to the people who you want to review/edit it. (Sharing documents is covered in Chapter 17, "Publishing and Sharing Pages, Numbers, and Keynote Documents.")

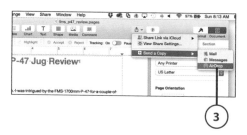

Being Edited Can Hurt... Sometimes It Hurts a Lot!

Through dozens of books and thousands of other types of writing projects, I've been involved in lots and lots of editing. I've worked with many different editors and reviewers in all sorts of roles. Sometimes receiving feedback on something you write is painful. A lesson I learned early on in my writing career is how to not take being edited personally—even though I'm quite attached to what I write. What I learned was that all the feedback you receive falls into one of two types. The first type is feedback that actually improves the document; as an author, this is the best case because ultimately it makes your work better. (It can still sting!) Because your work gets better as the result of other people's input, you win, so there's no reason to get bent out of joint. The second type is feedback that is not in line with what you are doing in the document, not aligned with your style, or is simply wrong. In this case, you can decline to make the suggested changes. There's really nothing lost to you in this case, so there's no need to take this type of editing personally either. I've been fortunate to have been edited by lots of really good editors and have learned everything I do is better with help from others!

Review and Respond Individually to Changes Made by Others in Pages Documents

When you receive a document with changes from others, you can review and accept or reject those changes:

1. Open the document that's been reviewed. You see the changes the reviewer made.

2. Click a change. The change box appears.

3. Read a description of the change, such as what was added or deleted.

4. To accept the change, click Accept. The change is saved into the document, the change tracking identification is removed, and the change box closes.

5. To reject the change, click Reject. The content is returned to what it was before the change was made, the change tracking identification is removed, and the change box closes.

6. To move to the next change without taking any action on the current one, click the right-facing arrow; to move to the prior change without any action on the current one, click the left-facing arrow.

7. Repeat steps 3 through 6 to address the next change. If you accept or reject a change, you need to manually move to and select the next change to review it.

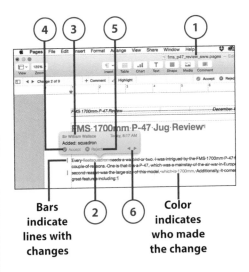

Bars indicate lines with changes

Color indicates who made the change

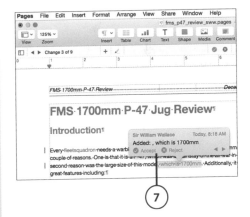

Use the Comments & Changes Pane and Bar to Address Changes in Pages Documents

The Comments & Changes pane and bar are more efficient tools to address changes in a document.

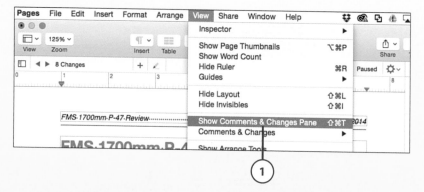

1. Choose View, Show Comments & Changes Pane. In the pane, you see each of the changes made in the document.

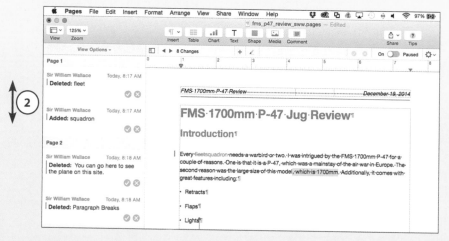

2. Browse the changes you see.

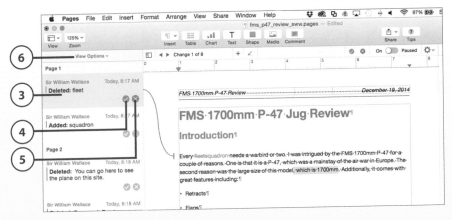

3. Hover over a change. It is highlighted, and a line points to the change in the document.

Can't See a Change on the Page?

If the change over which you are hovering isn't visible on the page, the line points off to the screen toward the top or bottom. Click the change to jump to its location in the document.

4. To accept the change, click the check mark. The change is included in the document, and the change tracking marks are removed.

5. To reject the change, click the x. The change is removed, and the change tracking marks are removed.

6. Click View Options.

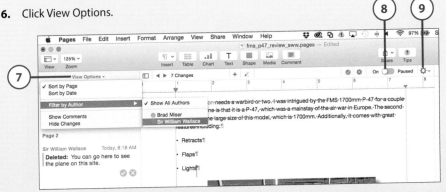

7. Use the options on the menu to configure how you are viewing changes; these work the same as they do for comments (see "Use the Comments Pane to Address Comments in Pages Documents").

8. To disable change tracking, move the switch to Paused (set it to On to resume change tracking).

9. Click the Gear icon.

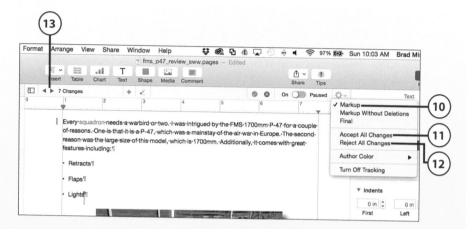

10. Choose the view you want to use. Markup shows all changes, Markup without Deletions shows only additions, and Final shows the document as it would be if you accepted all changes.

11. To accept all the changes in the document without reviewing them individually, choose Accept All Changes.

12. To reject all the changes without reviewing them individually, choose Reject All Changes.

13. To move to the next or previous change, respectively, click the right- or left-facing arrow.

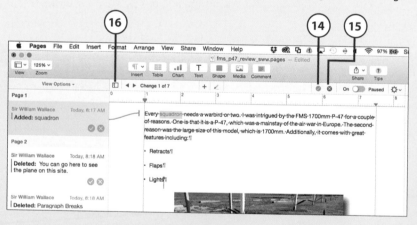

14. Click the check mark to accept the change.

15. Click the x to reject the change.

16. Click the Show/Hide button to close the Comments & Changes pane. (You can still use the bar to work with changes.)

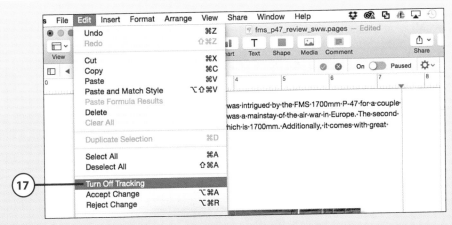

17. To turn off tracking, choose Edit, Turn Off Tracking. If there are changes you haven't accepted or rejected yet, you're prompted to accept or reject them all, which you must do before tracking can be turned off.

Create a New Version or Replace the Original?

When you send out a document for review, the document that is returned to you is a separate document from the original. You can either save it as a new version so you can retain the prior version, or you can replace the prior version with the reviewed one. Retaining the previous version is sometimes helpful if you want to refer back to it, but it also requires more work to manage multiple versions. Replacing the prior version with reviewed versions means you only have one version to deal with, but it also makes it harder to go back to prior versions if you need to.

Collaborate on Pages Documents via iCloud Sharing

Collaborating with comments and changes is useful, but it is a sequential process, meaning that the document moves from you to the reviewers, back to you, and so on until it is done. For true collaboration, you can share a document via iCloud and then work with others in real time.

You can use iCloud to collaborate with just about anyone because the people with whom you share don't have to have an iCloud account or the Pages app. All that is needed is the link to the document (which you send to them), a password (that you also provide), and a computer with a web browser and Internet connection.

First, share the document. Second, work with others on the document you have shared. Of course, you can stop sharing a document at any time.

Share a Pages Document via iCloud

To share a Pages document via iCloud, perform the following steps:

1. Open the Share menu and choose View Share Settings.

No Change Tracking for Shared Documents

Turn change tracking off before you share a document because you can't share it with change tracking enabled.

2. On the Permissions menu, choose Allow Editing if you want others to be able to change the document or View Only if you want them to be able to see, but not change, it.

3. Click Add Password.

4. Enter a password for the document in the Password and Verify boxes.

5. If you want to provide a password hint, enter it in the Password Hint box.

6. To have the password remembered in your keychain, check the check box.

7. Click Set Password.

8. Click Share Document.

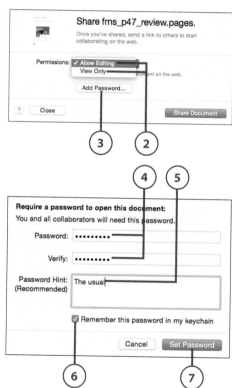

Sharing for the First, but Probably Not the Last, Time

The first time you share a document, you see a warning prompt explaining that you are about to share a document and that anyone can access it once shared—unless you've applied a password, in which case that password is needed to open it.

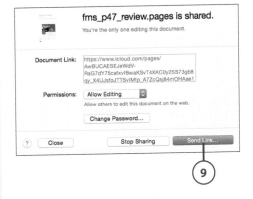

9. Click Send Link.

10. Choose how you want to share the link, such as via Mail.

11. Complete the sharing process using the method you selected in step 10. If you configured a password for the document, you need to provide that to the people with whom you are sharing it, but make sure you don't include it in the same information as the link in case that message gets intercepted along the way. (In other words, always communicate the link separate from the password.)

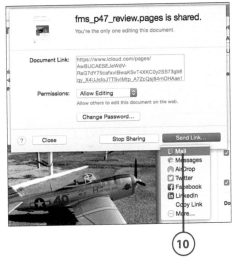

Start a Collaboration Session

To do online collaboration, you use the online version of Pages as follows:

1. Open a web browser and move to icloud.com.

2. Enter your Apple ID.

3. Enter your password.

4. Check the check box if you want to remain logged in.

5. Click the right-facing arrow. You move into your iCloud website.

6. Click Pages to move into the online Pages app.

7. Double-click the document you shared to open it.

8. Enter the document's password.

9. Click OK. The document opens.

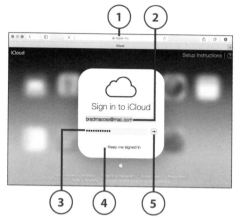

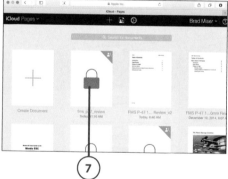

10. Collaborate after others open the same document. (See the next task.)

This document is shared

Use iCloud Sharing to Collaborate on Pages Documents

When the people with whom you've shared a document access the link you sent, they can open the document. It opens in a web browser (assuming they are able to provide the required password). To get started, let the people you want to collaborate know you are ready to get started. Open the shared document using the steps in the previous task, and wait until the others open it.

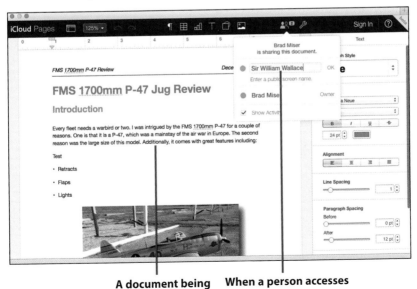

A document being shared via iCloud

When a person accesses a shared document, he provides a screen name

When someone uses the link you provide, he is prompted to provide the document's password. When he's done that correctly, he is prompted to provide a screen name, and he sees how many people are currently in the document.

Click to access sharing information

People currently sharing the document

Check to see activity as it happens

You can click the Sharing button to see who is currently sharing the document. When the Show Activity check box is checked, you see changes other people make in real time.

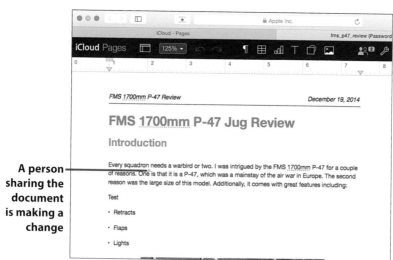

A person sharing the document is making a change

When someone else makes a change in the document, the change is marked with an upward-facing arrow. You see the changes as they are made.

It's Not All Good

Unfortunately, the location in the document that people are viewing isn't kept in sync. So if someone makes a change on a part of the document that you aren't currently viewing, you won't know it. It's a good idea to keep communicating with people as you collaborate to make sure you can see the changes other people are making.

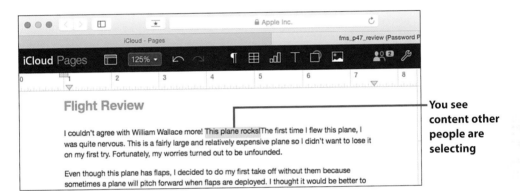

You see content other people are selecting

As people select content in the document, such as to delete it, you see it highlighted on the screen.

Because you are working live on the cloud, you don't need to worry about saving the changes because they are saved automatically.

When people are done collaborating, they can close their document windows. You see a notification when someone leaves the collaboration session.

When you're done with the document, close its window.

Be Stingy; It's Okay

To stop sharing, open the document and click the Share button on the toolbar. Then click View Settings, Stop Sharing. The document is no longer accessible to others via iCloud.

Create tables to
store, analyze, and
present information   Format cells   Format tables

Numbers   File   Edit   Insert   Table   Format   Arrange   View   Share   Window   Help

household_budget.numbers — Edited

View   Zoom   Formula   Table   Chart   Text   Shape   Media   Comment   Share   Tips   Format   Sort & Filter

Sheet 1   Table   Cell   Text   Arrange

	A	B	C	D	F
			Monthly Budget		
1	Category	Sub-category	Budgeted Amount	Actual Amount	Complete
8					
9	Fixed Expenses				
10		Mortgage	$2,000		
11		Taxes	$1,250		
12		Benefit Costs	$1,000		
13		401K Deduction			
14		Insurance	$560		
15	Total Fixed Expenses				
16					
17	Variable Expenses				
18		Food and Household	$1,200		
19		Utilities	$300		
20		Entertainment	$100		
21		Giving	$500		
22	Total Variable Expenses				
23					
24	Total Fixed and Variable Expenses				
25	Balance				

Table Styles

Headers & Footer

2   1   1

Table Name

Table Font Size   A   A

Table Outline

0.35 pt

Outline table name

Grid Lines

Alternating Row Color

▼ Row & Column Size

Row: 0.29 in   Fit

Column: 0.75 in   Fit

Category Calculations

In this chapter, you learn how to develop spreadsheets in the Numbers app. Topics include the following:

→ Create and Structure Tables in Numbers Spreadsheets

→ Enter and Format Data and Tables in Numbers Spreadsheets

Developing Numbers Spreadsheets

Numbers spreadsheets are really useful for any sort of numeric information you want to create, analyze, and report on. From basic household or project budgeting to complex business analysis, Numbers can help you make sense of the numbers you deal with. You can add all sorts of information to Numbers spreadsheets and then use the app's tools, such as formulas, to perform calculations using that information. You can also make your data more meaningful and visible using charts. Like the other iWork apps, Numbers offers lots of formatting tools you can use to make your spreadsheets look great. In this chapter, you learn how to set up a basic spreadsheet with data that you use in later chapters to perform calculations and to use other Numbers features.

Getting Started with Numbers

Like Pages and Keynote, you can start a new Numbers spreadsheet using one of its templates or "from scratch." (For information about starting new documents, see Chapter 1, "Working with iWork Documents.") The household budget spreadsheet used as the example in this and the following chapters is based on the Blank template. If you start a spreadsheet using one of the other templates, such as the Budget template, there are placeholders for your content. Templates can be a faster and easier way to build a spreadsheet, and the results may look better too!

Create and Structure Tables in Numbers Spreadsheets

A table is the basic object in a Numbers spreadsheet; you create a table for each set of data that you want to include in that spreadsheet. A table consists of the following elements. (See the last figure in the following task.)

- **Title.** The title is located at the top of the table and can be used to label the table's content or to describe its purpose. You can choose to delete a table's title if you don't want to use one for a particular table.

- **Rows.** Rows are the horizontal element of tables. Rows are identified by numbers on the far left of the table.

- **Header rows.** The top rows of a table are used for the column labels. Most tables have one header row, and some have multiple header rows. Header rows usually have special formatting to distinguish them from body rows.

- **Columns.** Columns are the vertical element of tables. Columns are identified by letters at the top of the table.

- **Header columns.** The column on the left side of a table provides the labels for the data presented in the table's rows. Most tables have one header column, but sometimes you use more than one header column. Header columns typically use formatting to distinguish them from body columns.

- **Cells.** Cells are located at the intersections of rows and columns. They are where you store data and perform calculations using formulas or where you store labels (row or column headers). Cells are identified by the intersection of the corresponding column letter and row number. For example, the first cell in a table is labeled A1, whereas the cell in the third column and fourth row is labeled C4. Cell identification is especially important because this is how you refer to cells when developing calculations.

- **Body rows and columns.** These rows and columns are where the data and calculations in a table are stored.

- **Footer row.** When used, a footer row is the last row in a table and is most typically used to summarize the results of the rows above it, such as the sum of a series of values.

Add Tables to Numbers Spreadsheets

To create a table in a Numbers spreadsheet, perform the following steps:

1. Click the Table button on the toolbar. The Table style sheet appears.

2. Click the left- and right-facing arrows to browse the table styles.

3. Click the table style you want to use for the new table. The table is created and is ready for your content.

4. Double-click the table title so it becomes editable.

5. Edit the table name.

6. Double-click in the first cell in the table.

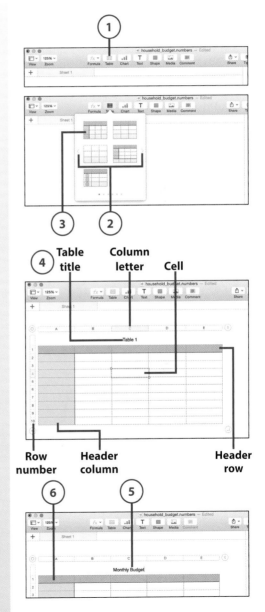

7. Type the label for the first column, which is the header column.

8. Press the Tab key to move to the next cell on the first row.

9. Enter the label for the second column.

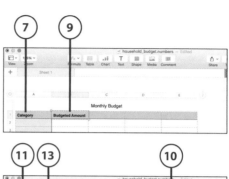

10. Repeat steps 8 and 9 until you've labeled all the columns in the table. Don't worry if there are extra columns you don't use because you learn how to delete columns later in this chapter. (If there aren't enough columns, see "Add Rows or Columns to Numbers Spreadsheets," later in the chapter, to learn how to add columns to a table.)

11. Double-click in the first cell in the second row of the table, and enter its label.

12. Press the Enter key to move to the next row.

13. Type the label for the next row.

14. Repeat steps 12 and 13 until you've entered a label in the last row in the table.

15. Press the Enter key once. A new row is added to the table, and you move into its first cell.

16. Type the label for the new row.

17. Repeat steps 15 and 16 until you've added all the rows you want in the table.

Enter Now; Format Later

Don't worry about formatting text or other information as you enter it or if you don't have the right number of header columns or rows. It's usually more efficient to set up the basic structure of the table and then tweak it before you start formatting it. Formatting usually depends on both the structure of a table and its contents, so it's better to get those two things set up first.

Moving Around

You can move around in a table using the left, right, up, and down arrow keys along with the tab and enter keys.

Your Mileage May Vary

The design of a table depends on the style you select when you add a table to a document. Styles can have different column and row headers, shading, and so on. This example shows a table with a single column and row header. If you selected a different style for your table, your results may look a bit different, but the app's tools work similarly.

Add Column or Row Headers or Footer Rows to Numbers Spreadsheets

In the event you realize you need more column or row headers, you can easily add them. In this example, I'm going to add more column headers because I want to show subtotals in the budget for the major subcategories.

1. Select the table. When it's selected, you see the column letters, row numbers, and selection handles.

2. If the Inspector isn't open, click the Format button to open it.

3. Click the Table tab.

4. To add a header column, open the first menu in the Headers & Footer section.

5. Choose the number of header columns you want in the table. Header columns are added (or removed) based on the number you select.

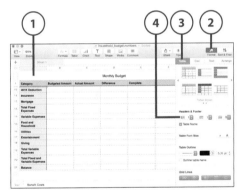

6. Choose the number of header rows on the second menu.

7. Choose the number of footer rows on the third menu.

8. To hide the table title, uncheck the Table Name check box.

New header column

Select Tables, Rows, Columns, and Cells in Numbers Spreadsheets

As you work with tables, it's important to be able to select tables and their elements (cells, rows, and columns).

1. To select a table, click it. You see the column letters, row numbers, and selection handles. This indicates the table is active and ready for you to work on.

2. To select a cell, click it. Its borders are highlighted and you see selection handles.

3. To select a range of cells, drag a selection handle.

4. When the box encompasses the cells you want to select, release the selection handle.

5. You can resize or move the selection box around to select a different range of cells.

6. To select a column, click its label (letter). Its heading box is highlighted, and you see the selection box around the column.

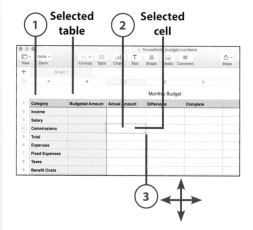

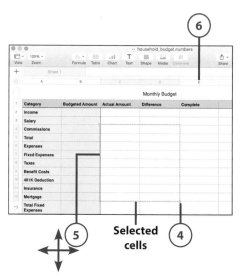

7. To select more columns, drag a selection handle to the left or right.

8. To select a row, click its label (number). Its heading box is highlighted, and you see the selection box around the row.

9. To select more rows, drag a selection handle up or down.

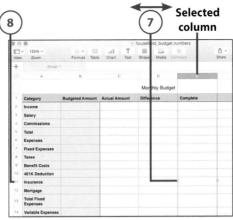

Move Cells, Rows, and Columns in Numbers Spreadsheets

You can move cells, rows, and columns within a table by dragging them.

1. Select the cells you want to move.

2. Drag the cells to their new location.

3. When the cells are in their new location, release them. Note that if you drag cells onto other cells that have content in them, that content is replaced with the content you are dragging, and you're not warned. (Of course, you can always choose Edit, Undo to undo a move.)

4. To move rows or columns, select the rows or headings you want to move.

5. Drag the rows or columns up or down (rows) or left or right (columns). As you move around rows or columns, the existing rows or columns spread apart to make room for those you are moving.

6. When the rows or columns are in their new position, release them.

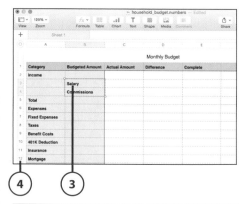

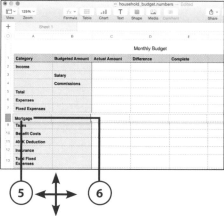

Add Rows or Columns to Numbers Spreadsheets

Earlier, you saw that rows are added automatically when you enter more data than can fit in the current table. You can add rows or columns to a table at any time as follows:

1. Click the row or column heading around where you want to add more rows or columns. When you select a row or column, you see a downward-pointing arrow, indicating a menu.

2. Click the downward-facing arrow.

3. Choose Add Row Above or Add Row Below to add a row above or below the current one, respectively, or Add Column Before or Add Column After to add a column to the left or to the right, respectively, of the current column. The row or column is added to the table.

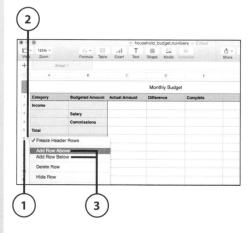

Number Selected Equals Number Added

When you select more than one row or column, the number of rows or columns added equals the number you selected. For example, if you want to add three columns, select three and then choose the appropriate add command from the menu.

Add Multiple Tables to the Same Sheet in a Numbers Spreadsheet

You can include multiple tables in a Numbers spreadsheet. For example, you might want to use one table for calculations while showing totals in cells in different table. This example shows creating a second table to calculate the expenses for specific categories in the monthly budget table.

1. Move to an empty space under the current table in the spreadsheet.

2. Click the Table button.

3. Choose the style for the new table. It is added to the spreadsheet.

4. Use the tasks earlier in the book to set up the new table.

5. Drag the table to where you want it to be in the spreadsheet.

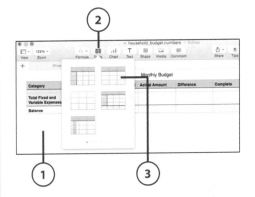

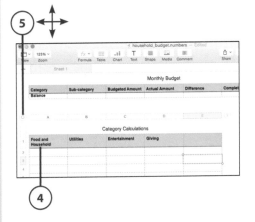

Enter and Format Data and Tables in Numbers Spreadsheets

With a basic table in place, it's time to start building it out. In this section, you learn about the following tasks:

- **Add data to cells.** You add data to the cells in a table to communicate information or perform analysis. There are two basic ways to add data. You can manually input data, which is covered in the next task. Or you can use a calculation or formula to add data; this topic is covered in Chapter 8, "Working with Calculations and Formulas in Numbers Spreadsheets."

- **Format tables.** You format a table in a number of ways, such as by choosing its style, setting the headers and footers, choosing a font size for the table, etc. The formatting you do at the table-level impacts the entire table.

- **Format cells.** You format the cells within tables in several areas. You can set the format for the data you are including in the cell; examples include currency, percentage, or fractions. You can also fill cells with color, gradients, or even images; in addition to filling cells for appearance's sake, you might fill cells to indicate ones that are data inputs to the table. You can also choose the borders for cells.

- **Format text.** You can use text formatting tools to format the text within cells. These are the same text formatting tools available in Pages.

- **Set row heights and column widths.** By default, row heights and column widths are set by the table design. You can increase or decrease heights or widths to make your table look better or to allow for more information.

- **Merge cells.** You can combine cells to make multiple cells into a single cell.

- **Set row heights and column widths.** You can remove rows or columns you no longer need.

- **Show or hide columns or rows.** You can show or hide rows or columns in a table. When you do this, you don't see the hidden rows or columns, but the data they contain is still active. For example, you might want to hide a column that contains values you use in a calculation but that aren't meaningful to someone viewing the table.

Add Data to Cells in Numbers Spreadsheets

You can manually add data to cells in a table as follows:

1. Click the cell in which you want to enter data.

2. Type the information you want to enter; you can type numbers or text in cells. You don't need to format it now because you can apply the formatting later. If you prefer to enter formatted information, set the cell format as explained in "Format Cells in Numbers Spreadsheets," later in the chapter, before entering the information.

3. Press the Enter key to move into the next cell down the column, or use an arrow key to move into a cell in a different direction.

4. Enter data in the next cell.

5. Repeat steps 3 and 4 until you have added all the information you want to include in the table; skip cells that you want to be calculated. (You learn how to work with calculations in Chapter 8.)

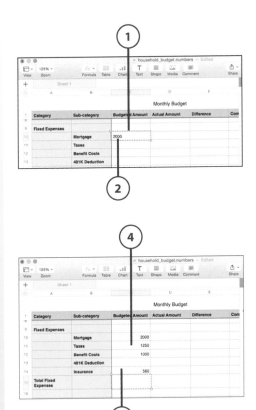

Format Tables in Numbers Spreadsheets

Use the following steps to apply formatting to an entire table:

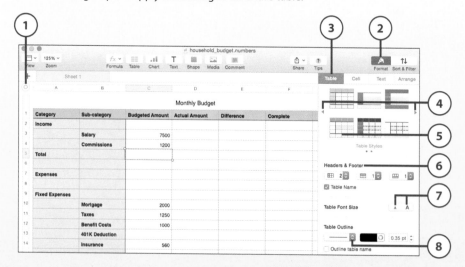

1. Select the table you want to format.

2. If the Inspector isn't open already, click the Format button.

3. Click the Table tab.

4. Use the left- and right-facing arrows to browse the styles available.

5. Click a style to apply it to the selected table. The table is reformatted according to the style you applied. This can impact header rows and columns and footer rows; if the style messed up your table design, undo it.

6. Use the Headers & Footer tools to configure header rows and columns, the footer row, and the table name. (See "Add Column or Row Headers or Footer Rows to Numbers Spreadsheets" earlier in this chapter.)

7. Click the smaller "A" to decrease the font size used for all the content in the table or the larger "A" to increase it. (To change the size of font in specific cells, use the text formatting tools instead as explained in "Format Text in Numbers Spreadsheets," later in the chapter).

8. Click the Table Outline menu.

9. Choose the line style for borders you use in the table.

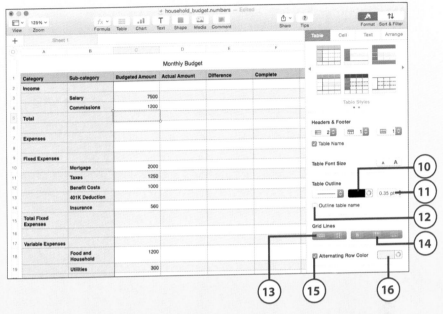

10. Use the Color tool in the Table Outline section to set the color of the borderlines.

11. Use the Thickness tool to set the width of the borderlines.

12. Check the Outline table name check box if you want the table's name to be enclosed in an outline.

13. Use the first two Grid Lines boxes to determine how borderlines are used in the body cells of a table; the button on the left shows or hides horizontal lines, and the button to its right shows or hides vertical lines.

14. Use the three boxes to show or hide borderlines in header columns, header rows, or footer rows, from left to right, respectively.

15. Check the Alternating Row Color check box if you want alternating rows in the body of the table to have a color.

16. If you use the alternating row color, use the Color tool to configure the color used in these rows.

Saving Styles

As you make changes on the Table tab, you are designing a custom style. You can save this style to use on other tables by browsing the table styles until you see a style box that contains the +. Click this box to save the style. You can apply custom styles you save just like default styles (in the current file only; these are not added back to the Numbers templates).

Format Cells in Numbers Spreadsheets

You can format the cells in a table as follows:

1. Select the cells you want to format; if you want to use the same format across multiple columns, select those columns or rows or any other group of cells.

2. In the Inspector, click the Cell tab.

3. Open the Data Format menu.

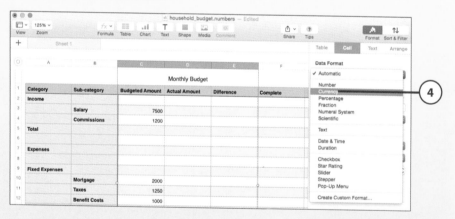

4. Choose the type of data in the selected cells. You can see that there are many options.

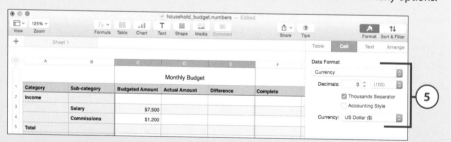

5. Use the options you see to configure the type of data you selected. This example shows the Currency type for which you can set the number of decimal places, the way negative numbers are formatted, if a comma is used to denote thousands, whether the Accounting style is applied, and the type of currency.

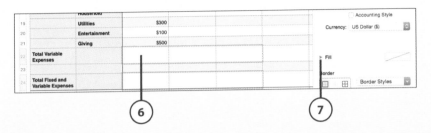

6

7

6. Select cells you want to fill.

Selecting Cells

You can select any cells in a table by holding down the ⌘ key while you click each cell you want to select.

7. Click the disclosure triangle next to Fill.

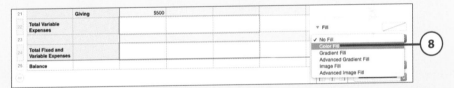

8

8. Choose how you want to fill the cells using the Fill menu.

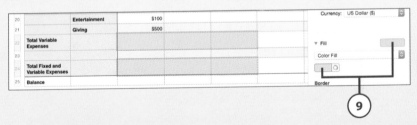

9

9. Use the tools that appear for the option you selected in step 8 to configure it. For example, when you select the Color Fill option, use the top Color tool to pick a default color or the Color Picker to choose a custom color.

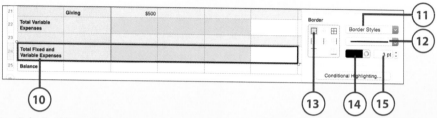

10. Select cells to which you want to apply borders.

11. Use the Border Styles menu to choose the style of border you want to apply; you can choose from different thicknesses or colors, or you can choose No Border to remove a border.

12. Choose the type of line you want to use on the lower menu; options include solid, dashed, or dotted.

13. Click the boxes corresponding to where you want borders used. You can choose the outline of the selected cells, no sides, all sides, or specific sides.

14. Use the Color tool to set the color of the borders.

15. Use the Thickness tool to set the thickness of the borders.

Format Text in Numbers Spreadsheets

You can format text in cells by doing the following:

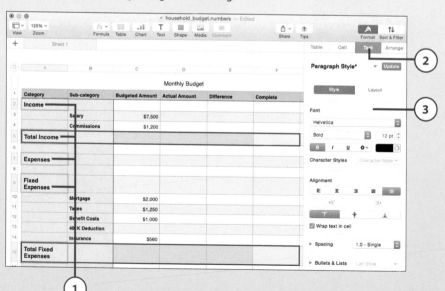

1. Select the cells containing text you want to format.

2. Click the Text tab in the Inspector.

3. Use the formatting tools to format the text; you can use text styles, format the text manually, or use any of the other tools you see. These tools work just like they do for text in Pages documents; see Chapter 2, "Working with Text in Pages Documents," for details.

Set Row Heights and Column Widths in Numbers Spreadsheets

You can adjust the heights of rows or the width of columns as shown in the following steps:

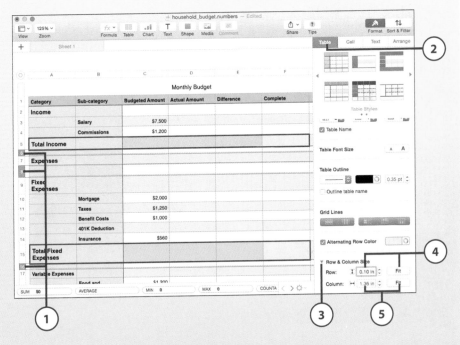

1. Select the rows or columns you want to resize.

2. Click the Table tab of the Inspector.

3. Expand the Row & Column Size section.

4. Use the Row Size box to set the height of selected rows, or click Fit to set the height based on the content of the cells in that row.

5. Use the Column Size box to set the width of selected columns, or click Fit to set the width based on the content of the cells in that column.

Resizing Is a Drag

You can also resize rows or columns by dragging. Hover over the edge of a row or column heading (letter or number) until the cursor changes to a line with arrows projecting out of it. Drag the edge to resize the row or column.

>>>Go Further

UNFREEZE HEADER COLUMNS OR ROWS

By default, header rows and columns and footer rows are frozen so that they remain on the screen as long as the table they are in does. This makes it easier to understand the table because these elements contain the headings that identify the information in the table. If you don't want them frozen, open the corresponding row or column menus and choose the Unfreeze command. You can freeze them again by opening the menu and choosing the Freeze command.

Merge Cells in Numbers Spreadsheets

At times, it can be useful to combine cells by merging them.

1. Select the cells you want to merge.

2. Choose Table, Merge Cells. The selected cells become one cell.

Be Separate

To unmerge cells, select the merged cell and choose Table, Unmerge Cells.

Delete Rows or Columns in Numbers Spreadsheets

You can get rid of rows or columns you don't want any more:

1. Select the columns or rows you want to delete.

2. Open the contextual menu for what you selected by clicking the arrow that appears in the heading of what you selected.

3. Choose the Delete command. The columns or rows you selected are deleted (along with any information in the cells they contain).

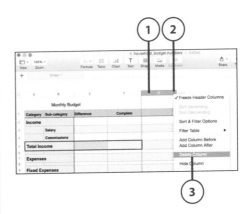

Show or Hide Rows or Columns in Numbers Spreadsheets

At times, it is useful to hide rows or columns; for example, you might want to hide rows or columns showing interim calculations that don't need to be seen.

1. Select the rows or columns you want to hide.

2. Open the contextual menu by clicking the arrow that appears in the columns or rows you selected.

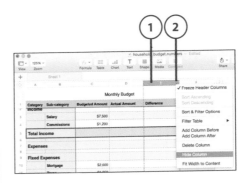

3. Choose the Hide Column or Hide Row command. The selected rows or columns are hidden. You can tell rows or columns are hidden because the column letters or row numbers "skip" the hidden columns or rows. For example, if the column letters go from D to F, you know that column E is hidden.

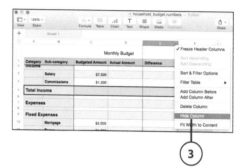

4. To show hidden rows or columns again, select the rows or columns surrounding the hidden rows or columns.

5. Open the contextual menu by clicking the arrow that appears in the columns or rows you selected.

6. Select the appropriate Unhide command, such as to unhide specific rows or columns or to unhide all hidden rows or columns.

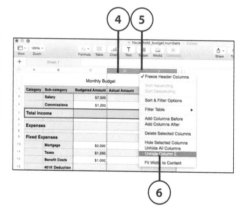

>>>Go Further

MULTIPLE SHEETS IN A SPREADSHEET

Each Numbers spreadsheet can have multiple sheets, and each sheet can have multiple tables. Each sheet within a spreadsheet is independent, or you can use the information on one in calculations on another.

Just under the toolbar, you see a tab for each sheet. Every spreadsheet has at least one sheet (tab), which is named Sheet 1 by default. To add more sheets, click the Add (+) button just under the View button on the toolbar. A new sheet is added. To rename a sheet, select its title, click the downward-facing arrow, choose Rename, enter the sheet's name, and press the Enter key to save it. To delete a sheet, select its title, click the downward-facing arrow, and choose Delete.

It's Not All Good

When you use multiple sheets, it is really helpful to be able to see more than one sheet at a time; for example, you might be using the data on one sheet in a calculation on another. Unfortunately, like the other iWork apps, Numbers doesn't allow you to have the same document open in more than one window. (Microsoft Excel allows you to do this.) This means you can't see more than one sheet at a time, making it much harder to work with than it should be. Hopefully, this major limitation in the iWork apps will be addressed in a future version. A workaround is to create separate spreadsheets instead and have each open in its own window.

Unleash the power of
Numbers with formulas
and calculations

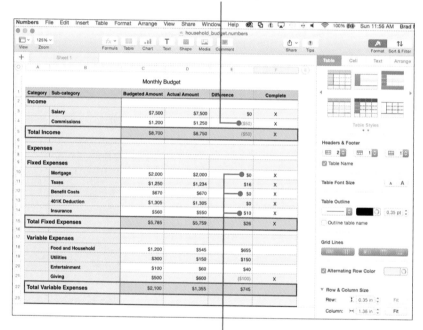

Numbers makes it easy to
reuse formulas multiple times

In this chapter, you learn how to add and configure calculations and formulas in Numbers spreadsheets. Topics include the following:

→ Understand Calculations and Formulas in Numbers Spreadsheets
→ Add Calculations to Numbers Spreadsheets
→ Add Formulas to Numbers Spreadsheets
→ Repeat Calculations in Numbers Spreadsheets

8

Working with Calculations and Formulas in Numbers Spreadsheets

The reason spreadsheets exist is to calculate numbers. The calculations they do can be basic calculations, such as adding a series of numbers, or quite complex, involving formulas and functions, such as IF statements. You can use Numbers to create spreadsheets containing calculations that are as simple or as complex as you need to get the information you want.

Understand Calculations and Formulas in Numbers Spreadsheets

When you perform a calculation manually, such as subtracting one number from another, you combine the numbers in an expression. An expression consists of the numbers (also called *values*) you are calculating and an operator that defines the action you are taking on those numbers, in this example, a minus sign (-).

A simple subtraction calculation might look like this:

100 - 37 = 63

If either of the numbers on the left side of the equal sign changes, you need to calculate the expression again, as in:

100 - 42 =58

Basic calculations like this are easy to do, especially with calculators, apps on mobile devices, or even pencil and paper.

Numbers spreadsheets can easily be used for these types of calculations, too, but that would be overkill. Where Numbers spreadsheets start to shine are when calculations get more complex, involving multiple numbers, more complex operators, or even statistical or other types of mathematical functions.

Numbers spreadsheets also excel when you want to repeat a calculation many times or over time. For example, if you are using a budget, you want to update your budget's balance regularly. Using a spreadsheet makes this much easier because you can change one or more values, such as the amount you've spent in a specific category, and the spreadsheet recalculates the balances for you automatically.

When you create a calculation in a spreadsheet, you store the values in that calculation in cells. You store the calculation itself in another cell. Recall from the previous chapter that cells are identified by their column (letter) and row (number) position, such as A6 or D127.

You tell Numbers that a cell contains a calculation by inputting = into a cell first. Numbers then uses anything following the = to calculate the result. When you view the cell, you see the result. When you select the cell, you see the calculation instead. (For example, you might want to make changes to it.)

Got Variables?

If you are familiar with the mathematical concept of a variable, you can think of cells in which you input data for calculations in a spreadsheet as variables. Calculations refer to cells by their location, but the values in those cells can change based on manual input or other calculations. This is similar to the variables in an equation because the variables represent values in that equation; those values can change depending on the other elements of the calculation being performed.

If the simple subtraction example earlier is put into a spreadsheet, it might be described something like this:

> Subtract the amount in cell B6 from the amount in A6 and put the result in C6.

In a mathematical expression, this would look like this:

> A6 - B6 = C6

You would input the number you want to subtract from in the cell A6. You would put the number you want to subtract in cell B6. The result would appear in C6 automatically. However, if you select cell C6, you would see the calculation being performed as =A6-B6.

To use this calculation, you would simply input the values you want to use into cells A6 and B6; Numbers would immediately subtract them and show the result in C6.

Using Numbers to perform calculations is much easier and less prone to mistakes than calculating things manually. It can take a little practice to start doing math the Numbers way, but you'll find the time you spend learning how will pay off many times over.

Finally, understand that there are two basic types of calculations you can do in Numbers spreadsheets: straight calculations and formulas.

A straight calculation involves basic mathematical operators, such as + (add), - (subtract), / (divide), and * (multiply). You can also use () to segment a calculation; parts of the calculation that are contained within () are done first. To use fewer words through the rest of this chapter, this type is called just a *calculation*.

A *formula* is a higher-level mathematical expression that is used for more complex operations. Formulas can include basic calculations plus *functions*. There are many different types of functions. A Logical function provides different paths for the operation depending on the values involved. One example of this type is an IF function, which says that if a condition is true, there should be a certain result, whereas if the condition is not true, there should be a different result. Statistical functions include things like the average of a range of cells, such as a column of values. When you access Numbers Function tools, there are many different types of functions you can use.

Math Is Fun

Because this is a chapter on Numbers and not on math, you won't find much other explanation of the mathematical concepts that Numbers implements. You can get lots of math help on the Web, and Numbers provides help for the functions you can use to make them easier to use correctly. Unless you are doing some complex scientific or other types of analyses, it is very likely that the information in this chapter will enable you to use Numbers for the math that you need to use in your spreadsheets.

Add Calculations to Numbers Spreadsheets

When you add calculations to a numbers spreadsheet, you have two options:

- **Manually create a calculation.** You can perform a calculation by manually entering all the cell references and operators into a cell. This enables you to do any sort of calculation you might want to do, but it does require more work from you because you are inputting everything directly and manually. If you've never used a spreadsheet before, I recommend you begin by doing all your calculations this way to better understand how calculations in Numbers work.

- **Use an Instant Calculation.** Numbers provides this tool to make entering calculations easier. For example, you can quickly total the amounts in a column by selecting a range of cells and using the Sum calculation instead of including each cell and the + individually. Instant Calculations are a great time saver, but you should understand what they do to make sure you get the correct result.

In the following tasks, you learn how to add both types to a spreadsheet.

Manually Create Calculations in Numbers Spreadsheets

To manually enter a calculation, perform the following steps:

1. Select the cell in which you want to see the result of the calculation.

2. Press the = key on the keyboard. (This tells Numbers you are entering a calculation rather than a value.) The Equation bar appears in the cell. (The Functions Browser appears in the Inspector pane; you learn about this later).

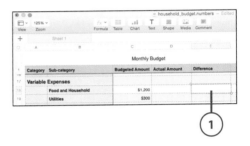

Equation bar

3. Click the cell containing the first value you want to use in the calculation. The cell reference (such as C18) or the column and row header labels (such as Budgeted Amount Food and Household) for the cell you clicked appears in the Equation bar.

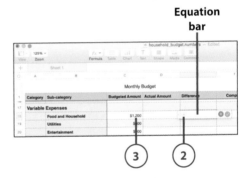

Empty Cells Work

You don't have to have values in the cells you use in a calculation before you enter the calculation itself. You can input the calculation first and then add values to the cells included in that calculation. Usually it's a good idea to start with values, though, because it's easier to tell if the calculation you are entering appears to be working correctly if it has values to act on.

4. Type the operator that you want to use on the value you selected in step 3, such as - to subtract a number from it or + to add a number to it.

5. Click the cell containing the next value you want to add to the calculation. The cell reference for that cell is added to the Equation bar.

6. Repeat steps 4 and 5 until you've added all the operators and values you want to include in the calculation.

Multiple Tables

The cells you use in a calculation don't have to be in the same table, or even sheet, as the calculation. You can click on a cell in a different table or sheet to add that cell to a calculation just like other cells in the same table.

7. Click the Save button (the check mark) to save the calculation. The Equation bar closes, and you see the results of the calculation in the cell you selected in step 1.

8. Add data to any cells that impact the calculation.

9. Check the results to make sure the calculation is working correctly.

10. Repeat these steps to manually create calculations in other cells. (You learn faster ways to replicate calculations in "Repeat Formulas in Numbers Spreadsheets" later in this chapter.)

Column and row header for the selected cell

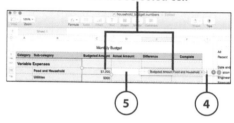

5   **4**

7

8   **Result of calculation**

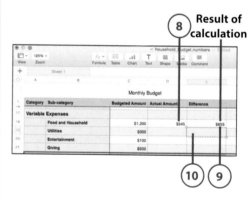

10   **9**

Makin' Mistakes

If you make errors in a calculation, Numbers flags the problem for you and offers suggestions about how to fix them. Sometimes these errors are warnings, such as when you divide by zero, which can indicate that the calculation itself is correct, but something is wrong with the values being used.

Add a Calculation for a Range of Cells in Numbers Spreadsheets

You often want to calculate the sum, average, or other amount for a range of cells, as shown in the following steps:

1. Select the cell in which you want to see the results of the calculation. This example shows summing the total of a column of expenses from the Category Calculations table in the Monthly Budget table. This is a good example of how you can combine data in multiple tables. In this case, you can enter individual expenses in the Category Calculations table while seeing their total in the Monthly Budget table.

2. Click the Formula button on the toolbar.

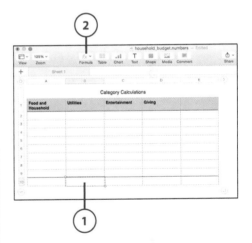

3. Click the function you want to use; this example shows the Sum function, which is useful for totaling the values in rows, columns, or any other group of cells. The function is inserted into the cell. Numbers selects the range of cells on which the function acts based on its "best guess" depending on where the calculation is stored. For example,

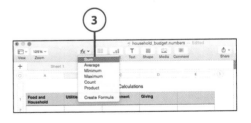

if you select a cell in a footer row, Numbers assumes you want to sum the cells above it. The cells Numbers selected for the formula are highlighted, and you see the current formula in the Formula bar.

4. Click outside the cell you selected in step 1. This saves the calculation, and you see any results; you see 0 if there is no data in the cells being used.

5. Add data to the cells used in the calculation. The results of the calculation appear in the cell you selected in step 1.

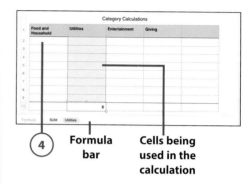

Formula bar **Cells being used in the calculation**

Data used in the calculation

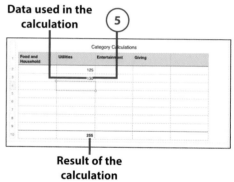

Result of the calculation

Add Instant Calculations to a Cell in Numbers Spreadsheets

You can use Instant Calculations in Numbers to create calculations faster and more easily than creating them manually. This example shows using the sum of the values in a column in one table in a different table.

1. Select the cells containing the data you want to use in the calculation. The Instant Calculation tool appears. You see a variety of calculations, such as the sum, average, minimum value, and so on, for the range of cells you selected.

2. Drag the calculation you want to from the Instant Calculations bar to the cell where you want the result to appear.

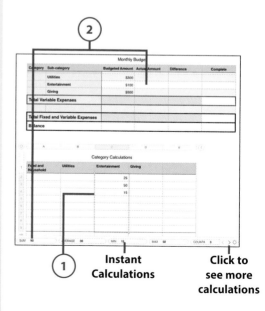

Instant Calculations **Click to see more calculations**

3. When the cell in which you want to store the calculation is high-lighted, release it. The calculation is stored in that cell, and you see its current results. When you change the data in the range of cells you selected in step 1, the result changes immediately and automatically.

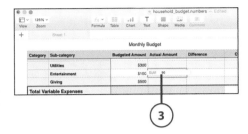

Change Calculations in Numbers Spreadsheets

You can edit existing calculations. How you do this depends on the specific calculation you are changing, but the following example illustrates this process:

1. Double-click the cell containing the calculation you want to change. The Equation bar appears and displays the current calculation.

2. Use the Equation bar to make changes to the calculation, such as changing the function used (click the current one to select a different one) or the range of cells on which the calculation acts. You can also add operators, include more values, and more.

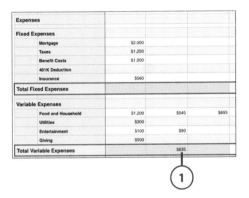

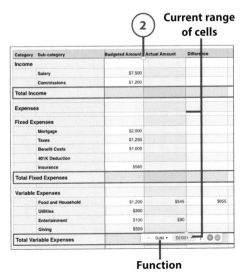

Current range of cells

Function

3. To change the range of cells used, for example, drag the selection handle so the range you want to be used is highlighted.

4. To save the calculation, click the Save (check mark) button.

5. To discard the changes, click the Cancel (x) button.

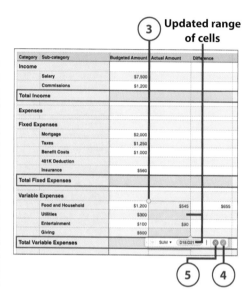

Delete a Calculation

To delete a calculation, select the cell in which it is stored and press the Delete key.

Add Formulas to Numbers Spreadsheets

The calculations you've seen so far involve fairly basic mathematics, such as addition and subtraction, and basic statistics, such as the average of a group of numbers. When you need to do more complex calculations, you can create formulas that use functions.

There are many different types of functions available in Numbers; examples include Date and Time, Duration, Engineering, Financial, and Logical & Info. You access functions through the Functions Browser.

Creating formulas is a bit more complex than performing basic calculations because the functions have different structures and sometimes involve more advanced concepts. And all functions have a specific syntax that must be used. The good news is that the Functions Browser includes help you can access to understand and use functions.

The example formula used in the next several tasks calculates different percentages of savings based on an amount of commission income. The outcome of the formula should be the following:

- For commission income less than $500, save 5%.

- For commission income greater than $500, save 15%.

To create this type of formula, you use a logical function that includes an IF statement. The syntax of an IF function looks like this:

IF(if-expression, if-true, if-false)

You can interpret this as follows:

- IF indicates the IF function is being used on whatever is enclosed in the ().

- if-expression is the expression for the condition that is used to determine whether the true or false result is used.

- if-true is the result when the expression is true.

- if-false is the result when the expression is false.

Each of these elements is referred to as an argument.

Other functions have different syntaxes; you can refer to the Functions Browser help information to understand the syntaxes and variables involved.

Build Formulas in Numbers Spreadsheets

To build the savings calculation formula described in the previous section, perform the following steps:

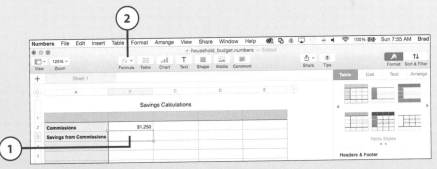

1. Select the cell where you want to create the formula.

2. Click the Formula button on the toolbar.

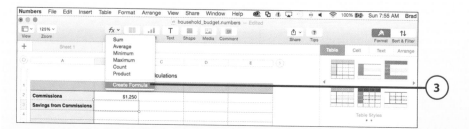

3. Choose Create Formula. The Formula Editor opens, and the Functions Browser appears in the Inspector.

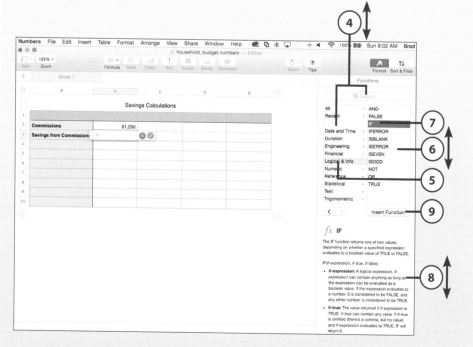

4. Browse or search the Functions Browser to find the category of function you want to use.

5. Click the category of function you want to use.

6. Browse the functions available in the category you selected.

7. Click the function you want to use. An explanation of the selected function appears at the bottom of the Functions Browser.

8. Read the information about the selected function; you can browse up and down in the help area to see all of the explanation. Pay particular attention to the syntax of the function because you must follow a function's syntax to use it correctly.

9. Click Insert Function. The selected function is added to the Formula Editor. In shaded ovals, you see the arguments for each component of the function as required by its syntax.

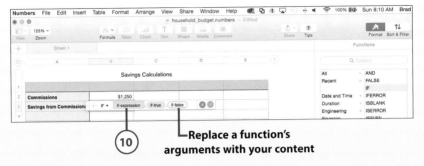

──Replace a function's arguments with your content

10. Select the first argument you want to replace; in this example, it is the if-expression, which we want to see if the amount of commissions is less than $500.

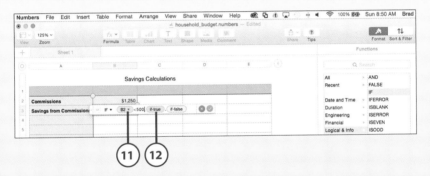

11. Create the if-expression using the techniques you learned earlier to create a calculation. In this case, the if-expression checks the value in cell B2, which is the amount of commissions, to see if it is less than $500.

12. Select the next argument in the function.

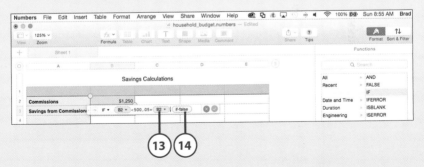

13. Replace the argument with a value or calculation. In this case, the value when the if-expression is true should be 5% of the value in cell B2.

14. Select the next argument in the function.

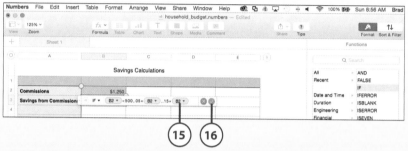

15. Replace the argument with a value or calculation. In this example, the value when the if-expression is false should be 15% of the value in cell B2.

16. Click the Save button. The formula is saved in the cell you selected in step 1, and you see the current result of the formula in the cell.

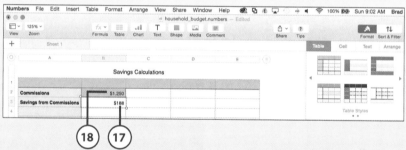

17. Check the result of the formula based on the current input. In this case, the commission amount is $1,250, so the savings amount should be $187.5 (15% because $1,250 is greater than $500). (The format of the cell is set to not include decimals, so the result is rounded to $188.)

18. Change the input amount to test the formula. In this case, you'd want to input a value less than $500 to make sure the calculation is done using 5% instead of 15%.

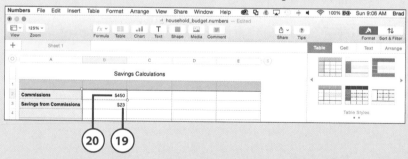

19. Check the result to make sure it is correct for the amount input in step 18. With the commission amount set to $450, the savings amount should be $22.5 ($450 x 5%), which it is (rounded to $23).

20. Repeat steps 17 through 19 until you are sure the formula is working correctly.

Change Formulas in Numbers Spreadsheets

As with other calculations, you can change formulas to make them work differently or to correct errors:

1. Select the cell containing the formula you want to change. The formula appears in the Formula bar at the bottom of the screen.

2. Check the formula to see what changes need to be made.

3. Click the cell containing the formula. The Formula Editor appears.

4. Use the Formula Editor to make changes to the formula. You can replace arguments or values, change cell references, and so on. (Note that when the Formula Editor is open, you see the current result of the formula in the Formula Result bar at the bottom of the screen.)

5. To save the changed formula, click the Save button. The updated formula replaces the previous one.

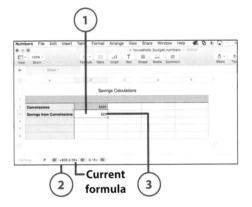

Current formula

Current result

Repeat Formulas in Numbers Spreadsheets

One of the great things about spreadsheets is that it is easy to repeat formulas. So you can set up a formula once and then reuse it in multiple locations.

There are two basic ways to repeat a formula: Autofill or copy and paste. When you Autofill a formula, you select a cell and then repeat the formula in that cell in the range in the cells below, above, to the left, or to the right of the cell containing the formula. When you use copy and paste, you can copy a formula and paste it in one or more cells next to the one containing the formula or in other areas of the spreadsheet.

As you reuse formulas, it's important to understand the two types of cell references: relative or fixed. A relative cell reference changes as you reuse a formula in a different field, whereas a fixed reference always points back to a specific cell. Both types are useful.

You can define relative or fixed references for either the column, the row, or both.

Use a relative reference when you want the cell references to stay "relative" (and thus the name) to the cells in which you are reusing a formula. For example, in the budget worksheet used as the example in this chapter, there is a Difference column to calculate the difference between the Budgeted Amount and the Actual Amount, which are stored in the two columns to the left. The cell references in the formulas in this column are relative because they always refer to the columns to the left of the current one.

If, on the other hand, you wanted to calculate a series of numbers based on the same percentage, you would use a fixed reference back to the cell containing the percentage you want to use in the formula because you want that percentage to be used every time you repeat that formula in a cell. You input the percentage in one cell, and it is used everywhere the formula referring to it is used.

As you repeat formulas, you need to understand which type of reference you want to use because using the wrong type ends up in formulas that don't do what you want. By default, formulas use relative references. Make sure you are using the correct type before you repeat a formula; you learn how to change the reference in the next task.

Once you've set up a formula with the correct reference type, it's easy to repeat it using Autofill or copy and paste, as shown in the last two tasks in this chapter.

Set Up Formulas with Relative or Fixed Cell References

To change the type of cell reference used in a formula, perform the following steps:

1. Select the cell containing the formula in which you want to set the cell reference type. The calculation or formula appears in the Formula bar at the bottom of the window.

2. Click the cell containing the formula in which you want to set the cell reference type. The Formula Editor opens, and you see the current calculation.

3. Click the downward-facing arrow for the cell reference you want to configure.

4. Check the Preserve Row check box to fix the row reference. When you check the check box, a $ appears in front of the reference to indicate it is fixed.

5. Check the Preserve Column check box to fix the column reference. When you check the check box, a $ appears in front of the reference to indicate it is fixed.

6. Update other cell references as needed.

7. Click the Save button to save the changes to the formula. It uses the type of references you configured.

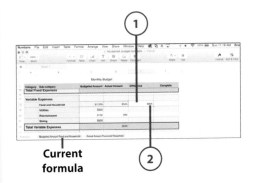

Current formula

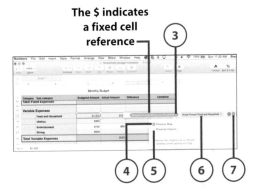

The $ indicates a fixed cell reference

Configuring References Manually

When you enter a cell reference manually, you can add $ before a reference to make it a fixed reference. For example, to cause a formula to always use the contents of cell A6, you would enter A6 when you add the cell reference to the formula.

Autofill Calculations in Multiple Cells in Numbers Spreadsheets

To repeat a formula using Autofill, use the following steps:

1. Select the range of cells in which you want to repeat a calculation with the first cell in the range containing the calculation you want to repeat.

2. Choose Table, Autofill Cells.

3. Choose the direction in which you want to fill cells. The formula is copied into each of the cells in the selected range.

4. Check the results in the cells in which you repeated the formula to make sure they are what you expect. If the results aren't what you expect, make sure the cell reference types are correct; it is easy to use a relative type when you meant to use a fixed type or vice versa.

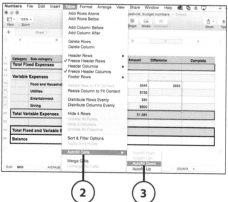

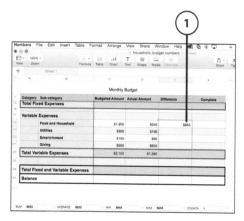

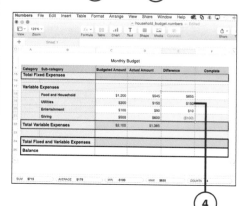

Copy and Paste Formulas into Multiple Cells in Numbers Spreadsheets

You can copy and paste formulas in spreadsheets just as you can other types of information in different apps:

1. Select the cell containing the formula you want to reuse.

2. Choose Edit, Copy.

3. Select the cells in which you want to repeat the formula you copied in step 2. You can select single cells, ranges of cells, or multiple cells located anywhere on the sheet.

4. Choose Paste to paste the formula and formatting, Paste and Match Style to paste the formula while retaining the current cell's formatting, or Paste Formula Results to paste only the results of the formula (instead of the formula itself). The formula or result is copied into the selected cells.

5. Check the results to make sure they are what you expect.

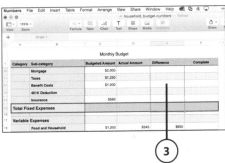

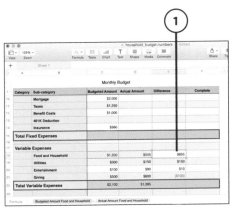

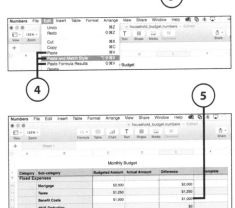

Use charts to display data graphically to make it communicate more clearly

Numbers offers many chart tools so you can customize charts to your heart's content

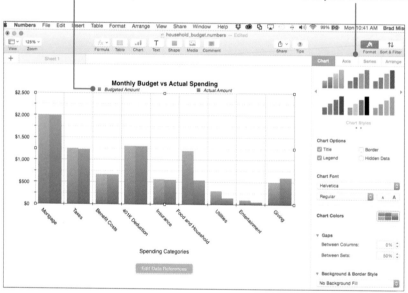

In this chapter, you learn how to add charts to and format charts in your Numbers spreadsheets. Topics include the following:

→ Add Charts to and Format Charts in Numbers Spreadsheets

→ Configure Chart Axes and Data Series in Numbers Spreadsheets

9

Working with Charts in Numbers Spreadsheets

Using charts to express the information in Numbers spreadsheets makes the data easier to understand and more visually appealing. Numbers enables you to create and format many different types of charts, including bar, pie, area, scatter, and bubble. Charts can be 2D or 3D. You can also create interactive charts so the viewer can choose how the data in a chart is presented.

Although many different types of charts are available in Numbers, you use similar tools and techniques to work with any of them.

There are lots of ways to create and format charts. You can start by selecting the data you want to display in the chart and then formatting it, or you can choose the chart first and add the data to it. There are also options for how and when you format chart elements depending on your personal preferences; you can do things in almost any order.

In this chapter, the example used for the tasks is a bar chart that compares budgeted spending versus actual spending for the monthly budget spreadsheet from previous chapters. This example gets you started in creating charts for your own spreadsheets.

Add Charts to and Format Charts in Numbers Spreadsheets

Like other objects in Numbers documents (and the other two iWork apps for that matter), you add a chart to a spreadsheet and then use the formatting tools in Numbers to make it look the way you want it to.

Add Charts to Numbers Spreadsheets

To create a chart in a Numbers spreadsheet, do the following steps:

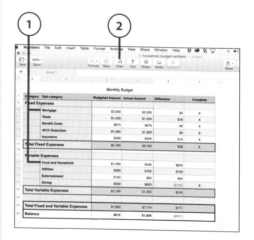

1. Select the cells containing the data you want to display in the chart. You can select individual cells, ranges of cells, or entire rows or columns. When you choose the data to display, make sure you include categories or other identification for the data you are selecting so that information appears in the chart. It can take some practice to select data so you get exactly the chart you want.

2. Click the Chart button on the toolbar.

Selecting Multiple Ranges of Cells

When choosing data for a chart, it can be useful to select multiple ranges of cells. To do this, select the first range. Then hold down the ⌘ key and drag through the next range of cells you want to select. You can repeat this process as many times as you need to include all the data you want to chart. This technique is especially useful when you have groups of data to chart that aren't located right next to each other.

3. Click 2D to create a two-dimensional chart, 3D to create a three-dimensional chart, or Interactive to create an interactive chart.

4. Browse to the left or right to see all the types of charts available for the option you selected in step 3.

5. Click the type of chart you want to create. The chart is created using the data you selected in step 1, and it's added to the bottom of the spreadsheet. Of course, you can move or resize it as needed.

6. Review the chart to see if it is what you had in mind. If it isn't, press the Delete key to delete the chart and repeat steps 1 through 5 until you get the basic chart you want. You can then format and edit it to get it just right.

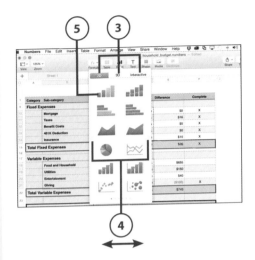

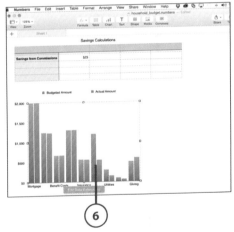

Resize and Move Charts in Numbers Spreadsheets

It is typical to need to move and resize charts as you format them. You can do this just like other objects in the other iWork apps.

1. Select the chart you want to resize or move. Selection handles appear at its corners.

2. Drag a selection handle in the direction in which you want to resize the chart. For example, to make a chart wider, drag one of the selection handles on the right side of the chart to the right. As you drag, the current dimensions of the chart are displayed.

3. When the chart is the size you want it to be, release the selection handle you were dragging. The chart is resized.

4. To move a chart, click on it and drag in the direction you want to move it; as you drag it, its current location is displayed.

5. When it is in the location you want, release it.

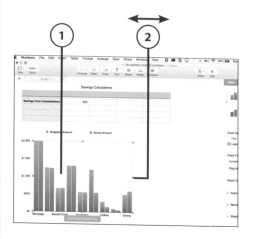

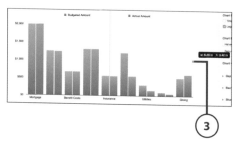

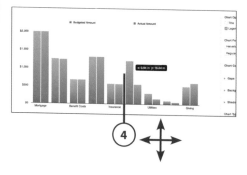

Format Charts in Numbers Spreadsheets

Formatting charts is similar to formatting other types of objects:

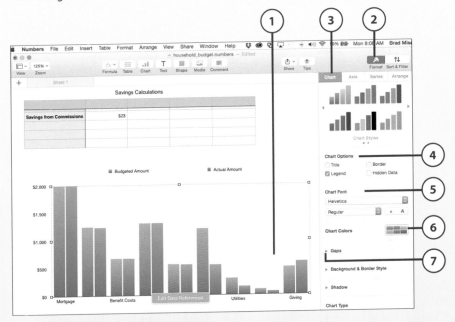

1. Select the chart you want to format.

2. If the Inspector isn't open, click the Format button on the toolbar to open it.

Charts with Style

Like tables, you can apply different styles to charts using the Chart Styles tool at the top of the Inspector. You can browse the available styles and then reformat a chart by clicking the style you want to apply. As with tables, you can save your custom chart styles by formatting a chart and then clicking + in an empty chart style box.

3. Click the Chart tab.

4. Check or uncheck the Chart Options check boxes to show or hide, respectively, the chart title, legend, border, and hidden data.

5. Use the Chart Font tools to configure the chart's overall font; you can choose the font and style on the menus and use the buttons to decrease or increase the relative size.

6. Use the Chart Colors tool to change the colors used in the chart.

7. Click the disclosure triangle for Gaps to expand that section.

Formatting Depends on Type

The formatting and other options you see in the Inspector depend on the type of chart with which you are working. This example shows the options for a bar chart.

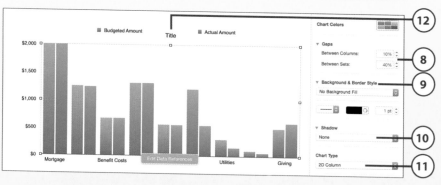

8. Use the two boxes in the Gaps section to control the amount of space between the columns (in this example, between the bars for Budgeted Amount and Actual Amount) and between the sets of data (for example, between the two Mortgage bars and the two unlabeled bars to their right).

9. Use the Background & Border Style tools to configure the chart's background and border. You can apply various kinds of fill, such as color or gradient, and choose the style of line around the chart if you want to use one.

10. Use the Shadow tool to apply a drop shadow to each series or to each group of data.

11. Use the Chart Type menu to change the chart's type; if you are going to do this, you should do it before formatting the chart because a chart's type determines the formatting options available for it.

12. If you added a chart title, double-click it.

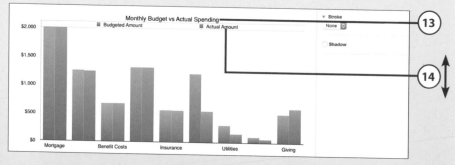

13. Type the chart's title.

14. Drag the legend so it doesn't interfere with the title.

Format Chart Text Elements in Numbers Spreadsheets

Charts can have different text elements, such as titles, legends, and more. To format these elements, perform the following steps:

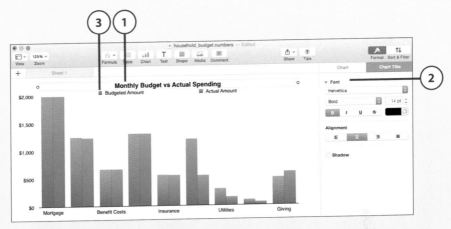

1. Select the element you want to format, such as the chart's title. When you select an element on a chart, the Inspector automatically displays tools for that element.

2. Use the tools on the Chart Title tab to format the title. These are the same text formatting tools you've seen elsewhere.

3. Select the next element you want to format, such as the legend.

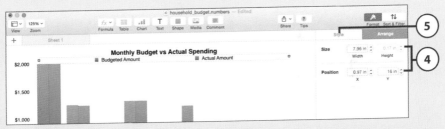

4. Use the Size and Position tools on the Arrange tab to set the size and position of the element, such as the legend, that you selected in step 3.

5. Click the Style tab.

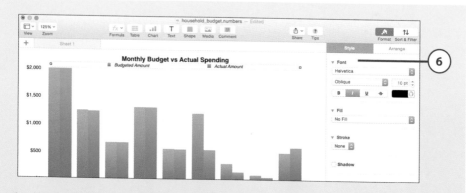

6. Use the Style tools to format the legend's text.

7. Repeat these steps for other text objects on the chart. (Axes and data series are covered in the next section.)

>>>Go Further
CHARTS IN PAGES AND KEYNOTE DOCUMENTS

Charts are a great way to display data in Pages documents and Keynote presentations. You can develop a chart in Numbers and copy it. Then move into a Pages document or Keynote presentation and paste the chart where you want to use it.

Configure Chart Axes and Data Series in Numbers Spreadsheets

A chart is all about presenting data clearly and in a meaningful way. One key to doing this is to make sure the chart axes and data series are configured the way you want them to be.

Configure the Axes on Charts in Numbers Spreadsheets

To configure the axes in a chart, perform the following steps:

1. Select the chart whose axes you want to configure.

2. Click the Axis tab.

3. Click the Value (Y) tab to configure the vertical axis.

4. To display a label for the axis, check the Axis Name check box. The placeholder "Value Axis" appears next to the axis on the chart. (If you include a label, double-click it and type the text you want to replace the placeholder with.)

5. To display a line for the axis, check the Axis Line check box.

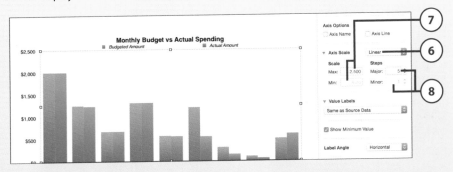

6. To change the scale of the axis, open the Axis Scale menu. Options include Linear and Logarithmic.

7. Use the Scale boxes to set the scale of the axis by inputting the maximum amount in the Max box and the minimum amount in the Min box. By default, both display Auto, which means Numbers selects values based on the amounts in the data you are charting.

8. Use the Steps boxes to configure the number of markers on the axis by inputting the number of major markers in the Major box and the number of minor markers in the Minor box. Based on your input, Numbers adds or removes markers and recalculates the values shown.

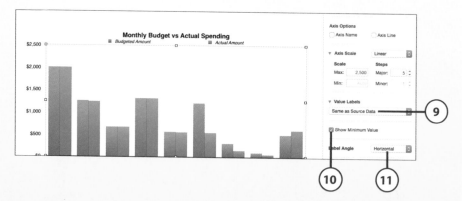

9. Use the Value Labels menu to choose the format of the data displayed. In most cases, you want to leave the option Same as Source Data selected, but you can choose and configure a different format if you wish.

10. If you don't want the minimum value to be displayed, such as 0, uncheck the Show Minimum Value check box.

11. Use the Label Angle menu to orient the text labels. For example, choose Left Diagonal to display the labels oriented at a 45-degree angle to the axis line. Choose Custom to be able to define a specific angle amount.

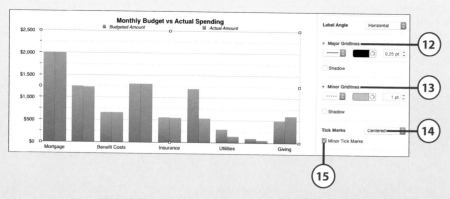

12. Use the Major Gridlines tool to configure lines at the major values on the axis.

13. Use the Minor Gridlines tool to do the same for the lines at the minor values on the axis.

14. To display tick marks on the axis, choose how you want the tick lines to be aligned with the axis.

15. Check the Minor Tick Marks check box to display tick marks on the minor values too.

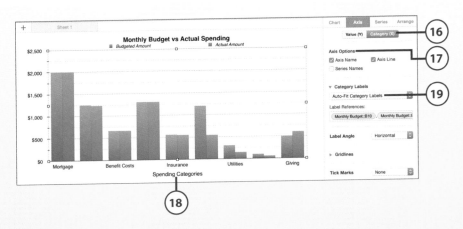

16. Click the Category (X) tab.

17. Use the Axis Options check boxes to show or hide the axis name, axis line, or series names.

18. If you show the axis name, double-click it, enter the name, format it, and then come back to the Category (X) tab.

19. On the Category Labels menu, choose how you want the data labels to be displayed; for example, choose Show All Category Labels to display all the labels, even if they overlap.

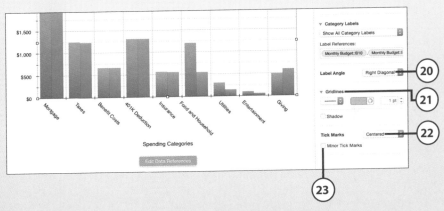

20. Set the orientation of the labels using the Label Angle menu.

21. Use the Gridlines tools to configure gridlines for the axis.

22. Use the Tick Marks menu to display tick marks on the axis and choose how they are oriented to the axis.

23. To show tick marks at the minor values, check the Minor Tick Marks check box.

Configure Data Series in Numbers Spreadsheets

You can make changes to the data series being used in a chart as follows:

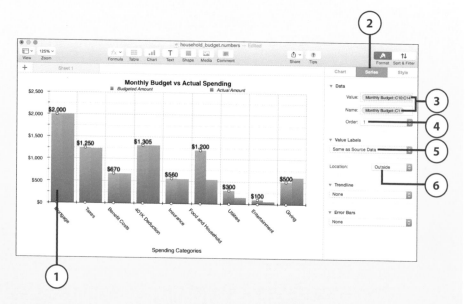

1. Select the data series you want to change.

2. Click the Series tab in the Inspector.

3. If you want to change the source of data in the series, change the cell references in the Value and Name boxes.

4. To change the order of the data series, select the order for the current series on the Order menu. For example, if the chart has two data series and you change the selected series from 1 to 2, the order in which the data series appear on the chart swaps.

5. To label the data on the chart, choose the option you want on the Value Labels menu. For example, if you choose Same as Source Data, you see the actual values on the chart. You can also choose a different format or None if you don't want the data to be displayed.

6. If you displayed data in step 5, choose where you want the data to be displayed on the Location menu.

Trendlines and Error Bars

You can add trendlines to a data series that show how the data is trending over time; for some types of data, a trendline helps interpret what that data indicates over a period of time more clearly than just seeing the individual data series. Error bars are used to indicate the uncertainty in data.

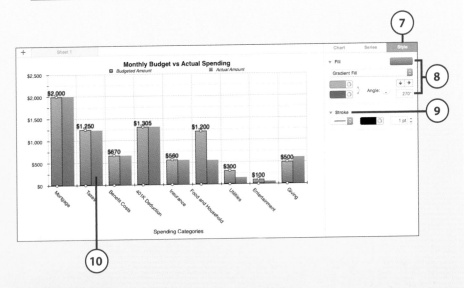

7. Click the Style tab.

8. Use the Fill tools to configure the fill for the series.

9. Use the Stroke tools to configure a line around the series.

10. Select and configure the other data series on the chart using these steps.

Collaborate with others using
comments or iCloud sharing

Use filters to hide
rows in a table

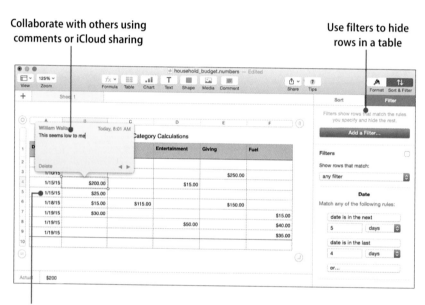

Sort tables to
configure the
order in which
rows appear

In this chapter, you learn how to sort and filter tables, check spelling, and involve others in your spreadsheets. Topics include the following:

→ Sort or Filter Tables in Numbers Spreadsheets
→ Check Spelling in Numbers Spreadsheets
→ Collaborate with Others on Numbers Spreadsheets

10

Finishing and Collaborating on Numbers Spreadsheets

After you've built a spreadsheet, you're ready to finish it off. You may want to sort and filter tables to change the way they are presented. Of course, you want to check the spelling in a spreadsheet before it's done. And, as with other iWork documents, you may want to collaborate with others on a spreadsheet.

Sort or Filter Tables in Numbers Spreadsheets

As you work with tables, you may want to sort or filter them.

You can sort tables to determine the order in which the rows of that table appear based on the values in specific columns. You can quickly sort a table by the values in any one of its columns, or you can create and use sorting rules when you want to sort a table by more than one column at the same time. For example, if you have a table of expenses, you may want to sort those expenses so the largest expenses appear at the top of the table. Or, you may want to sort a table of expenses by the date and amount.

When you filter tables, you limit the rows displayed for the table to only those that have specific values in selected columns. As with sorting, you can do a quick filter on a single column, or you can create filter rules for more complex filtering based on multiple columns at the same time. You can use filtering to help you focus on specific data in tables by hiding data that isn't currently of interest to you. (You can remove filters from tables to display all the data those tables contain.)

Sort Tables in Numbers Spreadsheets

To quickly sort a table by a single column, perform the following steps:

1. Select the table you want to sort.

2. Hover over the column by which you want to sort the table. The downward-facing arrow appears.

3. Click the downward-facing arrow.

4. Choose Sort Ascending to sort the table so that values get "larger" as you move down the table or Sort Descending to sort the table so values get "smaller" as you move down the table. Larger and smaller depend on the type of data you are working with. For example, when you are sorting a table by date, Ascending means older dates are placed at the top of the table.

After you make a selection, the table is sorted accordingly.

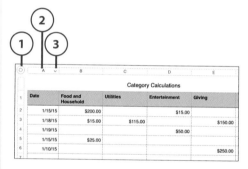

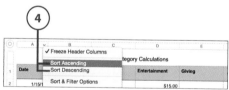

This table is sorted by date

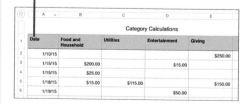

Use Sorting Rules to Sort Tables in Numbers Spreadsheets

Sorting rules enable you to sort tables by more than one column at a time. You can create sorting rules for a table for more sophisticated sorting.

1.   Select the table you want to sort.

2.   Click the Sort & Filter button on the toolbar. The Sort & Filter sidebar opens.

3.   Click the Sort tab.

4.   Click Add a Column.

5.   Choose the first column by which you want to sort the table.

Sort Selected Rows Only

You can sort specific rows within a table by selecting the rows you want to sort and choosing Sort Selected Rows on the menu on the Sort & Filter sidebar. If you configure the rest of the options as described in these steps, only the rows you selected are sorted.

6.   Choose how you want the sort to be done (Ascending or Descending).

7.   Click Add a Column.

8.   Choose the next column by which you want to sort the table.

9.   Choose the sort order for the column you selected in step 7.

10.   Repeat steps 6 through 8 to add additional columns to the sort. As you add and configure columns, the table is sorted.

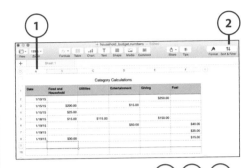

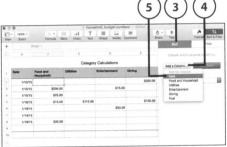

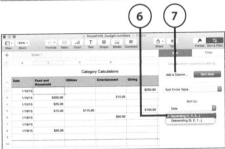

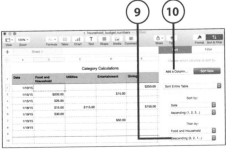

11. To change the order of the columns by which the table is sorted, hover over one of the sorting rules until the List button appears, and drag that button up or down the list of sorting rules. As you change the order of columns, the table is re-sorted accordingly.

12. To remove a sort rule, hover over it and click the Trash button. That column is removed from the sort, and the table is re-sorted.

13. To re-sort the table using the current sort order, click Sort Now. For example, if you add more rows to a table, you can click the Sort Now button to sort the table again.

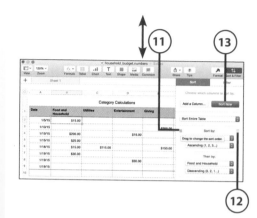

Filter Tables in Numbers Spreadsheets

You can filter tables based on a single value as follows:

1. Select the table you want to filter.

2. Hover over the column containing the information you want to use to filter the table. The downward-facing arrow appears.

3. Click the downward-facing arrow.

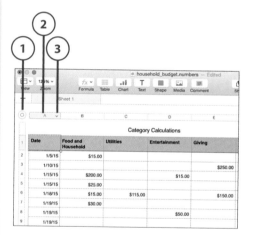

The Sorting Remains the Same

The Sorting rules for a table are saved for that table so that you can use or change them at any time. When you add more rows to a table, it is not sorted by the current sorting rules automatically. You have to click the Sort Now button to re-sort the table. You can have only one set of sorting rules for a table at a time. You can remove all the sorting rules for a table by clicking the Trash button next to each sorting rule.

4. Choose Filter Table. You see a list of all the values in the column you selected in step 2.

5. Choose the value with which you want to filter the table. All rows that don't contain the value you selected in step 4 are hidden.

6. To remove a filter from a table, hover over the column by which the table is currently filtered.

7. Open the column's menu.

8. Choose Filter Table.

9. Choose the data by which the table is currently filtered; this value has the check mark. The filter is removed, and you see all the table's rows again.

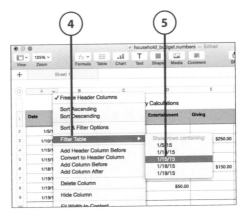

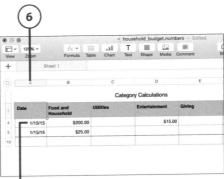

Only rows with the value selected as the filter are shown

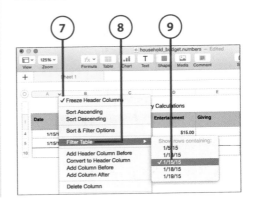

You Can't Add Rows to a Filtered Table

When a table is filtered, you can't add more rows to it. You need to remove the filter, add rows, and then add the filter again.

Use Filtering Rules to Filter Tables in Numbers Spreadsheets

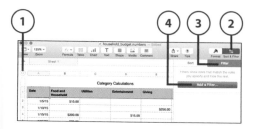

Similar to sorting, you can create filtering rules to filter the information displayed in a table using more complex criteria.

1. Select the table you want to filter.

2. Click the Sort & Filter button on the toolbar. The Sort & Filter sidebar opens.

3. Click the Filter tab.

4. Click Add a Filter.

5. Choose the first column you want to use as a filter. You're prompted to create a rule for the column you selected.

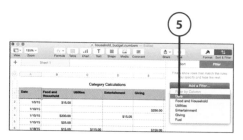

6. Click the tab for the type of information you are using in the filtering rule. This example shows a column containing dates, so the Dates tab is used. Each type of data has its own filtering options, but they are all configured similarly.

7. Select how you want to configure the filtering rule. The options you see depend on the type of data you selected in step 6. This example filtering rule shows filtering the table based on a range of dates using the date is "in the next" option. The configuration tools for the option you select appear in the sidebar.

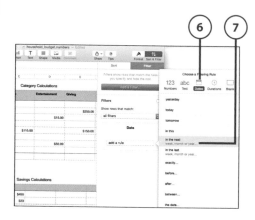

8. Configure the filtering rule, such as by entering a number of days.

9. Press the Enter key. The table is filtered according to the filtering rule.

10. To add more filters in the current filtering rule, click Or.

This table is filtered so that only rows with dates within the next five days are shown

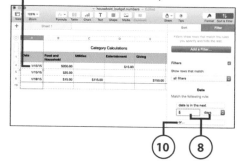

11. Select the type of data you are using in the filtering rule.

12. Select an option for the filtering rule.

13. Configure the filtering rule.

14. Press the Enter key. The table is filtered by the new filtering rule.

15. To filter by another column, click Add a Filter.

16. Choose the column you want to use in the filtering rule.

17. Select the type of data you are using in the filtering rule.

18. Select an option for the filtering rule.

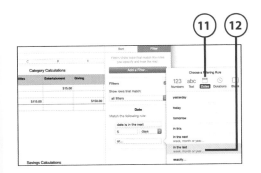

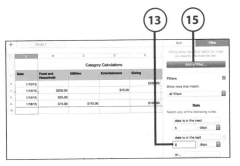

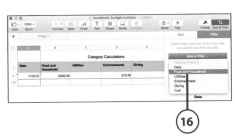

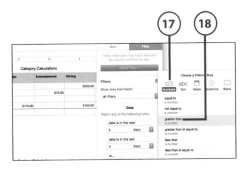

19. Configure the option you selected in step 18.

20. Press Enter. By default, the table is filtered by using all of the filtering rules, meaning that a row must meet all the criteria in the rules to be displayed in the table.

21. To show rows that meet one or more of the filtering rules, choose any filter on the Show rows that match menu.

22. To add more filtering rules, click Add a Filter and use steps 16 through 20 to configure them.

23. To disable a table's filtering rules, uncheck the Filters check box. All the rows are shown again. You can reapply the filtering rules by checking the check box again.

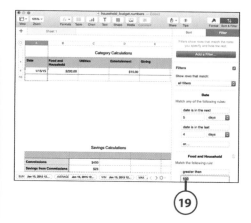

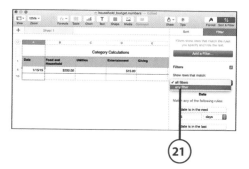

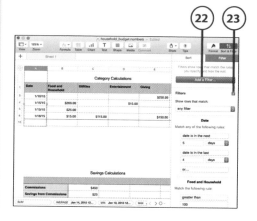

Deleting Filtering Rules

To delete a filtering rule, hover over the name of the column being used and click the Trash button. That filtering rule is removed.

Check Spelling in Numbers Spreadsheets

Most spreadsheets contain text along with numeric data. You can use OS X's spell checking tools to make sure the words in your spreadsheets are spelled correctly.

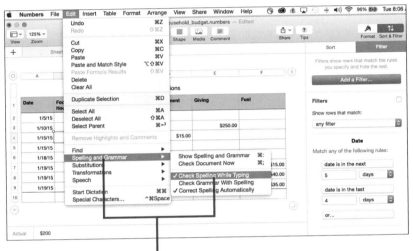

Use OS X's spelling and grammar tools
to check the text in your spreadsheets

Like almost all OS X apps, you access spelling and grammar tools on the Edit menu. You can have your spelling checked as you type, or you can check the spelling and grammar in a spreadsheet at any time. These tools work just as they do in the other iWork apps; details are provided in the section "Correct Spelling in a Pages Document" in Chapter 5, "Finishing Pages Documents."

Collaborate with Others on Numbers Spreadsheets

The iWork apps provide a consistent way to collaborate with others on your documents: comments and iCloud sharing.

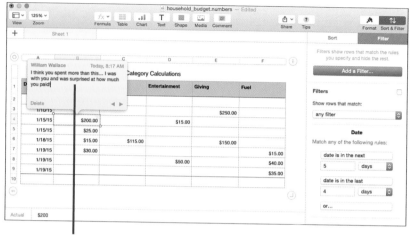

People can add comments to your Numbers spreadsheets just like your Pages documents

Comments allow others (or you) to add commentary to your Numbers spreadsheets.

To add comments, choose the cell to which the comment applies (you can only apply comments to individual cells), choose Comment on the Insert menu, and type your comment.

You can then review comments you or others have made and make changes to your spreadsheets accordingly (or not). Once you're done with comments, you can remove them.

Working with comments in Numbers spreadsheets is just like using them in Pages documents. See the section "Work with Comments in Pages Documents" in Chapter 6, "Collaborating with Others on Pages Documents" for detailed steps.

You can use iCloud to collaborate on Numbers spreadsheets in real time

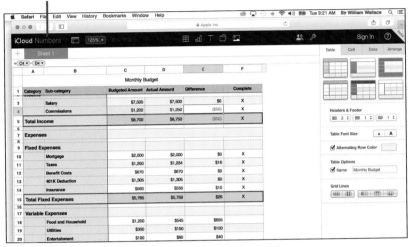

You can collaborate on spreadsheets with others in real time by sharing them using iCloud. Others can open the same spreadsheet you have open to review its contents and to make changes. This can be an effective way to polish spreadsheets you have created because you can incorporate other people's suggestions, or they can enter them directly into your Numbers spreadsheets.

This also works just as it does with Pages documents. For detailed steps, see "Collaborate on Pages Documents via iCloud Sharing" in Chapter 6.

But Wait; There's More

Printing, exporting, and other tasks that are common to all the iWork apps are covered in Chapter 17, "Publishing and Sharing Pages, Numbers, and Keynote Documents."

Create an outline for your
presentations to guide
their development

Use master slides to design
how the slides in your
presentations look and the
content they contain

In this chapter, you learn how to get started with Keynote presentations. Topics include the following:

→ Configure the Master Slides for Keynote Presentations
→ Build an Outline for Keynote Presentations

Developing Keynote Presentations

You can use Keynote to build effective and interesting presentations, which you can then deliver using a variety of means, such as a Mac, an iPad, or an iPhone. Like Pages and Numbers, Keynote offers lots of great features you can use to create compelling documents quickly and easily. If you read the previous chapters in this book, you are already familiar with many of these because Keynote uses the same toolsets for text, graphics, and other elements as Pages and Numbers. Of course, because Keynote creates its own unique type of documents (presentations as opposed to text documents or spreadsheets), it has a number of tools that are unique to it.

In this chapter through Chapter 16, "Presenting Keynote Presentations," you learn how to create, add content to, and present your Keynote presentations.

As you read this chapter, you learn how to develop a Keynote presentation by working with its master slides and creating an outline.

Presentations tend to have a greater number of design elements, such as backgrounds, colors, and text formats, than Pages documents or Numbers spreadsheets. Like those apps, Keynote includes a large number of templates (called themes) that you can start with as you create your own presentations. In most cases, you can save yourself a lot of time and end up with better results when you create your presentations using one of these templates. (See Chapter 1, "Working with iWork Documents," for information about creating a new document using a template.) This and the following chapters show a presentation created with the Slate template. Other templates look different but offer similar elements and features.

Configure the Master Slides for Keynote Presentations

Every slide you create in a Keynote presentation is based on a master slide that defines many aspects of how a slide looks and what type of content it contains. Because of this, it's important to understand what master slides are and how you can use them in your presentations.

Master slides typically include the following elements:

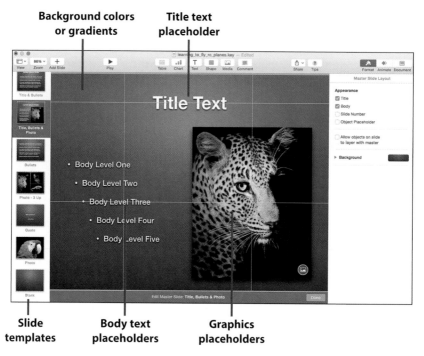

Background colors or gradients   **Title text placeholder**

Slide templates   **Body text placeholders**   **Graphics placeholders**

- **Background colors or gradients.** Master slides include background colors or gradients to set the overall look of your presentation.

- **Title text placeholder.** Many slides include a title at the top to identify the contents of the slide. The master slides include a title text placeholder that is formatted according to the template (theme) you selected when you created the presentation. When you create a slide, you replace the title text placeholder with the slide's actual title.

- **Slide templates.** When you add a new slide to a presentation, you can choose from various master slide templates available based on the presentation template you started with. Each template is designed for specific types of content, such as bullets, photos, or combinations of types of content. When you create a new slide, you should choose the template that best represents the content you are going to put on the slide. Note that you aren't limited to that type of content on a slide template because you can add more content of any type to a slide at any time.

- **Body text placeholders.** The most common type of text in a presentation is bulleted lists of text. Some slide templates include bulleted lists that are formatted according to the presentation's template (theme). When you create a new slide, you replace the body text placeholder with the slide's actual text.

- **Graphics placeholders.** Many slide templates include placeholders for graphics, such as photos. When you create a slide, you replace the graphics in placeholders with the slide's actual graphics, such as photos stored on your Mac.

Reviewing the master slides provided by the presentation template you are using can help you understand how your slides will look and what type of content they will contain. You can tweak the master slides to better suit your preferences and specific presentation. For example, you might want to change the font size of title text to be a bit larger or smaller than provided on the original master slide. You can change the master slides as much or as little as you like.

As you work with master slides, know that you aren't limited by them in any way. You can override the formatting and content from a master slide on any individual slide or add to it. For example, if you based a slide on a slide template with one placeholder for a graphic, you can add more graphics to that slide even though it has only one placeholder on it.

The primary purposes of master slides are to make your presentations look better and to give your presentations a more consistent and cohesive feel with less work on your part. Master slides don't limit your creativity.

In the following sections, you learn how to work with the master slides in a presentation. Start by viewing the master slides to make sure they are suitable for the presentation you are creating. As you view the master slides, you can make changes to their design; it's a good idea to do this before you start using them to create slides because that prevents you from having to do more work later.

View the Master Slides for Keynote Presentations

To see the master slides available in a presentation, perform the following steps:

1. Choose View, Edit Master Slides. In the center part of the window, you see the master slide for the slide currently selected. In the Sidebar on the left, you see the other master slides available based on the presentation template you selected when you created the presentation.

Be Warned

If slides in the presentation have content in them when you view the master slides, you see a warning that changing the master slides can impact the slides you have created. It's best to try to make changes on the master slides before using them to create content slides. If you change master slides after you use them to create content slides, carefully check the content slides to ensure the changes you made to the master slides didn't create problems.

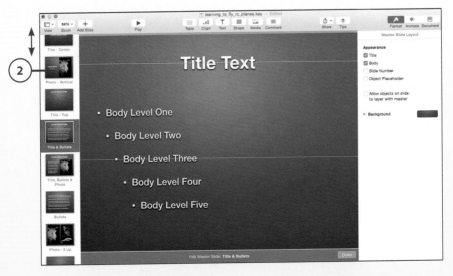

2. Browse up and down the master slide Sidebar on the left to see all the templates available.

3. Click a slide master you want to view. It appears in the center part of the window.

4. Review the slide master to see the type of content it contains and how that content is formatted.

5. View other templates available in the presentation.

6. Click Done when you are finished working with the master slides.

Change the Master Slides for Keynote Presentations

You can change the design of the master slides being used in a presentation; this allows you to completely personalize the presentations that you develop. After you change one or more master slides, any new slides you create use the updated design of the master slides on which they are based.

1. View the master slide you want to change.

2. If it isn't open already, open the Inspector by clicking the Format button. You see the Master Slide Layout tools in the Inspector.

3. Check the check boxes to add elements to or uncheck check boxes to remove elements from the master slide. You can add or remove title text (Title), body test (Body), slide number (Slide Number), or a placeholder for a table or chart (Object Placeholder).

Object Placeholder

An object placeholder can be used to preset a table or chart (such as one you created in Numbers). The size and shape of the placeholder determines the size and shape of the table or chart, as those objects fit the placeholder automatically. You can only add one object placeholder per master slide.

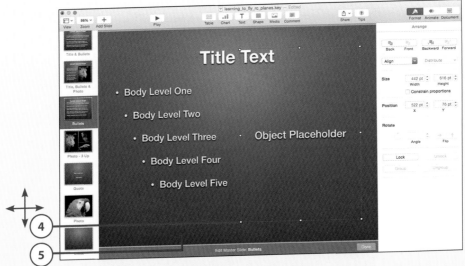

4. If you added an object placeholder, resize and position it on the slide using its selection handles just like other objects.

5. If you selected an object placeholder, click outside it to return to the Master Slide Layout Inspector.

6. If you want to be able to layer objects with objects on the master slide, check the Allow on slide to layer with master check box.

7. To change the master slides' background, click the Background disclosure triangle and use the resulting tools to change the color, replace the background with your own image, edit the gradient, and so on. In most cases, you'll probably want to stick with the background from the template, but you can change it if you want to.

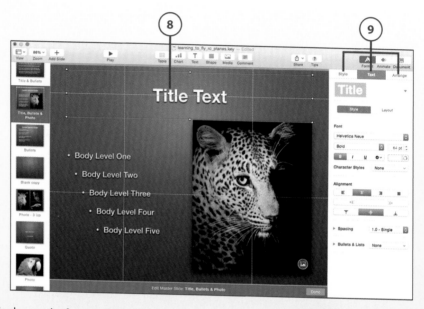

8. To change the format of text on the slide master, select the text placeholder whose format you want to change.

9. Use the tools in the Inspector to change the text box's style (Style tab), the format of the text in the text box (the Text tab), or the way the text box is aligned with and layered on the slide (the Arrange tab). These tools work just like they do in Pages and when you are working with text on a slide. (This topic is covered in later chapters.)

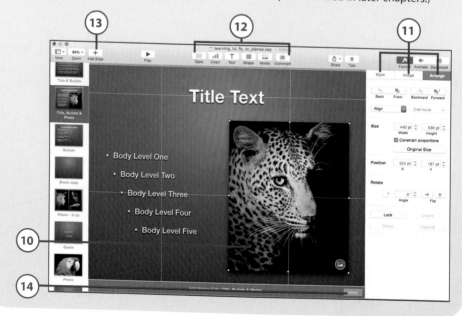

Deleting Master Slides

You can get rid of a master slide by selecting its thumbnail and pressing the Delete key.

10. You can select, resize, or reposition objects on a master slide by dragging their selection handles to resize them or dragging the objects themselves to move them.

11. Use the tools in the Inspector to reformat graphics placeholders on the page; again, these work just like when you manipulate objects on a slide. (The details are explained in later chapters.)

12. Use the content tools on the toolbar to add tables, charts, text boxes, shapes, or media (images, audio, or video) to the master slide. At the risk of being overly repetitious, the details of using these tools are provided in later chapters.

13. To add a new master slide, click Add Slide and click the master slide you want to start with. (You can choose a blank master slide to start from scratch.) A new master slide is created. You can design the new master slide using the same tools you did when changing an existing master slide.

Renaming Master Slides

To rename a master slide, double-click its current title (the text under its thumbnail) and edit the name as you see fit. It's helpful to use a name that makes choosing the correct master slide easier, such as a description of the type of slide for which you intend the master slide to be used.

14. When you're finished working with the master slides, click Done.

What Happens to Existing Slides When You Change the Master Slide?

When you change a master slide, any slides created using that master slide change accordingly. For example, if you move or resize a graphic placeholder on a master slide, any graphics on slides that use that master slide are also moved or resized. This can have unexpected consequences, so try to finalize your master slides before you create content slides in the presentation. If you make changes to master slides after you have added content slides, make sure you carefully review those content slides to ensure the changes you made to the master slide didn't negatively impact them.

Build an Outline for Keynote Presentations

Many people remember an outline from their school days as something one or more teachers tried to get them to create "just because." Rather than being a tedious task of little to no value, creating an outline is actually one of the most important steps in creating any kind of document; an outline defines the purpose, structure, and content of a presentation. You use the outline to guide you through the development of your presentation so that the end result achieves the purpose you had in creating that presentation. Creating a presentation without an outline is like trying to build a house without a plan. Even if it does end up being a house, which isn't likely, the process to build it will take a lot longer and be much more difficult than if a good set of plans were used.

To create an outline, you add a slide for each major "section" of content in the presentation. When you add a slide, you choose the master slide on which you want to base the slide you are creating; this determines the type of content that slide contains, so it's worth taking some time and thinking about what you want to do with each slide when choosing its master slide. When a slide contains a placeholder for title text, you should replace that placeholder with the slide's title. These titles become the "section titles" in your outline.

Once your outline is complete, you go through each slide adding its content, changing its design, and so on to fill out your presentation. (These tasks are covered in subsequent chapters.) As you do this, you may end up using multiple slides to complete the content represented by a single slide in your outline, which is to be expected.

At the risk of pummeling a deceased equine, get in the habit of spending time and brainpower to create an outline for a presentation before you start working on individual slides. Although it may seem you are "wasting" time, an outline actually makes the process go faster and easier while producing much better results.

Add Slides to Keynote Presentations

To add slides to a Keynote presentation, complete the following steps:

1. Click Add Slide.

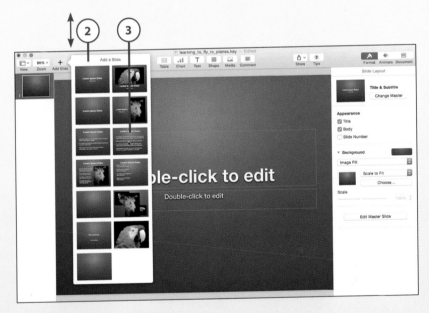

2. Browse the master slides available in the presentation.

3. Click the slide master from which you want to create the slide.

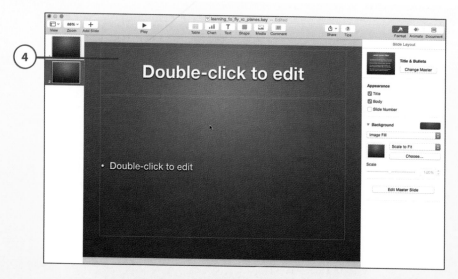

4. Replace content in placeholders with your content, add new content, and design the way the slide looks. (All of these tasks are covered in detail in this and subsequent chapters.) It's usually a good idea to build an outline by adding slides and titling them (see the next task) before completing each slide.

5. Repeat steps 1 through 4 until you've added all the slides you think you'll need in the presentation.

Building Slideshows Faster

To add slides to a presentation more quickly, add the master slides that you are going to use for multiple content slides. Exit the Slide Master mode and then select the slide built on a master slide you want to use more than once. Choose Edit, Copy and then Choose Edit, Paste to create a copy of the slide. Repeat until you have the number of slides you want. You can then reorder the slides as needed. (See "Reorder the Slides in Keynote Presentations," later in this chapter.)

Replace Text in Title Text Placeholders on Slides in Keynote Presentations

Many slides in a presentation have title text that identifies the content of those slides. When a slide includes a title text placeholder, replace the placeholder text with the slide's title as follows:

1. Double-click the title text placeholder.

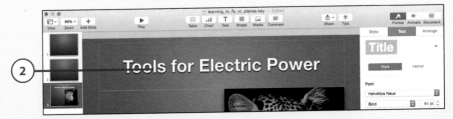

2. Type the slide's title.

3. Repeat steps 1 and 2 until you've titled all the slides in the presentation that have title text placeholders.

Change How You View Slides in Keynote Presentations

As you work with a presentation, it is useful to be able to view the slides in different ways based on the task you are performing. Keynote offers several different view options. To choose the view option you are using at any time, perform the following steps:

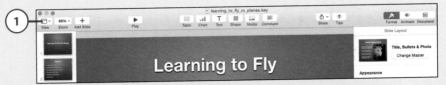

1. Click the View button.

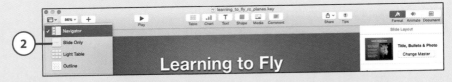

2. Click the view you want to use. The Navigator view comes up, unless it is already in that view. The view options are Navigator, Slide Only, Light Table, and Outline. A figure showing each view and a brief description of when the view is useful follow:

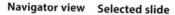

Navigator view   Selected slide

Slide   Drag to the left or right to
thumbnails   change the width of the Sidebar

Navigator is the default view; that's because it's probably the view you'll use most. In the Sidebar on the left, you can browse all the slides in the presentation. When you click a slide's thumbnail, it appears in the large center part of the window so you can work on it. You can change the size of the Sidebar by dragging its border to the left or right. This view is useful because it provides a good amount of room for you to work on a slide and makes it easy to get to the slides in the presentation.

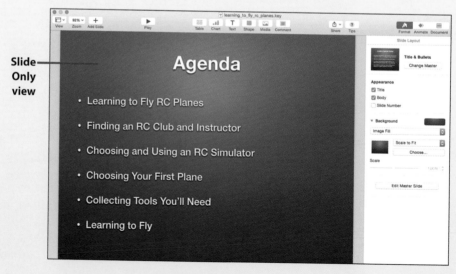

Slide
Only
view

In the Slide Only view, the current slide fills the window; of course, if the Inspector is open, you see it on the right side of the window. This view is useful when you need the maximum amount of space to work on a slide. You need to change to a different view to be able to select a different slide, so it is a bit cumbersome.

Light Table view

Current slide

Double-click a slide to work on it

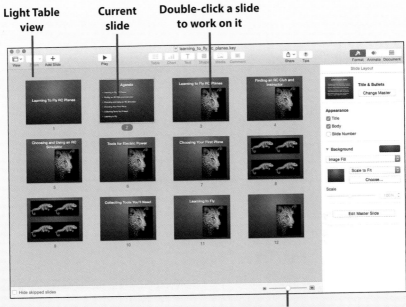

Drag to the left to make the thumbnails smaller or to the right to make them larger

The Light Table view shows thumbnails of all the slides in the presentation. You can browse up and down the window to see all the slides if there are too many to display in the current space. You can change the size of the thumbnails using the slider at the bottom of the window. This view is particularly useful for changing the order of slides, as you learn in the next task. You can work on a slide by double-clicking its thumbnail. It opens in the view you were most recently using, such as Navigator.

Outline view

Current slide

③

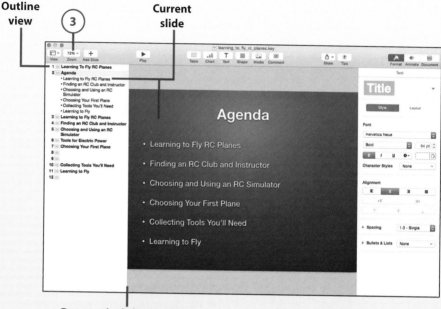

Drag to the left or right to change the width of the Sidebar

In the Outline view, you see the presentation's outline in the left Sidebar. As you might guess from its name, this view is particularly useful for working with a presentation's outline because you can see the titles of slides and an outline view of the text they contain. You can select a slide in the Sidebar to work with it. You can also change the text on slides by editing it directly on the thumbnails.

3. To change the size at which you are viewing the current slide, open the View menu. The current view size is marked with a check mark.

4. Choose the size of view you want or choose Fit in Window to have Keynote size the current slide so you can see all of it in the Keynote window. The larger percentage views are useful when you are working on details, whereas the smaller percentages are helpful when you are laying out a slide.

Reorder the Slides in Keynote Presentations

It is often useful to change the order in which slides appear in a Keynote presentation. You can do this in the Navigator, Light Table, or Outline views. The following steps show the Light Table view:

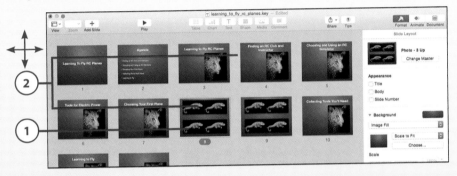

1. Select the slide you want to move.

2. Drag the thumbnail for the slide you want to move from its current position to where you want it to be. As you move a slide, surrounding slides spread out to make room for the slide you are relocating.

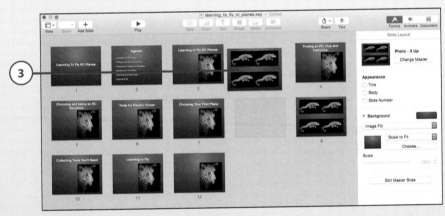

3. When the slide is in its new position, release it.

Change the Master Slide Used for Slides in Keynote Presentations

Earlier you learned how to work with master slides. You can also change the master slide currently applied to a slide in a presentation to change that slide's design:

1. Select the slide whose master you want to change.

2. Open the Inspector if it isn't open already. You see the Slide Layout pane. (If you don't see this pane, something on the slide is selected instead of the slide itself. Click a different slide to clear the selection and then return to the slide you want to work on.)

3. To change the master slide applied to the current slide, click Change Master.

Not So Hasty, Please!

Be aware that when you change the master slide applied to a slide, that slide's design and content can be changed significantly. It's usually a good idea to change a slide's master before you've done much with its content so you don't lose work. As you learn in this task, you can change the design elements for a slide without changing its slide master, which is useful because doing so doesn't eliminate the slide's content.

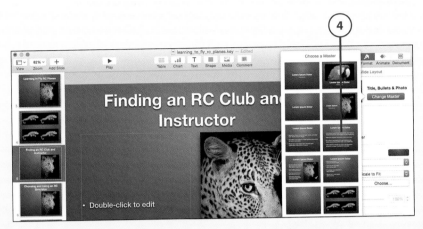

4. Click the master slide you want to apply to the current slide. The design of the slide is updated to reflect the new master slide.

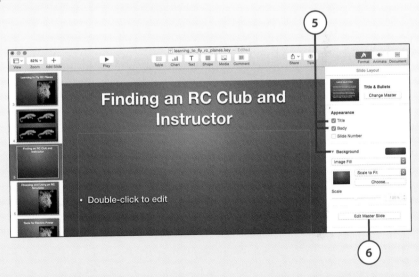

5. Use the Appearance check boxes and Background tool to add or remove elements or change the slide's background. These tools work just as they do when you are editing master slides except these changes impact only the current slide you are working on. (The master slide on which the current slide is based is not changed.)

6. To change the design of the master slide applied to the current slide, click Edit Master Slide and use the information in the task "Change the Master Slides for Keynote Presentations" earlier in the chapter. The changes you make this way affect all the slides that use the same master slide.

Add text with titles, bulleted
lists, text boxes, and shapes

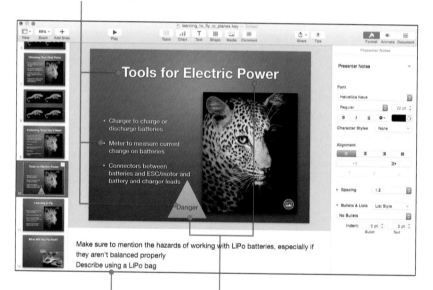

Use presenter notes to help
you make more effective
presentations

Format text
and objects
containing text

In this chapter, you learn how to add and format text on Keynote slides. Topics include the following:

→ Add Text to Keynote Slides
→ Format Text on Keynote Slides
→ Add Presenter Notes to Keynote Slides

Working with Text in Keynote Presentations

There are several types of text you're likely to use in your presentations, including the following:

- **Presentation titles.** In most cases, the first slide in a presentation contains the presentation's title, the presenter's name, the date, or other introductory information.

- **Slide titles.** Slide titles appear at the top of slides and should help the audience understand the purpose of the slide, such as its topic. A number of Keynote template slides don't include a placeholder for a slide title, but you can add one at any time. It is good practice to include a title on every slide both for the audience's understanding and to help you outline and develop your presentation.

- **Body text.** The body text contains the text you want the audience to see as you present. In most cases, body text consists of bulleted lists. Unlike Pages documents, the text in Keynote presentations is often just a summary of the information you are presenting. It's good practice to keep the text on slides relatively short and concise so the audience can read it quickly and easily. Its primary purposes are to reinforce the information you are presenting and to lead you and the audience through the presentation.

- **Shaped text.** You can include text in shapes, such as circles, triangles, and more. This can be useful to highlight key points and to make a presentation more interesting visually.

- **Captions.** Captions are used to label figures or other objects to help the audience understand what they are or to explain the purpose of the graphic.

- **Callouts.** Callouts are text that explains or highlights something on a graphic, such as a photo. A callout is a shaped text object with a pointer to a specific location on another object.

You can use the same tools to work with each of these types of text.

Add Text to Keynote Slides

There are a number of ways to add text to keynote slides, which include:

- **Replacing existing text in a text placeholder.** Many slides in Keynote templates include placeholders for titles or body text. Text placeholders display "Double-click to edit" so you can identify them.

- **Adding new text.** You can add more text to slides by adding a text box and then adding text to that box.

- **Adding a shape and including text within it.** You can include text inside shapes you add to slides.

- **Adding a callout (which is actually just a specific shape).** You add explanatory text inside callouts.

Examples of each of these are provided in the tasks in this section.

One unique thing about the text on Keynote slides is that all text is in a text box of some shape or size. Title text placeholders are usually relatively narrow rectangular boxes that expand across most of the slide's width. Body text boxes usually are tall enough to use most of the available height on a slide and fill either half the slide's width or all of it depending on the slide master being used.

Any text you add, using either the Text or the Shape tool, is also in a text box. You can see a text box by clicking once on the text; the resulting selection handles show you the size and shape of the text box.

Replace Text in Existing Text Boxes on Keynote Slides

In Chapter 11, "Developing Keynote Presentations," you learned how to replace text in title text placeholders. Replacing the text in any text placeholder is similar, as you see in the following steps:

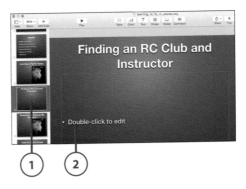

1. View the slide containing the text placeholder you want to replace with your own text.

2. Double-click the "Double-click to edit" text in the text placeholder. The "Double-click to edit" text disappears, and the cursor indicates where the text you are typing starts.

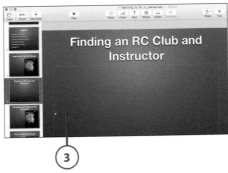

3. Type the text you want to add to the placeholder.

4. Use the same process to fill in the text placeholders in all the slides in the presentation.

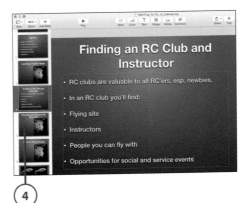

Other Ways to Add Text

Of course, you can use all of OS X's tools to enter text in Keynote presentations. You can dictate text directly onto Keynote slides. You can also copy and paste text from other documents onto slides. (When you paste content onto a Keynote slide, it's useful to use the Paste and Match Style command so that the text you paste uses the formatting of the text box in which you paste it.)

Add More Text Boxes to Keynote Slides

You can add more text to a slide using the Text tool as follows:

1. Move to the slide to which you want to add text.

2. Click the Text button. A new text box containing the word "Text" is added to the slide. The new text box is added to the center of the slide; it can be tough to see if there are objects, such as a graphic placeholder, under it.

3. Double-click the new text placeholder.

4. Type the text you want to add. Don't worry if it overlaps other objects or doesn't have the right size and shape; you'll fix that later.

5. Drag the text box to where you want it to be on the slide.

6. Format the text box and text it contains using the information in the section "Format Text on Keynote Slides" later in this chapter.

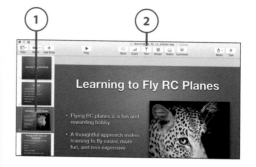

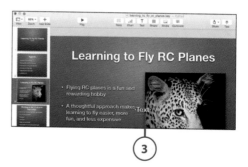

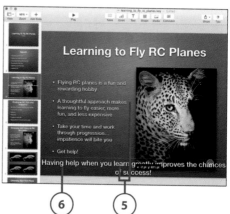

Add Shaped Text to Keynote Slides

It can be interesting and useful to add shapes to present text on a slide. Here's how:

1. Move to the slide to which you want to add shaped text.

2. Click the Shape button. The Shape palette appears.

3. Click the left- or right-facing arrows to browse the available shapes. Each page of shapes contains the same collection of shapes, just in different colors.

4. Click the shape you want to use. The shape is added to the center of the slide.

5. Double-click the shape. The cursor appears inside it.

6. Type the text you want to place in the shape. If you type more text than fits in the shape at its current size, you won't see the text as you type it. When you're done, you see the "+" at the bottom of the shape indicating there is too much text to fit in the shape at its current size.

7. Select the shape. When it's selected, selection handles appear.

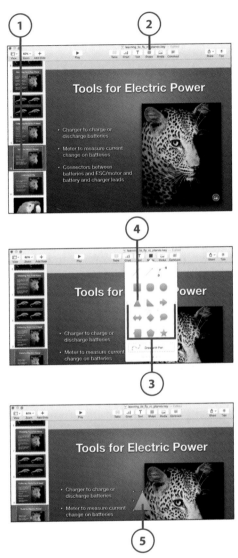

This indicates the shape ⑦ is too small to show the text it contains

8. Resize the shape so it accommodates the text it contains.

9. Move the shape to where you want it to be.

10. Format the shape and text it contains using the information in the section "Format Text on Keynote Slides" later in this chapter.

Add Callouts to Keynote Slides

Callouts are useful to point to specific areas of a graphic on a slide. For example, you might want to help the reader focus on a specific area of a photo to understand a key point. The following steps show how to add callouts:

1. Move to the slide to which you want to add shaped text.

2. Click the Shape button.

Style Matters

As you see in "Apply Formatting to Text on Keynote Slides" later in this chapter, you can use the text style tool to consistently and easily format text. It's a good idea to choose or create styles for specific types of text in your Keynote presentations as you enter that text on your slides. For example, if you are going to use a consistently shaped text element on your slides, maybe something like a caution triangle, it's a good idea to configure a style for that shaped text before you add those shaped text objects to your slides. This makes it easy to format your text because, by applying the style when you create the text object, you format it at the same time. More importantly, you can easily reformat all the text using that style throughout the presentation by simply changing the style.

3. Click a callout shape.

4. Drag the green reshape handle at the "pointed" end of the pointing line to point to the part of the slide that you want to call attention to.

5. Add text to, format the text in, resize, and place the callout just like other shapes.

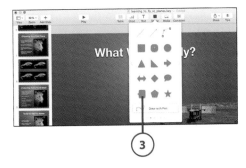

③

④

Rounding

The callout shape has sharp corners when you add it to a slide. You can round the corners by dragging the reshape handle that appears on one of the shape's corners to make the corners of the shape more or less round. Reshape handles are green while selection handles are white, so it's easy to tell which is which. Also, you see reshape handles only where you can reshape a shape, whereas selection handles appear on every "corner" of the shape. If you drag the corner's reshape handle, all the corners are rounded as you drag; you can also see the amount of radius you are using. When you drag the reshape handle as far as it can move, the callout shape becomes an oval.

⑤

Edit Text on Keynote Slides

You can use the following steps to edit any text on a slide:

1. Move to the slide on which you want to edit text.

2. Double-click where you want to start editing.

3. Edit the text by adding to it, deleting it, changing it, and more. If you add more text than can fit in the text box at its current size, the size of the font decreases until all the text fits in the text box. If you add text to a shape so that it can't contain all the text, some of the text disappears, and you see the "+" at the bottom of the shape. You need to resize the shape to display all its text.

Replacing Text

To replace all the text in a text box or shape, double-click inside it so its text becomes editable. Press ⌘-A (Select All), and all the text inside the text box or shape is selected. Type the new text, which replaces all the text that was in the text box previously. If you replace the text by pasting text you've copied, use the Paste and Match Style command instead of just Paste so that the text you paste assumes the formatting of the text currently in the text box.

Format Text on Keynote Slides

Like text in other iWork documents, you'll want to format the text on your Keynote slides. As you probably expect by now, you can use the same text formatting tools in Keynote that you can in Pages and Numbers. These tools include the following:

- **Style.** You use Keynote's Style tools to format the container (such as a text box or shape) in which text is displayed.

- **Text.** The Text formatting tools are used to apply or configure text styles, design the font used, set alignment and spacing, and so on.

- **Arrange.** The Arrange tool enables you to arrange text on a slide, such as layering text objects, rotating them, and so on.

Like the other iWork apps, you use the Inspector to format the text on Keynote slides.

Master Your Formatting

In Chapter 11 you learned about master slides. If the formatting changes you made should apply to all the slides that use the same master slide, format the master slide instead of making changes on the individual slides. For example, suppose you decide that the font size of the first level in a bulleted list should be a bit bigger on all your slides. Change the font size on the master slide, and that font size is changed on all the slides using the same master slide. When you make a format change on an individual slide, it applies only to that slide.

Apply Styles to Text Boxes or Shapes on Keynote Slides

Like text boxes in Pages, you can apply styles to text boxes in Keynote. Here's how:

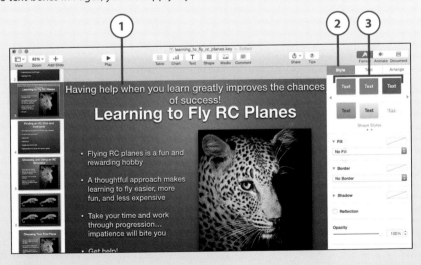

1. Select the text box you want to restyle.

2. Click the Style tab on the Inspector.

3. Use the Style tab's tools to change the text box's style, fill, border, shadow, reflection, or opacity. These tools are described in the task "Style Text Boxes in Pages Documents" in Chapter 2, "Working with Text in Pages Documents."

4. Style other text boxes on the same slide.

5. Style text boxes on other sides.

Apply Formatting to Text on Keynote Slides

You'll want to format the text on slides to make it look appealing and to enable the audience to read it easily.

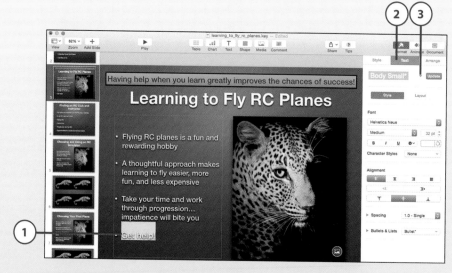

1. Select the text you want to format. You can select a text box or shape to apply formatting to all of its text or select a subset of the text to format words, sentences, and so on.

2. Click the Text tab on the Inspector.

3. Use the text formatting tools to format the selected text. Like text in other apps, you can define and apply styles or use the other tools to manually format text. Details of formatting text are provided in Chapter 2.

Format Bulleted Lists on Keynote Slides

The most common text in presentations is in the form of bulleted lists; many of the master slides include body text in bulleted list format; however, they have only a single "level" of bullets, and it is often useful to have two levels so you can organize content more effectively. Detailed steps to add a second level to a bulleted list follow:

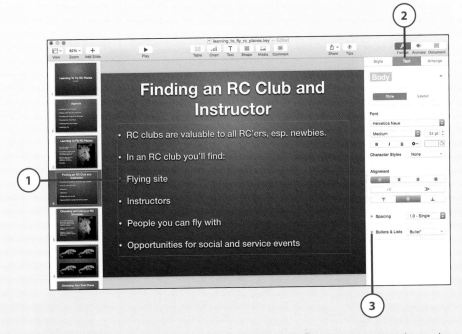

1. Position the cursor so that it is at the start of the first bullet that you want to be on the second level of the list.

2. Click the Text tab on the Inspector.

3. Click the disclosure triangle in the Bullets & Lists section to reveal its tools.

Make Bulleted Lists Your Own

You can use these steps to change the formatting of any bulleted list items. For example, you might want to adjust the first level of bullets to change the type of bullet being used or change other formatting. Just place the cursor in a first-level bullet in step 1. You don't need to create a new style for the first-level bullets; you can just update the current one (called Body in most templates).

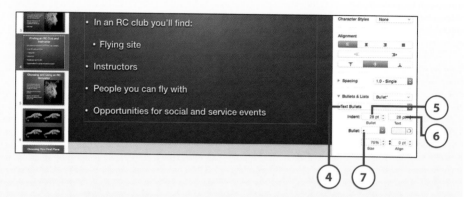

4. Choose the type of bullets you want to be on the second level using the menu directly below the Bullets & Text heading. The options are No Bullets, Text Bullets, Image Bullets, and Numbers. This example shows the Text Bullets option, but you can work with the others similarly.

5. Use the Bullet Indent box to set the amount of space before the bullet. Typically, you want each level in a bulleted list to be indented, with the bullet usually lining up with the text in the level above it. (In other words, the bullet in a second-level list item lines up with the start of the text in the first level.)

6. Use the Text Indent box to configure the amount of space between the bullet and the text.

7. Open the Bullet menu.

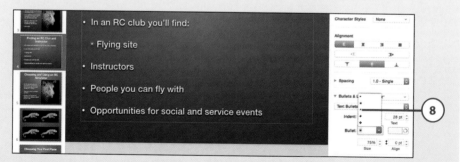

8. Click the type of bullet you want to use. In most cases, you want each level to have a different style of bullet to help the audience make the distinction easily.

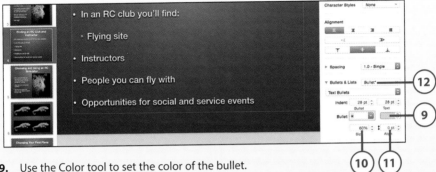

9. Use the Color tool to set the color of the bullet.

10. Use the Size box to set the size of the bullet.

11. Use the Align box to align the horizontal centerline of the bullet with the horizontal centerline of the text. When the Align value is set to 0, the centerlines are aligned. There may be cases in which you want to offset the bullet from the text for design purposes.

12. When you have the list item formatted the way you want it to be, click the List Style menu at the top of the Bullets & Lists section.

13. Click the Add (+) button. This creates a new list style based on the list item you are working with.

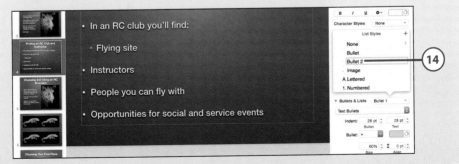

14. Type the name of the bullet list style you are creating. It's a good idea to include the level of the bullet list style in the name, as in Bullet 2 for a second-level bullet.

15. Press the Enter key. The new style is saved and marked with a check mark indicating that it is the style currently applied to the text.

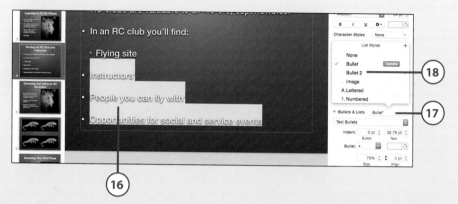

16. Select the other items on the list that should be at the level whose style you just created.

17. Open the Bullets & Lists menu.

18. Choose the bullet style you created. The selected items are reformatted, and all the list items at the same level have the same bullet formatting options.

>>>Go Further
GOING FURTHER WITH BULLETED LISTS

The Bullets & Lists style applies only to the bullets. The style of the text is determined by the text style applied. For example, if the text style is Body, it remains Body even after you apply a different Bullets & Lists style. So, while you change the bullet itself using the Bullets & Lists style, the text format remains the same. If you also want to change the format of the text in each level, use the same process as configuring the styles for any other text. It's a good idea to use a different text format for each level of a bulleted list because that also helps the audience understand the structure of the information more easily.

To create a new text style for a level in the bulleted list, place the cursor in the bulleted list item you want to format. Use the Text Inspector to format it, such as changing the font size, spacing between the lines, and so on. Open the Text Style menu, click the Add (+) button, name the new style, and press the Enter key. Now the bullet has the style you created for it, while the text has the style defined by the text style you created. Formatting additional list items using these two styles requires you to apply both the text style and the bullet style as separate steps.

Arrange the Text on Keynote Slides

You can change how objects on slides relate to the slide and to each other using the Inspector's Arrange tab as follows:

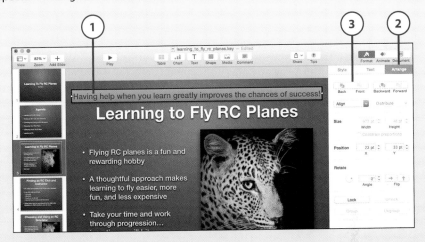

1. Select the text you want to arrange.

2. Click the Arrange tab in the Inspector.

3. Use the Arrange tools to determine how the text aligns with the slide and with other objects on the slide. The Arrange tools work just like in other apps; for the details of using these, see "Arrange Text Boxes in Pages Documents" in Chapter 2 and "Add Photos and Other Graphics to Keynote Presentations" in Chapter 13, "Working with Graphics and Other Objects in Keynote Presentations."

Add Presenter Notes to Keynote Slides

Presenter notes enable you to add any information about your slides that you want to have available without including that information on the slides themselves. Presenter notes are typically used to help you remember key points on the slide that you want to communicate during your presentation. For example, you might want to include notes about an anecdote related to the slide's topic, tips and tricks, reminders to yourself to help you avoid bad presentation habits, timing reminders, and more.

When you present a Keynote slideshow with your Mac connected to two displays (such as the internal display on a MacBook and a projector), you can choose to display different windows on each device. Usually the Keynote window you show to the audience displays the slides (and only the slides) in Presentation mode, whereas the window you see shows such things as the slides, presenter notes, and timing information.

You can add and format presenter notes for your slides with the following steps:

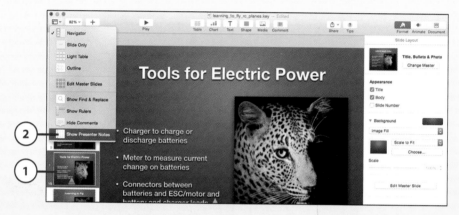

1. Move to the slide to which you want to add presenter notes.

2. Open the View menu and choose Show Presenter Notes. The Presenter Notes pane opens at the bottom of the Keynote window.

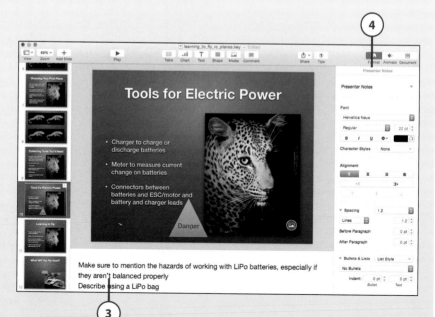

3. Type the notes you want to add to the slide.

4. Use the Inspector's Presenter Notes sidebar to format the notes. You have similar formatting options as with other text, such as text styles, bullets, and so on.

Please Make a Note of It

Keynote includes a default text style for presenter notes called, cleverly enough, Presenter Notes. If you make changes to the format of text in presenter notes, click the Update button that appears next to Presenter Notes on the Text Styles menu. This changes the Presenter Notes style to match the text you are formatting. Any text already formatted with the style is reformatted using the new definition, and any new text you enter in that style also uses this format.

The Inspector provides
lots of tools you can use to
format the graphics you use
in your presentation

Use shapes or groups of shapes
to drive home your points

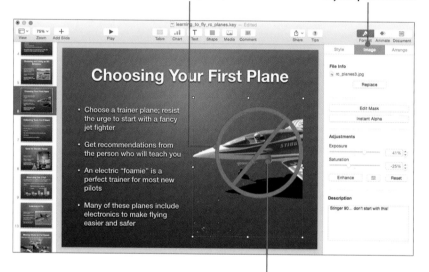

Add photos to presentations
for clarity and visual interest

In this chapter, you learn how to add and format various types of graphics in Keynote presentations. Topics include the following:

→ Add Photos and Other Graphics to Keynote Presentations
→ Add Charts to Keynote Presentations
→ Add Shapes to Keynote Presentations

Working with Graphics and Other Objects in Keynote Presentations

Presentations are seen as well as heard, so the graphics you include in your Keynote presentations are very important for both effectively informing the audience about your topic and making your presentations more interesting (which is also tied to making them effective). You can add a variety of graphics to your Keynote presentations, including the following:

- **Photos.** You can easily add photos from iPhoto or Aperture to Keynote presentations. Adding photos stored elsewhere on your Mac isn't much harder.

- **Other graphics.** You can use any graphics file, such as drawings, floor plans, and blueprints, in presentations similarly to the way you use photos.

- **Charts and tables.** Charts are an excellent way to communicate various types of information, especially if you are comparing information or showing trends over time. You can use Keynote's tools to create charts and tables, or you can create them in Numbers and copy and paste them into your Keynote presentations.

- **Shapes.** In the previous chapter, you saw how you can add shaped text to presentations. You can also include shapes without text.

- **Video or audio.** You can include videos or audio files on slides to play them during your presentation. Both can be useful to improve how the audience receives the information you are presenting and to make your presentations more appealing. For example, if you are explaining how to accomplish a task, a video demonstrating the steps can be effective.

You find tasks detailing how you can work with these types of content throughout the rest of this chapter.

Add Photos and Other Graphics to Keynote Presentations

Many slide masters include placeholders for graphics. You can replace the placeholder with your photos or other types of graphics. You can also add photos and graphics without using a placeholder.

There are two sources for the photos and other graphics you use in your Keynote presentations. If the graphic you want to add is in your iPhoto or Aperture library, you can use the Media Browser to add it to a slide. If it is stored on your computer in a different location, you can add it with just a bit more work.

Once it's added to a slide, you can then format and arrange the graphic on your slide.

Replace Placeholders with Photos in iPhoto or Aperture on Keynote Slides

To insert a photo or graphic in your iPhoto or Aperture library into a placeholder on a slide, perform the following steps:

1. Click the Media Browser button on the graphic placeholder in which you want to place your graphic. The Media Browser opens.

2. Click the Photos tab. On the left side of the browser, you see the hierarchy in your iPhoto or Aperture photo library.

3. Browse or search in the available photos to find the image you want to add to the slide.

4. Click the photo or graphic you want to add to the slide. The photo or image you selected replaces the image in the placeholder.

5. Size, mask, format, and arrange the graphic. (These actions are all covered in later tasks.)

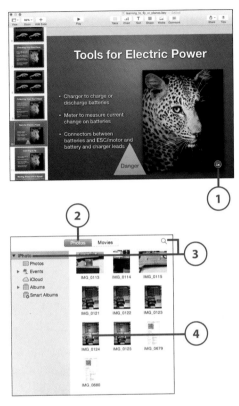

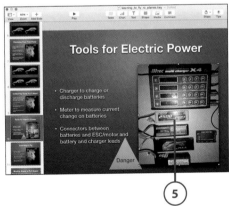

It's Not All Good

The Media Browser labels the photo library as iPhoto when you are using iPhoto or Aperture. Just ignore the iPhoto label if you use Aperture.

Replace Placeholders with Photos on Your Mac's Desktop on Keynote Slides

To insert a photo or graphic not stored in iPhoto or Aperture into a placeholder on a slide, do the following:

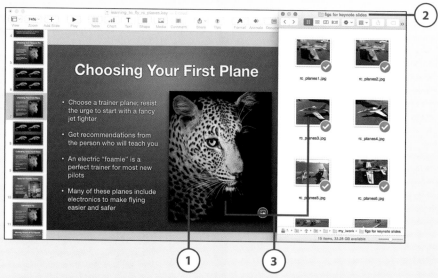

1. Move to the slide containing the placeholder that you want to replace.
2. Open a Finder window showing the graphic you want to use on the slide.
3. Position the two windows so that you can see the placeholder and the folder containing the graphics file.

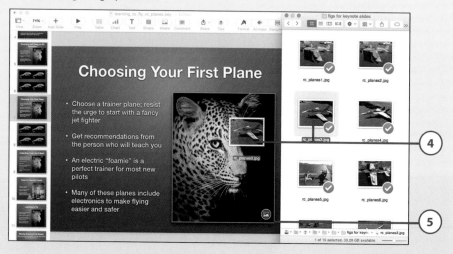

4. Drag the image from the Finder window onto the placeholder.

5. When the placeholder is highlighted in a blue box, release the image. The image fills the placeholder.

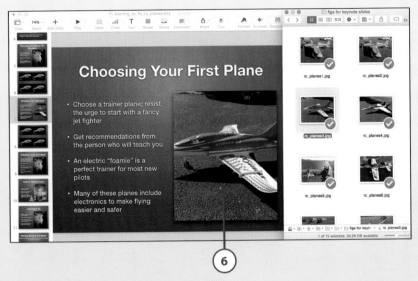

6. Size, mask, format, and arrange the graphic. (These steps are all covered in later tasks.)

Add More Graphics to Keynote Slides

Many slide masters have only one image placeholder on them. You might want to have multiple images on the same slide, or you might want to use images in locations and at other sizes than defined by placeholders. Fortunately, you aren't limited to adding photos or graphics only using placeholders, as the following steps illustrate:

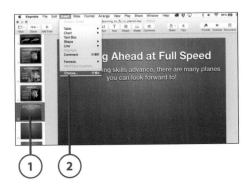

1. Move to the slide on which you want to place a graphic.

2. Choose Insert, Choose. The Select File sheet appears.

3. Move to and select the file you want to add to the slide.

4. Click Insert. The graphic is added to the slide. It is added at its default size so it may cover the slide.

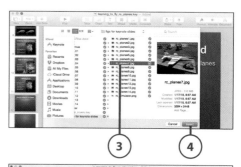

5. Select the graphic you added to the slide if it isn't selected already.

6. Resize the graphic until it is the size you want it to be.

7. Add the rest of the graphics to the slide.

Adding Graphics Is a Drag

Like replacing a graphic in a placeholder by dragging it there, you can add graphics from a Finder window to a slide by dragging them from the Finder onto the slide.

Mask Graphics on Keynote Slides

You can determine which part of a graphic is displayed by masking it as follows:

1. Double-click the image you want to mask. The full image is displayed with the part that is currently not shown being grayed out. You also see the masking tool.

2. Click the Mask button to adjust the mask.

3. Drag the slider to the right to increase the size of the image being displayed in the mask or to the left to decrease it.

4. Drag the image around inside the mask to change the part of the image that is displayed.

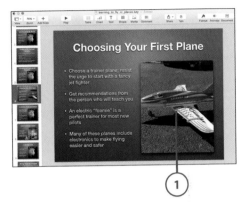

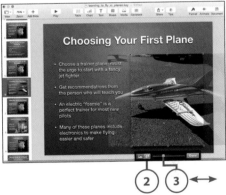

5. Click the Size box to change the size of the image on the slide. (This is selected automatically when you perform step 4.)

6. Drag the slider to change the size of the image.

7. Drag the resized image around to change the part that is shown in the mask.

8. Click Done to close the Mask tool. You see the image as masked and sized on the slide.

9. If the image isn't quite right, repeat steps 1 through 8 until it is.

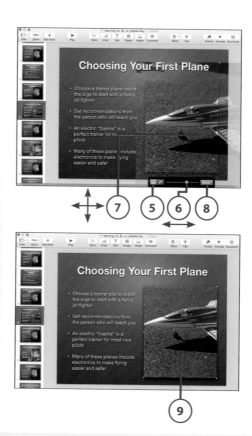

Format Graphics on Keynote Slides

Like other objects, you can format the graphics on slides using the following steps:

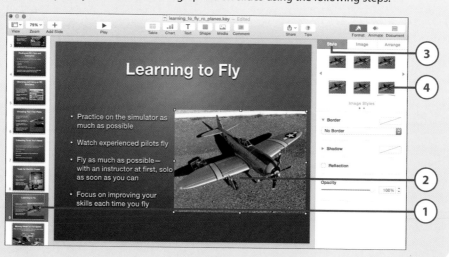

1. Move to the slide with the graphic you want to format.

2. Select the graphic.

3. Click the Style tab of the Inspector. (If the Inspector isn't shown, click the Format button on the toolbar to open it.)

4. Click a style to apply it to the image. Styles can include all the options you see on the tab, such as borders and shadows.

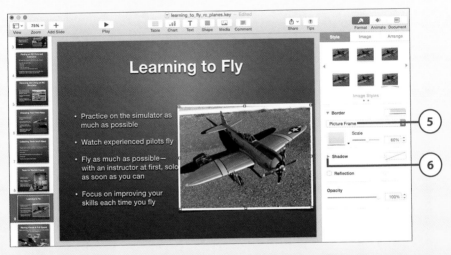

5. Use the Border tools to apply a border or to modify the current border. (If you applied a style that doesn't include a border in step 4, the box for the Border tool shows a red line through it, indicating that no border is currently applied. This doesn't stop you from modifying the border. You can click the box and choose a border to apply.)

6. Expand the Shadow section by clicking its disclosure triangle. (If you applied a style that doesn't include a shadow in step 4, the box for the Shadow tool shows a red line through it, indicating that no shadow is currently applied. Like the border, this doesn't stop you from modifying the shadow. You can click the box and choose a shadow to apply.)

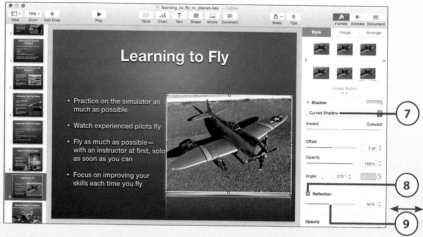

7. Use the Shadow tools to apply and configure a shadow for the image. There are many options from which you can choose, such as Curved, Offset, and Color.

8. Apply a reflection by checking the Reflection check box.

9. Use the slider to set the amount of reflection.

10. Use the Opacity slider to set the opaqueness of the image.

Saving Styles

As with Pages and Numbers, you can save the style settings you use on a graphic so that you can easily apply those same style options to other images. Configure the style options you want to save. Click the right-facing arrow in the Image Style section until you see a style containing the Add button (+). When you click the Add button, the current style options are saved as a new style. You apply the same options to other images by selecting them and clicking the custom style you created.

Adjust Graphics on Keynote Slides

You can change many aspects of graphics you use on the Image tab of the Inspector.

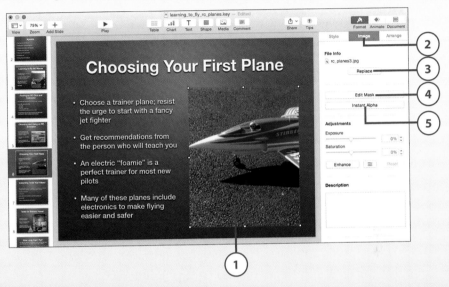

1. Select the graphic you want to adjust.

2. Click the Image tab of the Inspector.

3. To replace the graphic, click Replace and use the resulting sheet to choose the graphic with which you want to replace the current one.

4. To change the size or the mask of the image, click Edit Mask. This does the same thing as double-clicking the image. (See "Mask Graphics on Keynote Slides," later in this chapter.)

5. To remove background or specific colors from the image, click Instant Alpha. The Instant Alpha tool appears, its cursor is a large square that magnifies the color/background it is over.

6. Drag over the area that you want to remove from the image. As you drag, the color/ background that will be removed is highlighted, and the percentage is indicated on the screen.

7. When the part of the background/color you want to remove is highlighted, release the cursor. That part of the image assumes the color of the slide's background. (In other words, it becomes invisible.)

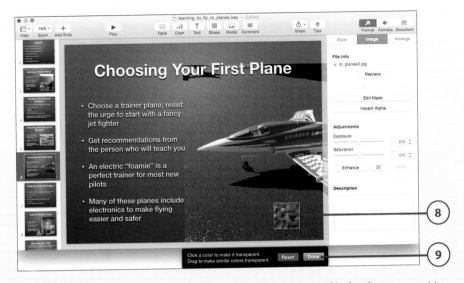

8. Repeat steps 6 and 7 until you've removed all the background/color that you want to get rid of.

9. Click Done. You see the image as you have changed it.

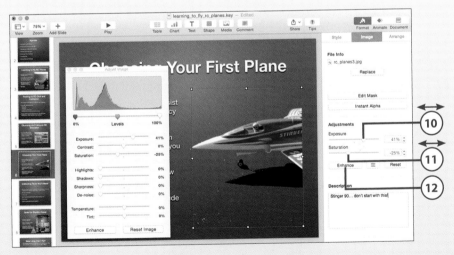

10. Use the Exposure slider to increase or decrease the exposure level.

11. Slide the Saturation slider to the left or right to decrease or increase, respectively, the saturation level of the colors in the image.

12. Click Enhance to have Keynote automatically enhance the photo. Sometimes this makes improvement, sometimes its impact isn't noticeable, and in some cases, it makes the image worse.

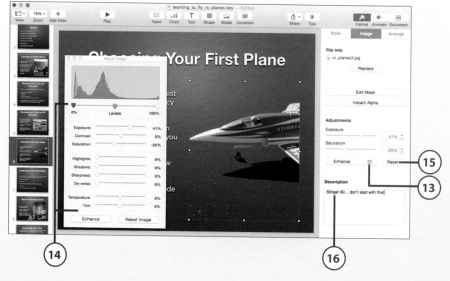

13. To make more precise adjustments, click the Adjust Image button. The Adjust Image tool appears.

14. Use the sliders on the Adjust Image tool to make changes to the image.

15. Click Reset to remove the changes you've made.

16. If desired, enter a description of the photo.

Don't Bother

When you are using the Instant Alpha tool, you see the entire image, including the parts outside the mask. Unfortunately, you can't tell which part of the image is visible when the Instant Alpha tool is displayed. If you have masked the image, you don't need to use the Instant Alpha tool on the areas that aren't visible. It's a good idea to click the Done button every so often to make sure you aren't wasting time removing parts of the image that won't be seen because of the mask.

Arrange Graphics on Keynote Slides

Arranging graphics on slides is very useful, especially if you have more than one image on the same slide.

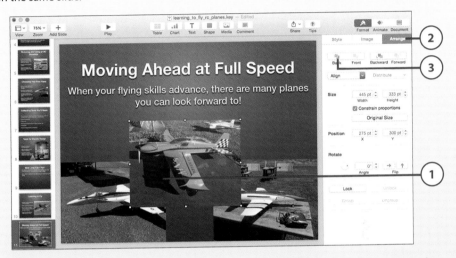

1. Select the graphic or graphics you want to arrange. If you select more than one graphic, the changes you make are applied to all the selected graphics at the same time.

2. Click the Arrange tab of the Inspector.

3. Use the position buttons and menus to determine how the selected graphics relate to the slide and to each other. For example, to position a graphic in the back, click Back, and any graphics that currently overlap it move to be in front of it.

4. Use the Align menu to choose how selected images align with each other.

5. Use the Distribute menu to distribute selected images evenly. For example, choose Horizontally to spread selected graphics evenly across the width of the slide.

6. Use the Size tools to set the size of the image. (Of course, you can drag its selectvion handles, too.)

7. Use the Position tools to set the image's position on the slide. (You can also drag it around the slide.)

8. Use the Rotate tools to rotate the image or to flip it vertically or horizontally.

9. To prevent changes to the image, click Lock. This is useful when you will be working near the image and don't want to accidently change it. The image can't be changed until you unlock it by clicking the Unlock button.

Group It

It can be useful to be able to act on multiple images as if they were one image. For example, you might create an image by using multiple shapes, or you might add a callout to an image and want the callout to remain in place when you move the image. Select the images you want to group and click the Group button on the Arrange tab. The images become one object. To separate them again, select the group and click Ungroup.

Add Charts to Keynote Presentations

Charts are an effective way to communicate a variety of information, especially data that compares items to each other, trend data, and so on. You can easily add charts to your slides to enhance their effectiveness and to make slides more interesting to your audience. After you've created charts, you can format and arrange them to design the way they look on the slide.

Create Charts on Keynote Slides

To create a chart, perform the following steps:

1. Move to the slide on which you want to create a chart.

2. Click the Chart button.

3. Use the tabs and left- and right-facing arrows to browse the available chart types.

4. Click the type of chart you want to create. A placeholder for the chart appears.

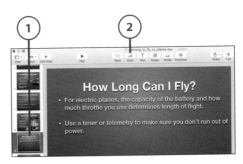

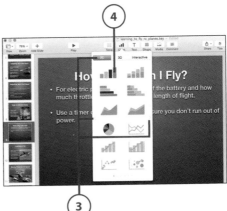

5. Size and place the chart to be approximately what you want it to be on the slide.

6. Click Edit Chart Data. The Chart Data window appears.

7. Enter the data you want to show on the chart. The quantity and type of data you can enter depends on the type of chart you selected in step 4.

8. When you've entered all the data, close the Chart Data window. The chart shows the data you entered.

9. Format and arrange the chart. (See the next task for details.)

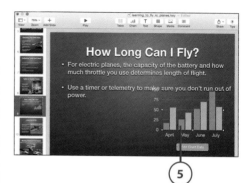

5

6

7 8

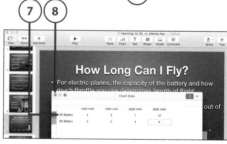

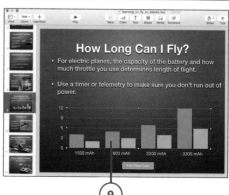

9

Format and Arrange Charts on Keynote Slides

Formatting and arranging charts is similar to other objects, as you can see in the following steps:

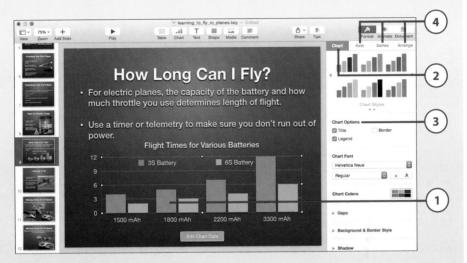

1. Select the chart you want to format.

2. Click on the Chart tab in the Inspector.

3. Use the Chart tools to apply a style, set chart options, choose a chart font, and more. These tools are the same as when you work with charts in Numbers; see Chapter 9, "Working with Charts in Numbers Spreadsheets," for details.

4. Use the Axis, Series, and Arrange tabs to configure those aspects of the chart. These tabs are also the same as when you work with charts in Numbers; see Chapter 9 for details.

>>>Go Further

ADDING TABLES AND CHARTS TO KEYNOTE PRESENTATIONS

You can also create tables in Keynote by clicking the Table button on the toolbar. Choose the table style you want and then add data to its cells. You can format the table using tools on the Inspector. This works similarly to creating tables in Numbers. See Chapter 7, "Developing Numbers Spreadsheets," for details.

Speaking of Numbers, it can be better to create tables and charts in Numbers because it is designed to work with these objects. For example, you can add calculations to tables, whereas the tables in Keynote are intended more for just entering data. You can copy and paste tables and charts from Numbers spreadsheets onto slides in a Keynote presentation, so there isn't much additional work to use Numbers for tables and charts and copy them into a presentation.

Add Shapes to Keynote Presentations

In the previous chapter, you saw how you could use Keynote's Shape tool to create shaped text. You can also add shapes to slides without text, as follows:

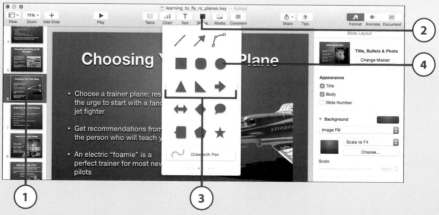

1. Move to the slide to which you want to add shapes.
2. Click the Shape button on the toolbar.
3. Browse the available shapes.
4. Click the shape you want to add to the slide.

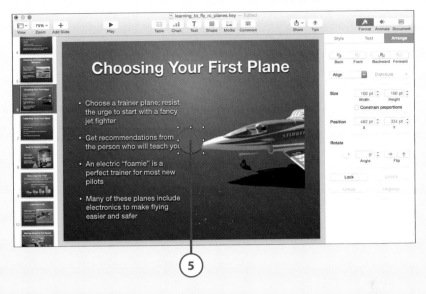

5. Move and size the shape to be what you want.

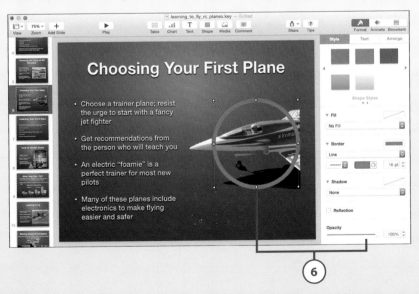

6. Use the tools on the Inspector to format the shape. These are similar to the tools for other objects.

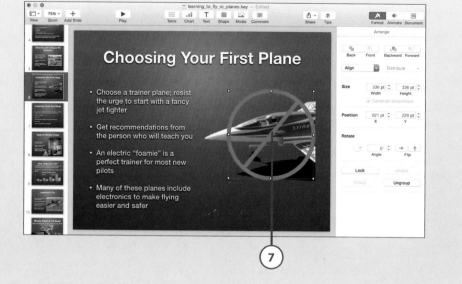

7. Add, format, and combine shapes if the default shapes aren't exactly what you want.

>>>Go Further

ADD MOVIES OR AUDIO TO KEYNOTE PRESENTATIONS

You can add movies or audio to slides using steps that are similar to adding images. Videos can be a good way to help the audience really get the point of a slide or just to add variety to your presentation. Audio can be used for interest (such as playing an audio quote instead of just showing it on the screen), for humor, or other reasons.

To add audio or video content that is stored in iPhoto or iTunes, click the Media button, click the Music or Movies tab, find the file you want to add, and click it. To add audio or video files stored in other locations, just drag them from a Finder window onto a slide.

The options for formatting and configuring audio and video on a slide are a bit more complicated than the options you have for static images. For movies, you can use the Style and Arrange tabs similarly to other objects. On the Movie tab, you can edit the movie to determine the part that plays during the presentation, determine if it starts playing when you click it, and so on. For audio files, you can use the Audio tab to edit it, set it to repeat, or choose how it starts.

When you use video or audio on your slides, try to keep the playing time for each video or audio segment relatively short. Long videos or audio playback can be awkward in a presentation scenario. (This is especially true for audio without video because the audience has nothing to look at.) The audience is expecting to hear from you, not just watch videos they could watch on their own. Video and audio can effectively supplement a presentation, but you need to be careful that the video or audio doesn't become "the star of the show." Using video or audio on slides also makes the playback of presentations more complex and introduces more opportunities for technical problems.

Add transitions to make your
slides flow more smoothly
with more visual appeal

Configure actions for objects,
such as having items on bulleted
lists appear one by one

Use the Build Order tool
to create a "script" for a
slide's animation

Move objects
around on the
screen

Animating Keynote Presentations

Keynote presentations help you communicate more effectively by enabling the audience to see information you are presenting while they hear you speak about it. The visual experience the audience has is important for two reasons. The first is that it can help you reinforce the information you are communicating by providing a second means to communicate it. (Hearing and seeing information enables people to better retain it.) The second is that it enables you to communicate the information more effectively; facts and figures are much better seen than just heard.

A key to effectively communicating during a presentation is keeping your audience engaged with what you are presenting. In previous chapters, you learned some techniques for this, such as including photos and other graphics, which add both information and visual interest.

In this chapter, you learn about animation, which is another technique you can use to make your presentations more visually interesting to and, thus, more engaging for, the audience. As implied by the term, when you animate slides, you add motion to them. The types of animation you learn how to incorporate into your Keynote presentations follow:

- **Transitions between slides.** Transitions are dynamic effects that are seen when you move from one slide to the next; Keynote offers many types of transitions you can use in your presentations. Transitions are easy to add to presentations, and they make presentations more interesting. They also provide a signal to the audience that you are moving to the next set of information.

- **Motion of objects on slides.** You can move objects on to, off of, or around slides. This can be useful from the visual interest standpoint, but it can also help you emphasize key points or make the relationship between objects more clear.

- **Builds of objects on slides.** A build is when the information on a slide appears over time instead of all at once when the slide is first shown. For example, you can have each item on a bulleted list appear as you speak about it. Or you might want a series of photos to appear one by one.

  In addition to being interesting to the audience, builds are effective in focusing the audience on specific information. This is because people tend to read an entire slide as soon as it appears, which may distract them from listening to you talk about specific points. When you use a build, you control what the audience is reading because you determine when each part of the slide appears.

You might find adding animations fun because of all the options that Keynote provides. However, when it comes to animation, less is more. It is all too easy to overwhelm audiences with animation so that the motion in the presentation is what they pay attention to most, and the information you are trying to communicate is lost. When you use too much of it, animation becomes a distraction for the audience instead of making your presentation more effective. You want to strike a balance between enough animation to make your presentation more interesting and effective but not so much that the animation becomes the star of the show. That balance point is likely toward less animation than you might be tempted to use.

Along with the quantity of animation in your presentation, keep the types of effects you use to a reasonable level. For example, don't try to make the motion on each slide different. Instead, limit the types of transitions between slides to just a few per presentation instead of trying to use a different transition between each slide to lessen distraction for the audience.

The Ransom Note Effect

In the early days of word processing, people often got carried away because they could apply all kinds of formatting options to text, such as fonts, sizes, and colors. This led to documents that looked sort of like ransom notes, which consist of individual letters cut out from magazines or other publications pasted together to form words and sentences. This overuse of formatting options became known as the Ransom Note Effect. Presentations can suffer from an analogous problem when too many different types of animations are used. The animations become distracting to your messages instead of supplementing them. Just because you can add animation doesn't mean you should. Use animation conservatively to enhance your ability to communicate. Subtle animation is often the most effective kind.

Add Magic Move Transitions to Slides in Keynote Presentations

Keynote's Magic Move feature does most of the work of animating slides for you automatically. To create a Magic Move transition, define how you want a slide to start the animation and how you want it to end the animation. Keynote automatically creates the transitions and builds to move between the two versions of the slide.

Creating a Magic Move is simple. Create the slide (the starting state) to which you want to apply a Magic Move transition. Duplicate the slide; this copy becomes the slide's final state. Then perform the following actions on either slide:

- Reformat text or objects (resize, mask, and so on).

- Add text or objects.

- Move text or objects.

- Remove text or objects.

When you apply the Magic Move transition to the two versions of the slide, Keynote transitions objects from their starting state (such as position or size) to their ending state, which might be a different location on the slide. For example, if you move an object to a different location on the copy of the slide, Keynote animates the motion of that object; it moves from its starting location on the first slide to its final location on the copy of the slide. If you add or remove objects from one of the slides, Keynote uses motion as those objects appear or disappear.

Out of Order?

I've presented the Magic Move transition first in this chapter because it is the easiest way to get started. However, it can be a good idea to learn how to animate your slides manually so you better understand what the options are. You may want to jump to the section "Animate Transitions Between Slides in Keynote Presentations" and read through the rest of the chapter. Then come back here to learn how the Magic Move transition works.

Add a Magic Move Transition

To add Magic Move transitions to a slide, perform the following steps:

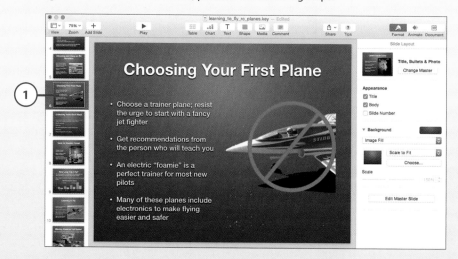

1. Select the slide to which you want to add a Magic Move transition.

Creating Slides for Animation

It's a good idea to create slides that you are going to animate in their most com-plex state, meaning with all the objects you're going to include on them at their largest sizes. That's because it's a lot easier to animate, to remove objects, or to make them smaller than it is to add objects or to make them larger. When you animate objects onto a slide, you can run into layout problems that cause you to have to resize, move, or reformat existing objects. If you start with a slide that is as complicated as it is going to get, the animation process goes more easily.

2. Press ⌘-D to duplicate the slide. A copy is created. The first version of the slide is its start state. The duplicate becomes the end state.

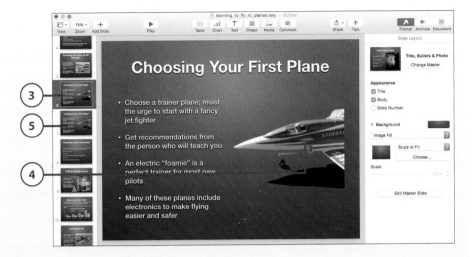

3. Select the starting version of the slide.

4. Make the changes to the slide so that the animation starts the way you want it to. (If you compare this figure to the previous one, you see I removed the red circle with the slash from the plane photo in the first version of the slide. The animation causes the red circle and slash to appear over the plane, emphasizing that it is a type that shouldn't be used to learn to fly.)

5. Select the ending version of the slide.

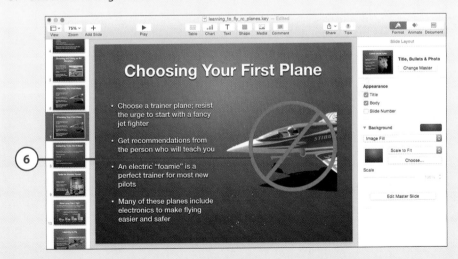

6. Make changes to the slide so that the animation ends as you want it to.

7. Select the first slide in the animation.

8. Click the Animate button. The Transitions pane in the Inspector appears.

9. Click Add an Effect.

Try Before You Buy

To see what the animation will look like, click Preview. A preview of the animation plays.

10. Click Magic Move. The transition is applied to the slide you selected, using the selected slide as the starting point and the duplicate slide as the ending state. The Magic Move pane appears in the Inspector. Use the tools on this pane to configure the transition.

I Remember the First Time

The first time you apply a Magic Move transition, you see a warning sheet that explains what it does. Check the check box so this doesn't appear the next time you use a Magic Move, and click OK to close it.

11. Drag the Duration slider to the left to make the transition play faster or to the right to slow it down, or set the duration's time by entering it into the box or using the up or down arrows.

12. To have objects that aren't on both slides fade in or fade out, check the Fade Unmatched Objects check box.

13. Choose the way you want the slides to be matched. Choose By Object to match the slides by their objects, By Word to match text by the word, or By Character to match text by the character.

14. Open the Acceleration menu.

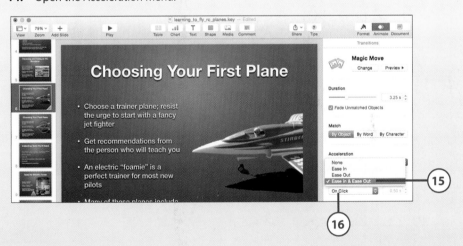

15. Choose the rate at which you want objects to be animated. Choose Ease In to have them appear slowly, Ease Out to have them disappear slowly, Ease In & Ease Out to have gradual fades in each direction, or None if you want the objects to just pop into or out of existence.

16. Open the Start Transition menu, which shows On Click by default.

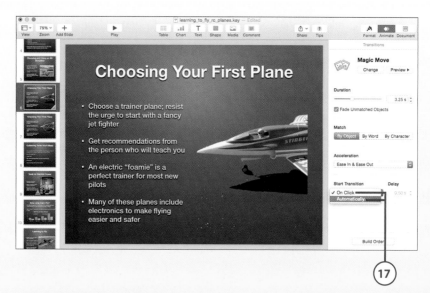

17. Choose the way you want the transition to start. Choose On Click to have it start when you click the mouse or Automatically to have the presentation automatically use the transition to move to the next slide.

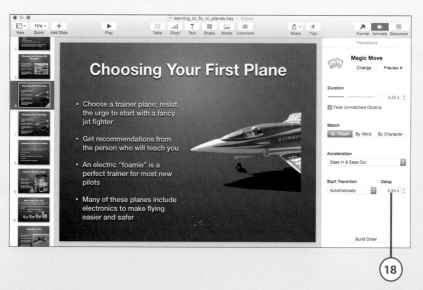

18. If you selected the Automatically option in step 17, use the Delay box to enter the delay between when you show the slide and when the transition starts to play. This is the amount of time you have to speak about the slide before the transition plays and the next slide appears.

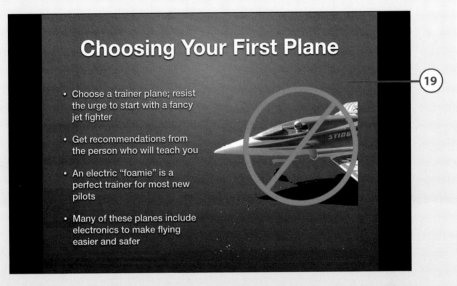

19. Preview the transition. (Details about playing presentations are provided in Chapter 15, "Finishing and Collaborating on Keynote Presentations.")

20. Using the Magic Move pane, make changes to the transition until it is what you want it to be.

>>>Go Further
MAKING THE MOST OF MAGIC MOVES

Here are a few tips to help you make magic with the Magic Move transition:

- When a slide has a Magic Move (or any other) transition applied to it, its thumbnail is marked with a blue triangle in the lower-right corner.

- Try to make sure you've corrected any mistakes in a slide before you apply the Magic Move transition. The copy you make is separate from the original, so when you fix a mistake on the original, you also have to fix it on the duplicate. If you don't, the transition treats the correction just like other differences, so the mistake reappears on the slide through the animation.

- You can also add builds to slides using the Magic Move transition. Builds are covered in "Build Objects on Slides in Keynote Presentations" later in this chapter.

- To remove a Magic Move transition, select its slide. On the Magic Move pane, click Change and choose None. The transition is removed. You also need to deal with the duplicate version of the slide, such as by deleting it.

Animate Transitions Between Slides in Keynote Presentations

Transitions between slides serve a couple of purposes. The first is that they make the changes between topics (slides) more obvious. The second is that transitions make these changes more visually interesting to the audience than simply jumping from one slide to the next.

You can add transitions between slides in a presentation, or you can change (or remove) existing transitions. Both of these topics are covered in the following tasks.

Create Transitions Between Slides in Keynote Presentations

To add a transition between slides, do the following:

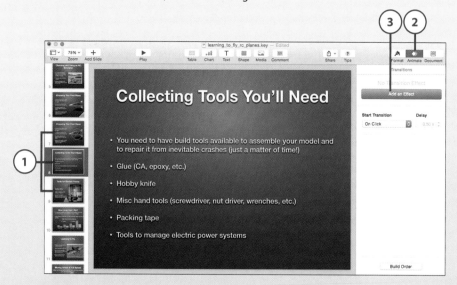

1. Select the slides to which you want to apply a transition. The transition is applied after the first slide you select through the last slide you select.

2. Click the Animate button. The Transitions pane of the Inspector appears.

3. Click Add an Effect. The list of effects appears. This list includes a number of sections, including Appear & Move; Flip, Spin & Scale; and more.

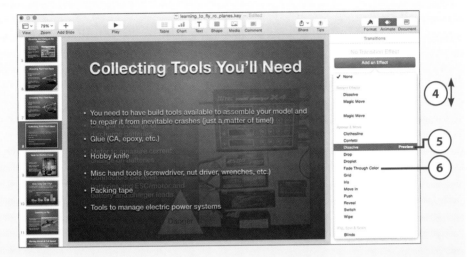

4. Browse the list until you find an effect you are interested in.

5. Click Preview. A preview of the effect plays in the center pane.

6. Continue previewing effects until you find the one you want to apply.

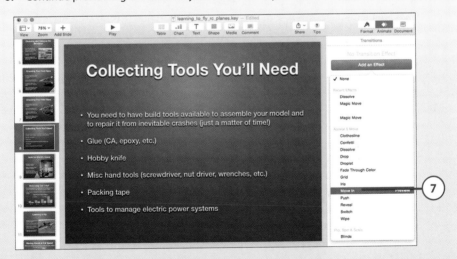

7. Click the effect you want to apply to the selected slides. The effect is applied, and the slide thumbnails are marked with a blue triangle to indicate that they have a transition. In the Animate pane, you see the controls for the transition that you applied. Each effect has its own set of controls. This example shows the options for the Move In effect; configuring the options for other effects is similar.

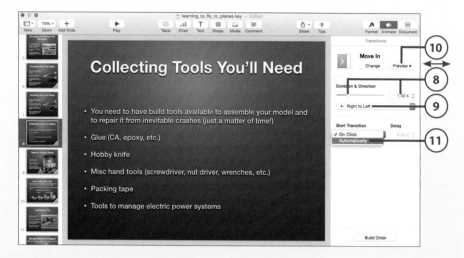

8. Use the Duration & Direction slider and input box to set the speed of the transition.

Different Slides, Different Options

The effect options you set apply to all the slides you have selected. To use different options for individual slides, select the slides to which you want to apply specific options, and then configure those options. After that, select the next slides you want to configure until you've done them all. You can apply different effects to the same transition for different slides. For example, you can have some slides move in from the left while others move in from the right.

9. Use the Duration & Direction menu to choose the effect's direction.

10. Click the Preview button to see a preview of the effect as it is configured.

11. On the Start Transition menu, choose On Click to have the transition start as soon as you advance to the slide or Automatically to have the presentation use the transition to automatically move to the next slide after a specific time that you configure. In most cases, you'll want to use the On Click option so that you can control the timing of the presentation to allow for variances in how long it takes you to talk about each slide.

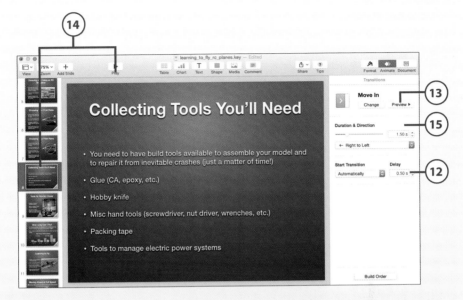

12. If you selected Automatically in step 11, use the Delay box to configure the time after which the transition should be used to move to the next slide.

13. Continue configuring and previewing the effect until you are happy with it.

14. Select the first slide you've configured, and click the Play button to watch the presentation with the transition. (Details about playing presentations are provided in Chapter 15.)

15. Use the Animate pane to make changes to the transition as needed.

Change or Remove Transitions Between Slides in Keynote Presentations

You can modify existing transitions as described in these steps:

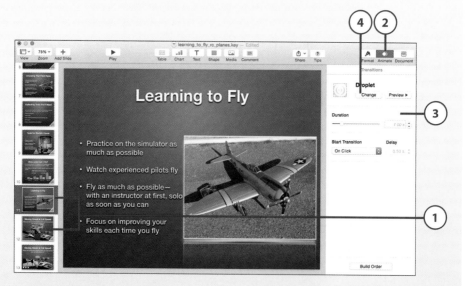

1. Select the slides on which there are transitions that you want to change.

Seeing Multiples

If the slides you select have different transitions applied, the title of the Animate pane is Multiple Effects to indicate that you've used different transitions on some of the slides. When you are making changes to transitions, it's better to ensure you have selected slides that use the same effect, or you may end up with unexpected consequences of changes you make. However, you can make some changes, such as the Start Transition setting for a group of slides that have different effects applied.

2. Click the Animate button if the Animate pane isn't open already.

3. Use the controls in the Animate pane to make changes to the effect, such as to the duration or direction.

4. To change the type of effect or to delete the effect, click Change.

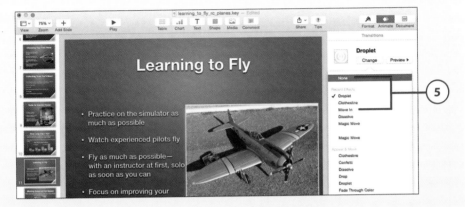

5. Choose a different effect to apply to the selected slides, or choose None to remove the effect.

Recent Effects

In the Recent Effects section, you see the effects you've used recently, which helps you easily select effects you've used elsewhere. As explained earlier, you don't want to use too many kinds of effects in the same presentation, so this list becomes a good way to make sure you limit the variety of effects you use.

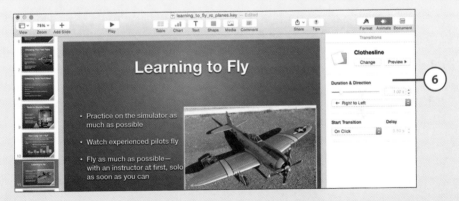

6. If you applied a different effect in step 5, use the Animate pane to configure it.

Animate Objects on Slides in Keynote Presentations

There are several options for animating objects on slides, including the following:

- Move objects onto or off of slides.
- Move objects around a slide.
- Use a build to present objects on a slide.

You can also change or remove existing animations.

Each of these animation techniques is explained in the following tasks.

Move Objects Onto or Off of Slides in Keynote Presentations

It can be useful to have objects move onto or off of slides. Here's how to accomplish this:

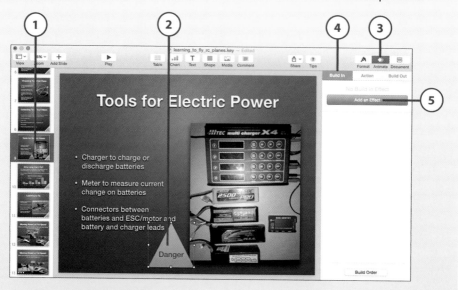

1. Select the slide containing objects you want to move onto or off of a slide.
2. Select the object you want to move.
3. Open the Animate pane if it isn't open already.
4. To move the object onto the slide, click Build In.
5. Click Add an Effect.

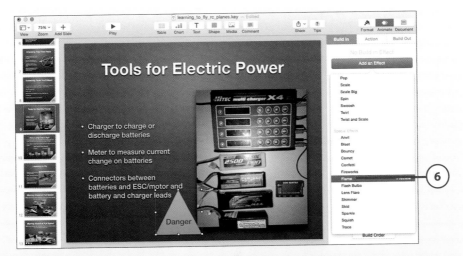

6. Preview and choose the effect you want to apply to the object. The list is the same as with slide transitions. The Animate options for the effect you selected appear.

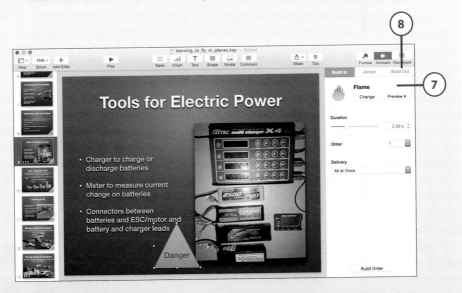

7. Use the options you see to configure the effect, such as to set its duration and direction.

8. Click Build Out and use similar steps to configure the object's exit from the slide. (You don't have to have a Build In and a Build Out; you can use only one or the other for an object.)

Move Objects Around Slides in Keynote Presentations

To move objects around on a slide, perform the following steps:

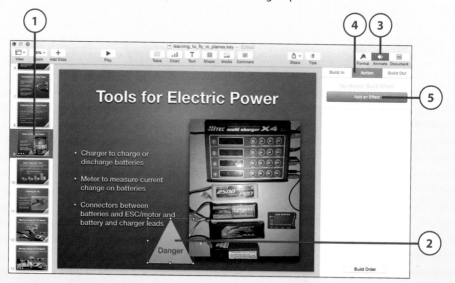

1. Select the slide containing objects you want to move around a slide.
2. Select the object you want to move.
3. Open the Animate pane if it isn't open already.
4. To move the object on the slide, click Action.
5. Click Add an Effect.

6. Browse and preview effects until you find the effect you want to apply.

7. Click the effect you want to apply to the object. The controls for the effect you select appear in the Animate pane. The rest of these steps show the Move effect, which causes the object to move along a path you define.

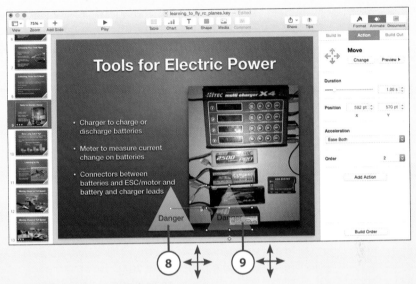

8. Place the object in its starting position.

9. Drag the object to its final position.

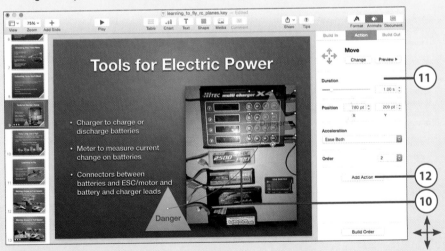

10. Drag the selection handles on the path line to reshape its path, such as to make it move along a curve instead of in a straight line.

11. Use the controls on the Animate pane to configure the motion, such as to choose its duration (which is speed for a Move effect).

12. To add an action to the current effect, click Add Action.

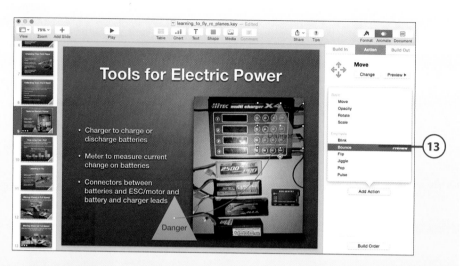

13. Click the action you want to apply.

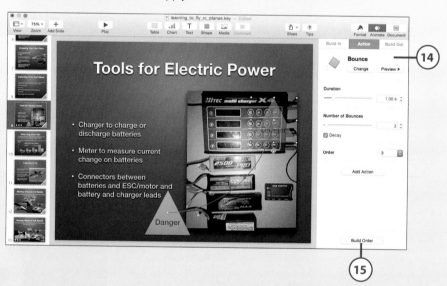

14. Configure the action using the controls on the Animate pane.

15. Click Build Order. Use the Build Order tool to configure how the effects play and how they relate to each other.

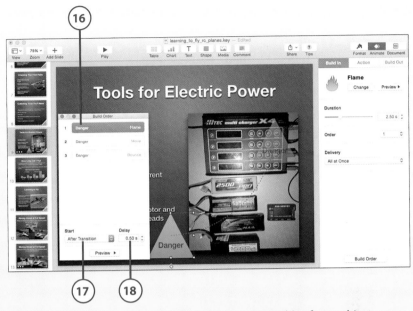

16. Select the action you want to configure, such as the Build In for an object.

17. On the Start menu, choose when you want the action to start. For example, if you want it to start automatically when you move to the slide, choose After Transition. When the slide's transition finishes, the effect plays automatically.

18. Set the delay between when the transition finishes and the action starts.

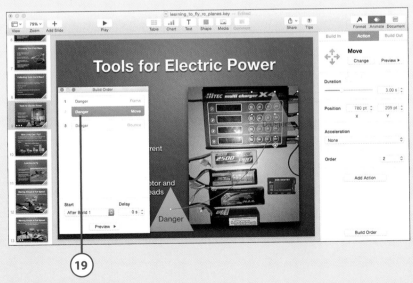

19. Select the next action.

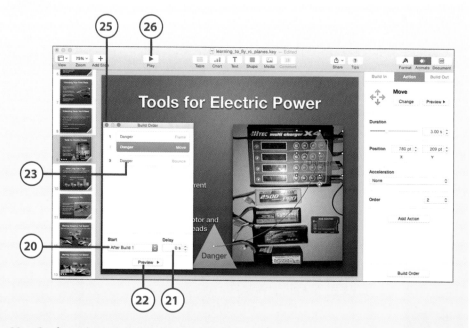

20. Configure how and when the transition starts. For example, to have it immediately follow the previous action, select After Build *X*, where *X* is the number of the action it follows.

21. Set the delay between the current action and the one before it.

22. Click Preview to preview the effects.

23. Select the next action, and use steps 20 through 22 to configure and preview it.

24. Repeat step 23 until you've configured all the actions for the object.

25. Close the Build Order tool.

26. Play the slide to see the motion in all its glory.

Be an Explorer

As you can see, Keynote offers many effects and options you can use to animate your slides. You should explore these options to see which you think will help you communicate most effectively (which is the point after all). The details of the effects vary, but you will be able to use any of them by following a pattern similar to what you see in the steps in this chapter.

Build Objects on Slides in Keynote Presentations

A build is useful because it helps you focus the audience on the information you are discussing. The most common use for this is to build a bulleted list so each item on the list appears on the screen, one at a time, so that you can talk about each point when it appears. You can use similar steps to add builds to any slide, such as to have photos appear one at a time. Here's how to add a bulleted list build to slides:

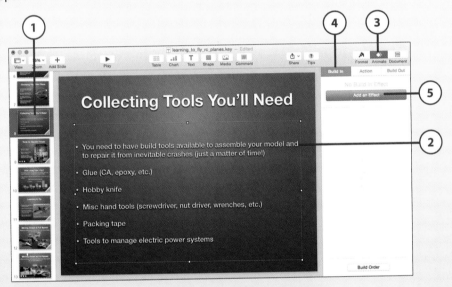

1. Select the slide containing a bulleted list that you want to build.

2. Select the text box containing the bulleted list.

3. Open the Animate pane if it isn't open already.

4. Click Build In.

5. Click Add an Effect.

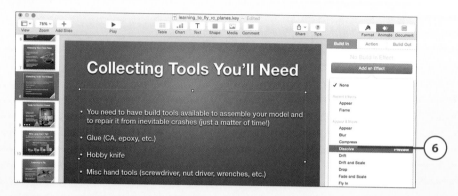

6. Choose the effect you want to use for the build.

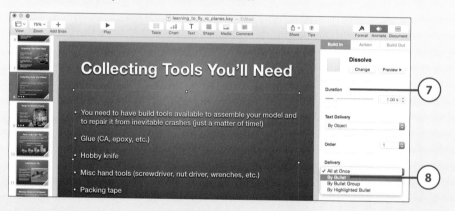

7. Use the effect's tools to configure it, such as to set its duration (speed).

8. On the Delivery menu, choose By Bullet.

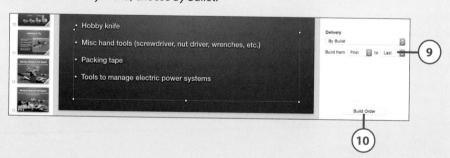

9. Use the Build from menus to choose the order for the build. In the case of a bulleted list, you usually want it to build from the First bullet to the Last bullet.

10. Click Build Order. The Build Order tool appears, and you see each of the bullets listed because each has an action applied to it. All the actions are selected by default.

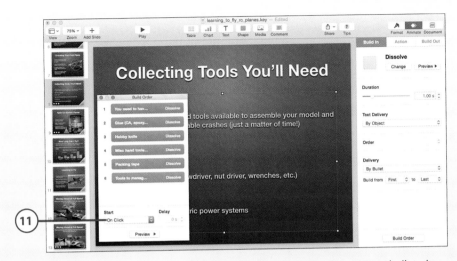

11. On the Start menu, choose the way you want all the actions to start. For a bulleted list, you most often want to use the On Click option so you can determine when each bullet appears, usually as you start talking about it. You might want to have the build happen automatically if you plan to have the presentation run by itself.

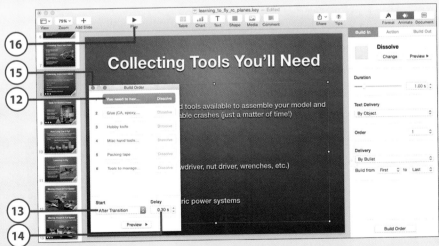

12. To make the first bullet appear automatically, select it. (This is useful because you don't have to do anything to make the first bullet appear; instead, you can start talking about it immediately when you get to the slide.)

13. On the Start menu, choose After Transition.

14. Using the Delay setting, set the delay between when the slide appears and the first bullet appears.

15. Close the Build Order tool.

16. Play the slide to see the results of your work.

Change or Remove the Animation on Slides in Keynote Presentations

You can modify animations like so:

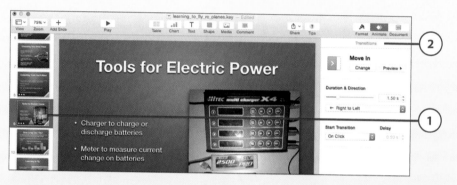

1. Select the slide that includes the animation you want to change or remove.

2. If you want to change the transition effect for the whole slide, use the tools on the Transitions pane. (If you don't see the Transitions pane, click the Animate button to open it.)

Lost in Transition

To remove a slide's transition effect entirely, change it to None. The transition is deleted from the slide.

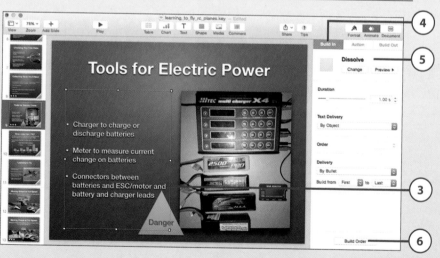

3. To change the animation for an object, such as a bulleted list, select the object instead. The controls in the Animation pane change to reflect whatever is currently selected.

4. Click the tab for the type of animation you want to change, such as Build In to change the Build In effect.

5. Use the tools on the Animate pane to change the effects applied to the selected object.

6. To change the way the animation on the slide occurs, click Build Order. The Build Order tool appears, and you see all the effects on the current slide. The order in which the effects are listed is the order in which they play during the presentation. The steps of the effect that are currently selected are highlighted.

7. Use the Start menu and Delay box to make changes to the effect's timing.

8. To change the order in which effects play, select the effect or effects you want to move in the sequence. In this example, I want the first bullet to appear and then the Danger icon to appear and move on the screen.

9. Drag the effect up or down the list until it is located in the sequence where you want it to play.

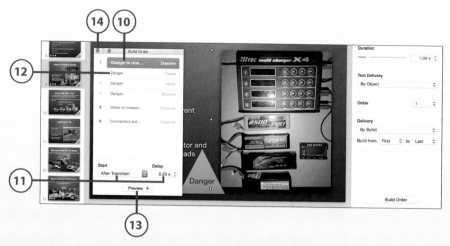

10. When the effect is where you want it, release it.

11. Set the effect's start and delay. In this case, I want the first bullet to automatically appear .2 seconds after the slide does.

12. Use similar steps to configure the rest of the effects in the series.

13. Preview the animation, and make changes if it isn't what you want it to be.

14. When you're finished, close the Build Order tool.

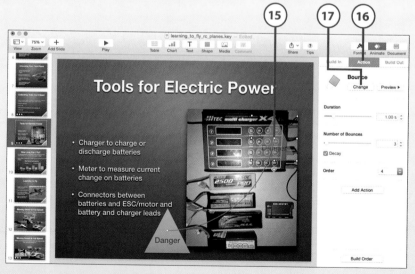

15. To remove an effect, select the object it is applied to.

16. Click the tab for the type of animation you want to remove, such as Action to change an action you've applied to the object.

17. Click Change.

18. Choose None. The selected animation is removed from the slide.

19. Repeat steps 15 through 18 to remove other effects from the slide.

Preview a presentation to see
it as your audience will

Use comments and iCloud
sharing to collaborate on a
presentation

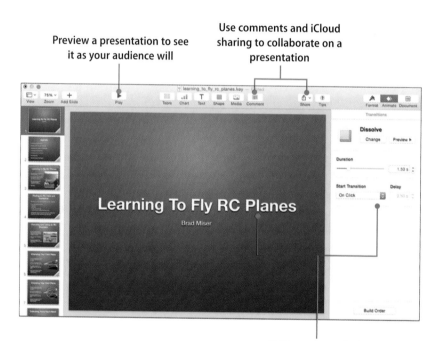

Edit a presentation's
content and animation to
finalize it

In this chapter, you learn how to finalize a presentation and prepare it for delivery to an audience. Topics include the following:

→ Finish Keynote Presentations
→ Collaborate with Others on Keynote Presentations
→ Prepare Keynote Presentations for Delivery

Finishing and Collaborating on Keynote Presentations

After you've built your presentation by adding content, formatting slides, and adding animation, finish it so that it is ready to deliver to an audience. It's tempting to gloss over this part of the process because it's likely you've spent a lot of time and effort getting the presentation "done." However, spending a few more minutes ensuring the presentation is ready to be seen by others can prevent embarrassing problems that you really don't want to discover when you are delivering it to an audience. Effective presentations require that you be confident. Ensuring that your presentation is as good as you can make it goes a long way toward helping you feel more confident.

Finish Keynote Presentations

As you develop presentations, you work on individual slides by adding content, formatting, and animating them. Now it's time to work with a presentation as a whole, from start to finish. You should preview the presentation as your audience will see it to discover problems you need to fix or improvements you want to make. This is usually an iterative process and requires multiple passes through the presentation to make sure it is "just right."

As you preview a presentation and find problems or identify improvements needed, you have a couple of options. You can stop the preview and fix the problem or make the improvement immediately. (This method is described in the following task.) Or you can use the Comment feature to make notes about changes that you need and then resume the preview; later, you can go through the presentation and address all the comments you made. (This process is covered in the task "Collaborate with Others on Keynote Presentations" later in this chapter.)

Each method has its benefits, so you should try both to see which works best for you.

Preview and Improve Keynote Presentations

To preview a presentation, perform the following steps:

1. Move to the first slide in the presentation.

2. Click the Play button. Keynote switches into presentation mode and displays the current slide. Any animations that are set to play automatically play according to their delay settings.

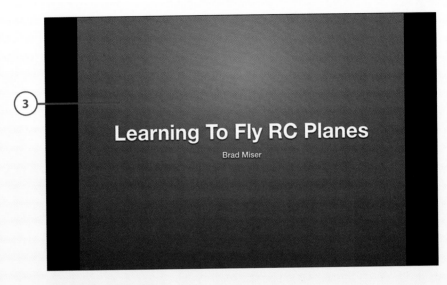

3. View the content of the slide.

4. If it has builds or animations that are set to start when you click the mouse button, do so until you've seen all the slide's content and animation.

5. Click the mouse button or press the right-arrow key to move to the next slide.

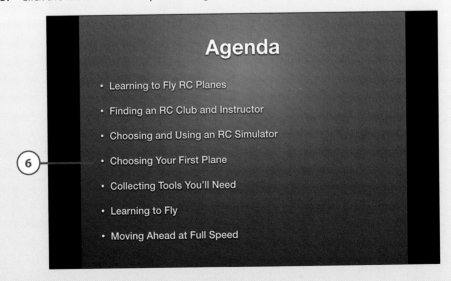

6. View the content and animation on the slide.

7. If there are problems that need to be fixed, exit presentation mode by pressing the esc key. Keynote returns to the previous view, and the slide on which you exited from the presentation is selected.

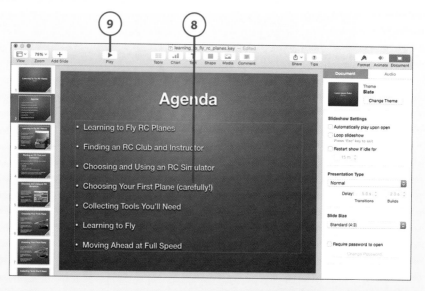

8. Make changes to the slide that needs to be improved or fixed. The techniques you use to make changes to content, format, and animation are provided in Chapter 11, "Developing Keynote Presentations," through Chapter 14, "Animating Keynote Presentations."

9. Click Play to resume the preview.

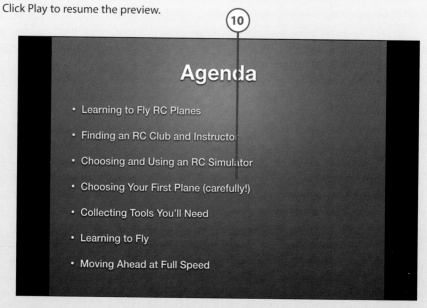

10. Check the slide to ensure the changes you made are "right."

11. Repeat steps 5 though 10 until you've seen the entire presentation at least once without having to stop to make changes.

Don't Forget About Presenter Notes

In Chapter 12, "Working with Text in Keynote Presentations," you learned how to add presenter notes to your presentation. These can be invaluable to you as references while you deliver your presentation to an audience. You can use presenter notes to remind yourself of key points you want to make on specific slides, facts, and figures you want to quote, or you can use them as reminders about effective presentation techniques (such as refraining from mumbling). As you preview a presentation, show the presenter notes pane (View, Show Presenter Notes) so that you can quickly add or change notes as you go.

Check Spelling in Keynote Presentations

To ensure the spelling in a presentation is correct, do the following:

1. Choose Edit, Spelling and Grammar, Show Spelling and Grammar. The Spelling and Grammar tool opens and shows the first word not found in the dictionary. A list of words that might be the correct spelling is shown in the window at the bottom of the tool.

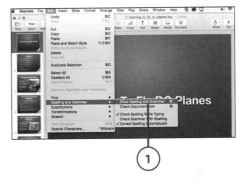

2. Review the word the Spell Checker thinks is misspelled.

3. If the word is spelled correctly and you don't want to take any action on it, click Find Next. The Spell Checker skips the current word and finds the next potential misspelling.

4. If the word is spelled correctly and you don't want it to be flagged again in the current document, click Ignore. The Spell Checker skips the current word and finds the next potential misspelling.

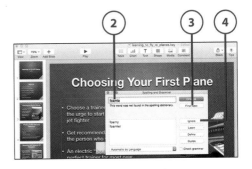

5. If the word is spelled correctly and you want to add it to the dictionary so that it is recognized as being a correct spelling in a future document, click Learn. The Spell Checker adds the word to the dictionary and moves to the next potential misspelling.

6. If the word isn't spelled correctly, double-click the correct spelling on the list of suggestions. The misspelled word is replaced with the one on which you double-clicked, and the Spell Checker moves to the next potential misspelling.

7. If the word isn't spelled correctly and you don't want to choose a suggested spelling, type over the misspelled word and click Change. The misspelled word is replaced with the one you typed, and the Spell Checker moves to the next potential misspelling.

8. When you've corrected, learned, or ignored all the misspellings in the document, close the Spelling and Grammar tool.

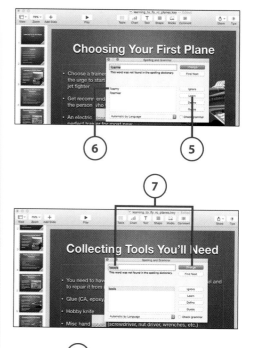

Endless Loop of Misspelled Words

If you don't take action on a misspelled word by replacing it, ignoring it, or learning it, it continues to be flagged as a potential misspelling, and the Spelling and Grammar tool keeps pointing out the same misspelling as long as you keep clicking Find Next. When you get back to the first misspelling you didn't take action on, you can just close the Spelling and Grammar tool. It's usually better to take action, even if it is only to ignore all the "misspelled" words so you don't see them flagged again.

Skip Slides in Keynote Presentations

You can skip slides in a presentation so that they aren't displayed to the audience but remain in the presentation for your use. Here's how to do this:

1. Select the slide you want to skip.

2. Choose Slide, Skip Slide. The slide collapses in the Sidebar indicating that it won't be displayed when you play the presentation, but it remains in case you want to show it again, make changes to it, and so on.

3. To cause a skipped slide to play again, select the skipped slide.

4. Choose Slide, Don't Skip Slide. The slide expands in the Sidebar and is shown when you play the presentation.

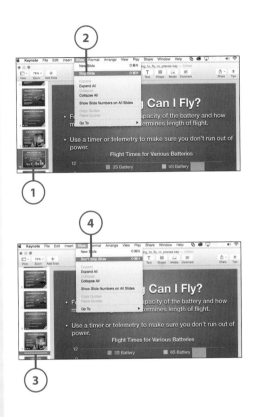

Delete Slides from Keynote Presentations

Some slides just don't work the way you'd hoped and need to be removed. If a slide is beyond all hope of being useful, delete it using the following steps:

1. Select the slide you want to delete.

2. Press the delete key. The slide is deleted from the presentation.

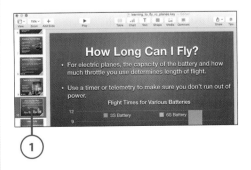

Collaborate with Others on Keynote Presentations

Collaborating with others on Keynote presentations can often help you find and fix problems or make improvements that you might not be able to come up with working on your own. Like other iWork documents, comments enable others to make notes in a presentation; you can review those notes and make any changes necessary. You can also share presentations via iCloud for real-time collaboration.

Add Comments to Keynote Presentations

To add comments to slides in a presentation, first ensure the correct author name is set, and then you can make comments that are associated with your name:

1. Ensure your name is associated with comments you make by choosing Keynote, Preferences. The Keynote Preferences dialog appears.

2. Click the General tab.

3. Enter your name in the Author field.

4. Close the Preferences dialog.

5. Choose View, Comments, Author Color, and the color you want to associate with comments you make.

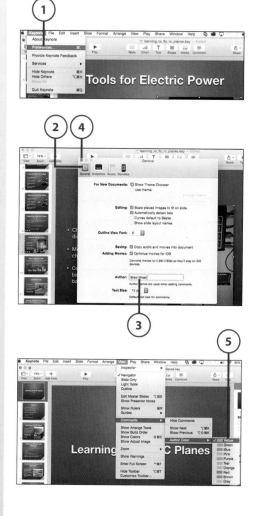

Set Once… or Not?

You need to perform steps 1 through 5 only when you want to change the name of or color associated with the person making comments in the presentation. Keynote retains the author name until you change it. However, if you want to use a different name or perhaps have someone else review the presentation using your computer, you may need to change the author name occasionally.

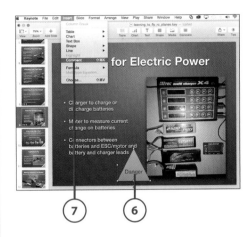

6. Select the object about which you want to comment. You can select an entire text box, specific words, graphics, or shapes.

7. Choose Insert, Comment or press shift+⌘+K.

8. Type your comment about the selected object.

9. Repeat steps 5 though 7 to add more comments to the presentation.

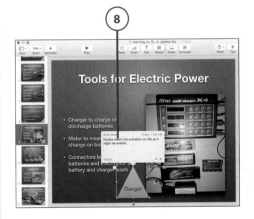

Review and Act on Comments in Keynote Presentations

To review and address comments in a presentation, perform the following steps:

1. Choose View, Comments, Show Next. The next comment from your current location in the presentation is shown in the Comment dialog.

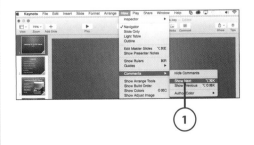

2. See whom the comment is from and when it was made.

3. Read the comment.

4. To move to the next comment, click the right-facing arrow; to move to the previous comment, click the left-facing arrow.

5. To delete the comment, click Delete. The comment is deleted, the Comments box closes, and you end up on the slide on which the comment was made.

6. To view a comment, you can also click the marker indicating a comment has been made. The Comment dialog appears.

7. Use steps 2 through 5 to deal with the comment.

Comments While Presenting

Comments aren't shown when you play a Keynote presentation. You can leave them in for future reference, and your audience won't see them when you play the presentation.

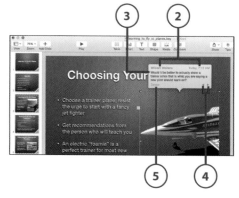

Use iCloud to Share Keynote Presentations

You can use iCloud to share presentations with others in real time, as described in the following steps:

1. Choose Share, View Share Settings. The Sharing sheet appears.

2. On the Permissions menu, choose the option you want people to have for the deck. Choose Allow Editing to allow people to make changes or View Only if you want them to only be able to view it.

3. Click Share Presentation. The presentation is shared, and you see its link.

4. Click Send Link.

5. Choose how you want to share the link. People can use the link you send to access the presentation via iCloud.

For the First Time

The first time you share a presentation, you see a dialog explaining what you are about to do. You can read this information and then dismiss it. You won't see it when you share in the future. Also, if you haven't stored the presentation on the cloud, which this book assumes is the case, you're prompted to move the document you are sharing to be stored there. Any documents you share with iCloud must be stored on the cloud.

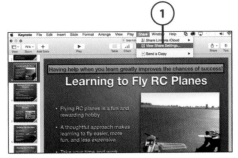

Password

You can use the Add Password button to apply a password to the presentation. More details on this are provided in Chapter 17, "Publishing and Sharing Pages, Numbers, and Keynote Documents." If you create a password, make sure you communicate it to the people with whom you are sharing the presentation.

More on Collaboration

Details on using iCloud collaboration to review documents in real time are provided in Chapter 6, "Collaborating with Others on Pages Documents."

Old-Fashioned Rehearsal?

It's great to use comments and iCloud sharing to collaborate on a Keynote presentation, but one of the best ways to finalize a presentation is to practice delivering it in front of others. It can be a challenge to get people together and have the setup (such as two displays) to do this, but it is time well spent. There's just no substitute for rehearsing a presentation in front of a live audience. That practice will reveal the good and the bad like no other method. If you can't get people together in a room, you can use an online delivery, such as WebEx, or you can use the iCloud sharing process you learned about in the previous task. These methods work almost as well. To get the most benefit, the rehearsal method you use should match the final delivery method (in person or online).

Prepare Keynote Presentations for Delivery

When the content and animation in your presentation is "ready for prime time," you can configure settings related to its delivery. Keynote's Slideshow preferences control certain aspects of how the presentation is displayed on the screen and how you interact with it while it is. You can also customize the presenter display you use during delivery of the presentation to match the information it provides to your preferences.

One Screen or Two?

In most cases, when you deliver a presentation to a live audience, you'll be using two displays. A common setup is to connect a MacBook Pro or Air to a projector or large screen display. You usually view the MacBook's display while the audience views the second display. Keynote is designed for this configuration because it provides a presenter display with information and controls that are useful to you while showing the slides in full screen on the second display that is viewed by the audience. If you have access to a second display, it's a good idea to use it as you finalize your presentation. When you think your presentation is "done," preview it using a two-display setup so that you can view it exactly as you will during the presentation. If you have only one display available, you'll have to make due with that. Try to get to the presentation venue early enough so that you can run through the presentation a time or two with the same setup you will use when you are "live."

Configure Slideshow Preferences in Keynote Presentations

To configure Keynote's Slideshow preferences, use the following steps:

1. Choose Keynote, Preferences.

2. Click the Slideshow tab.

3. Ensure the Scale slideshow to fit the display check box is checked. This causes the presentation to fill the screen on which it is presented while maintaining the correct proportion of its slides.

4. Check Apply motion blur to animations if you want Keynote to blur objects as they move in the screen. The best way to decide if you want to use this or not is to play the presentation with it enabled and with it disabled to see which you prefer.

5. Check Enable Presenter Display if you are going to be using two displays when you present.

6. Click the Show pointer only on slides with links or movies radio button if you want the pointer to appear only when slides have this type of content or the Show pointer when using the mouse or trackpad radio button if you want to be able to use the pointer to point to things on the screen, such as bulleted list items.

7. If you include movies in your presentations, check the Show playback controls when pointer is over a movie check box to display a movie's controls to point to it. If you leave this unchecked, the controls are always visible.

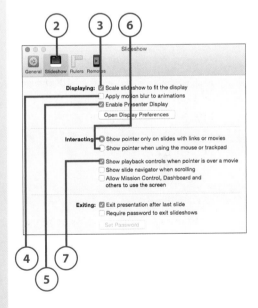

8. Check the Show slide navigator when scrolling check box if you want the slide Sidebar to appear when you scroll through slides.

9. Check Allow Mission Control, Dashboard and others to use the screen if you want these features to be active during a presentation. In most cases, you don't want other processes interfering with an active presentation, so you should leave this unchecked.

10. To automatically exit Presentation mode when you leave the last slide, check the Exit presentation after last slide check box. If you leave this unchecked, you remain in Presentation mode until you press the esc key.

11. To require a password to exit Presentation mode, check the Require password to exit slideshows check box and use the Set Password button to configure the password. This can be useful to prevent someone from accessing your computer if you step away from a presentation or if you are using a self-running presentation.

12. When you're done setting preferences, close the Preferences dialog box.

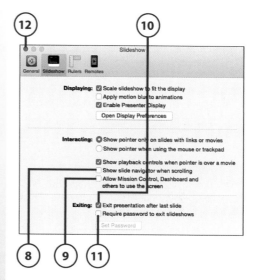

Customize the Presenter Display for Keynote Presentations

To configure the presenter display to match your preferences, perform the following steps:

1. Choose Play, Customize Presenter Display. The presenter display appears. You see the onscreen content along with the Customize Presenter Display dialog box.

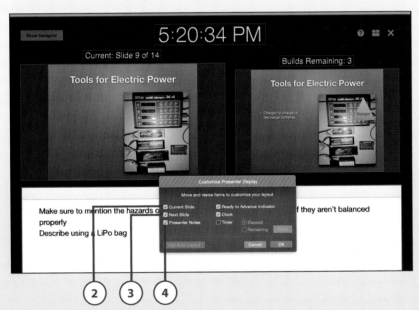

2. To display the current slide, check the Current Slide check box. If you uncheck this check box, the current slide isn't displayed for you, which might be confusing.

3. To display the next slide, check the Next Slide check box. This is helpful because you can see what is coming next. If the current slide has builds, you see the same slide with the next build instead of the next slide until you reach the end of the builds on the current slide.

4. Check the Presenter Notes check box to show the Presenter Notes pane. If you've added notes to your slides, check this check box to be able to view them while you present.

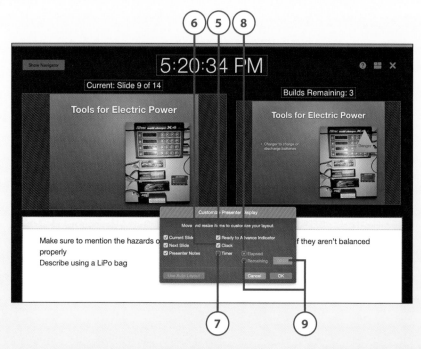

5. If you check the Ready to Advance Indicator check box, a green bar appears at the top of the screen when the animations on the current slide have played. This is useful to know so you don't "go too fast" and overrun the animations by advancing the presentation before the animations have completed.

6. Check the Clock check box to display a clock on the screen. This is very helpful to keep an eye on the time as you present.

7. Check the Timer check box if you want to see an onscreen timer.

8. If you enable a timer, check the Elapsed radio button to display the time the current slide has been displayed.

9. If you enable a timer, check the Remaining radio button to display a countdown from the time you enter in the box. (Note that you can enable the Elapsed or Remaining options for the timer, but you can't use both of them at the same time.)

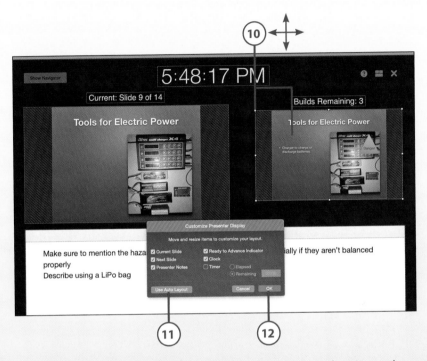

10. To change the size of a slide's preview window, drag it to a new location on the screen or drag its selection handles to change the size of the preview window.

11. Click Use Auto Layout to restore the presenter display to its default.

12. When you're done configuring the presenter display, click OK.

Use Keynote's presenter
display to help you deliver
your presentation more
effectively

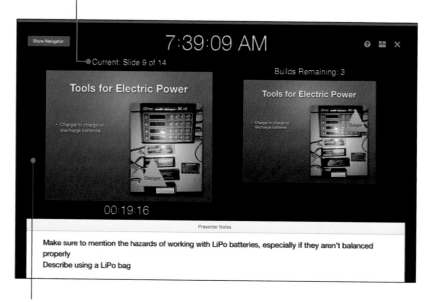

Use Keynote to rehearse
your presentation before
you deliver it

In this chapter, you learn how to show your presentation to an audience. Topics include the following:

→ Rehearse Keynote Presentations
→ Connect a Mac to a Second Display and Configure It for a Presentation
→ Run and Control Presentations on a Mac
→ Use an iPhone as a Remote Control During a Presentation

Presenting Keynote Presentations

Speaking in front of a group of people is often cited as one of the things people are most afraid of doing. Having a well-prepared presentation gives you confidence, which is a good way to help limit nervousness or fear. Using the information presented in Chapter 11, "Developing Keynote Presentations," through Chapter 15, "Finishing and Collaborating on Keynote Presentations," you're equipped to prepare an informative and entertaining presentation. In this chapter, you learn how to present your Keynote presentations to an audience.

Rehearse Keynote Presentations

Practice makes perfect; this cliché definitely holds true for delivering effective Keynote presentations. You should rehearse your presentation to make sure you can run through it smoothly and are extremely familiar with the animation in the presentation because it influences the timing of your speaking through it. Rehearsing a presentation enables you to identify and correct problem areas before you get in front of an audience, helps you check the timing of the presentation, and enables you to make sure you have and can deliver all the information you intend to provide. Additionally, rehearsing builds your confidence, which makes you a more effective speaker and helps decrease the anxiety you may experience when speaking in front of a group.

Assumptions

The most common way to deliver a Keynote presentation is using two displays. The benefit of this is that you can use the presenter display, which is a great tool to help you manage your presentations while you are making them. Because of this, this chapter is written with the assumption you will use this setup. If you plan to use only one display, you won't use the presenter display. Simply run the presentation as you do when you are creating it so that you see the slides in full screen on your display with no additional information or tools.

Display Defined

The term *display* used in this chapter indicates any device on which your Mac can show content. These devices include a MacBook Pro's internal display, a TV that accepts input from a computer, a traditional computer monitor, or a projector. The last three on this list can be configured and used for presentations as described in this chapter because once you connect one of these devices to your computer, you configure them for your presentation very similarly.

When you rehearse a presentation, what you see on your Mac screen is what your audience will see during an actual presentation, assuming you will present using two displays. One shows the presentation in full screen to the audience, and the other is for your use. The display that you see is the presenter display, which has controls and information for you as you run the presentation. (The audience doesn't see this screen.)

Using the Keynote Rehearse feature is nice because you can practice your presentations as if your Mac is connected to a second display without it actually being connected to one. This enables you to practice anywhere you have your Mac without the additional consideration of connecting it to a second display.

You can use Keynote to rehearse a presentation as follows:

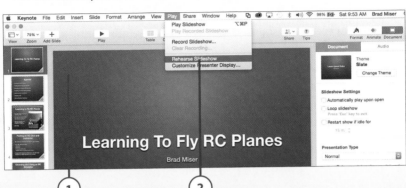

1. Open the presentation you want to rehearse.

2. Choose Play, Rehearse Slideshow. The presenter display fills the screen and presents the first slide.

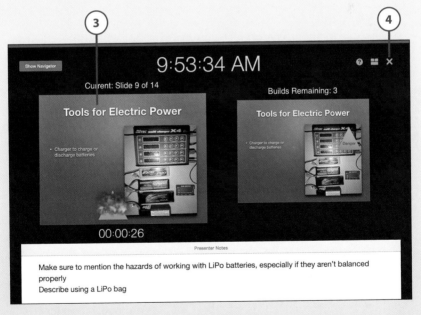

3. Control the presentation and use the presenter display to get information, such as to see your presenter notes, know when animations or builds have completed, and so on. Details for this are provided in the task "Run and Control Presentations on a Mac" later in this chapter.

4. To stop the rehearsal, click the Exit (X) button.

Customizing the Presenter Display

You can customize many aspects of the presenter display, including the
information you see and the layout of the screen. For the steps to customize
the presenter display, see the task "Customize the Presenter Display for Keynote
Presentations" in Chapter 15. Depending on how you configured your presenter
display, your screen may look a bit different from the one shown in these figures,
but the tools and information it provides should still be easily recognizable.

Connect a Mac to a Second Display and Configure It for a Presentation

As mentioned earlier, in most cases, you deliver a Keynote presentation using
two displays. Of course, to be able to do that, you need to connect your Mac
to a second display. The two most common options for connecting a Mac to a
second display are the following:

- **Use a cable.** As long as you have the right adapters (if required), using
  a cable to physically connect your Mac to a display is usually the easiest
  and least problematic option. The most important consideration when
  you use a cable is that you have the right connector to get output from
  your Mac into the display's input port. Modern Macs use Thunderbolt/
  Mini DisplayPort to output to a display. However, it is unlikely that a second display you use has a Thunderbolt/Mini DisplayPort input port, so in
  most cases you need an adapter to be able to connect your Mac to the
  display. You may not need an adapter if you are using a computer monitor as the second display because a number of newer displays provide
  Thunderbolt input (such as Apple's Thunderbolt display).

  There are adapters available for a variety of input ports for displays. The
  most common adapters you are likely to need are a Mini DisplayPort to
  VGA Adapter, a Mini DisplayPort to DVI Adapter, and a Mini DisplayPort
  to HDMI Adapter. The adapter you need depends on the input ports
  available for the display you are using. VGA is the oldest and most widely
  used input for projectors, whereas HDMI is commonly used for HD
  monitors (though these often also support VGA input). If you don't have
  access to the display you are going to use, try to find out which inputs
  it supports and make sure you have the required adapter to be able to
  connect to it.

You might also need a cable, but that might be provided along with the display you use. To be prepared, you should bring the cables you are likely to need with you. If you have an HDMI cable and a VGA cable, you'll probably have the cable you need (assuming you have the corresponding adapter too). It's best to find out exactly what you will need before you arrive at the speaking location. However, that isn't always possible, so it's a good idea to bring the cables and adapters you might need with you if you can.

Although using a cable is the simplest method from a technical standpoint, you are limited in the location from which you present by the length of the cable. This can be a problem if the end of the cable is at the back of the room in which you are presenting because it means you'll be behind the audience, which is definitely not desirable for a number of reasons.

- **Use AirPlay.** Using AirPlay, your Mac can wirelessly transmit video output to an Apple TV, which then displays the output on a monitor or an HD TV. AirPlay is nice because your Mac isn't tethered to a cable and can be easier to configure than using an external display (with regard to choosing the correct resolution). However, using AirPlay is more complex from a technical setup standpoint.

To use AirPlay, you must have an Apple TV that is set up for and connected to the display you want to use. And your Mac must be on the same Wi-Fi or Ethernet network as the Apple TV. Finally, the network you are using must allow AirPlay to operate, which isn't always the case (especially in a public venue such as a conference room in a hotel). These are several of the variables you have to account for when choosing to use AirPlay. If the network you are using doesn't support AirPlay, you'll need to get the provider of the network to change its settings, which can be difficult to do, especially if you have limited setup time.

Whether you use a cable or AirPlay for a second display, you need to first connect your Mac to the display and then configure your Mac to work with the display you are using. The steps for each option are slightly different, as you see in the following tasks.

Use a Cable to Connect a Mac to a Second Display and Configure It

To use a cable to connect your Mac to a second display and configure that display for your presentation, perform the following steps:

1. Connect the cable to a display port on your Mac (using an adapter if required). The Mac and display recognize each other, and your Mac starts transmitting a signal to the display.

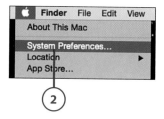

2. Open the Apple menu and choose System Preferences.

3. Click Displays. You see a Display window on each display. The Display window on your Mac is titled with the name of its display, such as Built-in Display when you are using a MacBook Pro or MacBook Air, and has three tabs: Display, Arrangement, and Color. (If you don't see the Arrangement tab, your Mac is not recognizing the second display. Check to make sure the display's power is on and that the cable between it and your Mac is properly connected.)

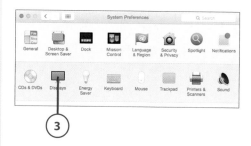

4. Click the Arrangement tab. On this tab, you see a thumbnail of each display. The thumbnail with the white menu bar across its top is your Mac's display, whereas the other represents the second display.

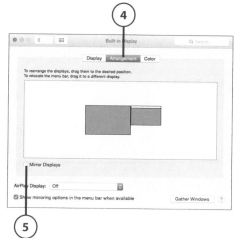

5. For presentation purposes, ensure that the Mirror Displays check box is not checked. (If you check this check box, you won't see the presenter display, but the slides play in full screen on both displays.)

6. Move to the Display window on the second display, which is titled with the name of the display to which your Mac is connected. This window has two tabs: Display and Color.

7. Click the Display tab.

8. Ensure the Default for display radio button is checked. This usually provides the best video quality.

9. Play your presentation to make sure it is displayed properly. (See "Run and Control Presentations on a Mac" later in this chapter.)

10. If the presentation displays properly, you're done and you can skip the rest of these steps. If not, continue on to adjust the resolution of the display you are using. Changing the resolution is the most common solution to display problems.

11. Click the Scaled radio button. The controls expand so you can choose specific resolutions.

12. Click one of the resolutions you see. If the video quality improves to be what you want it to be, you're done and you're ready to present.

13. If there are still problems, repeat step 12 until you've achieved the video quality you need. You may have to try several resolutions until you find the one that works best.

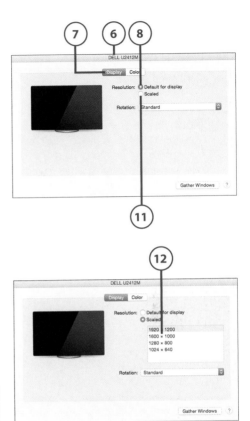

Technical Difficulties Stink

If you are going to use a second display with which you aren't familiar, such as one in a conference room you are using for the first time, the highest risk of technical problems is connecting and configuring the second display for your use. Most of the time, this goes smoothly and isn't a big deal. Sometimes you run into a technical issue that needs to be resolved before you deliver your presentation. Whenever possible, get to the location and set up your Mac to present well ahead of when your presentation is supposed to start to allow time to solve problems should they occur. If everything goes smoothly and you're good to go with time to spare, you'll be more confident and relaxed for your presentation. If it doesn't go smoothly, at least you have time to try to solve the issue.

Use AirPlay/Apple TV to Connect a Mac to a Second Display and Configure It

Using AirPlay to connect your Mac to a second display to show your presentation can be accomplished with the following steps:

1. Connect your Mac to the same network as the Apple TV that is connected to the display you want to use; you can do this via Wi-Fi or Ethernet. (Depending on the network configuration, you may have one or both options.)

2. Ensure the Apple TV and display are powered up and that you see the Apple TV's output on the display.

3. On your Mac, open the AirPlay menu. If you don't see this menu, your Mac is not able to communicate with an Apple TV, and you won't be able to use its display. You need to troubleshoot the issue until you see this menu. The most likely issue is that the Mac and the Apple TV can't access the same network or that the network doesn't allow AirPlay.

In either case, you'll probably need
help from the people supporting the
network to be able to resolve the
issue.

4. Choose the Apple TV that is
    connected to the display you want
    to use. Your Mac connects to the
    display through the Apple TV.

5. Open the AirPlay menu, which is
    now blue, indicating that your Mac
    is using AirPlay.

6. Ensure that Extend Desktop is
    selected. (If Mirror Built-in Display is
    selected, you won't see the presenter
    display; both displays will show the
    slides in full screen.) You're ready to
    display your presentation.

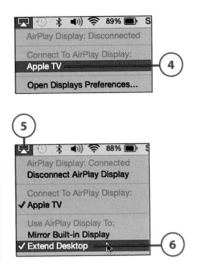

Run and Control Presentations on a Mac

To run and control a presentation on a Mac, use the following bullets:

Click to start a presentation

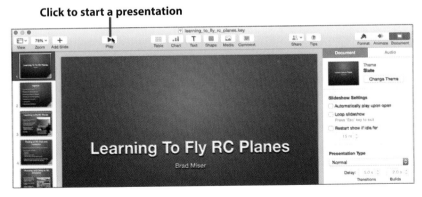

- Open the presentation and click the Play button. The current slide appears
  (the first slide, if you just opened the presentation) in full screen on the
  second display while you see the presenter display on the Mac's screen.

Customizing the Presenter Display

You can customize many aspects of the presenter display, including the information you see and the layout of the screen. For the steps to customize the presenter display, see the task "Customize the Presenter Display for Keynote Presentations" in Chapter 15. Depending on how you configured your presenter display, your screen may look a bit different from the one shown in these figures, but the tools and information it provides should still be easily recognizable.

- When you're ready to advance to the next slide, press the right or down arrow key. The slide being shown advances. To move back to the previous slide, press the left or up arrow key.

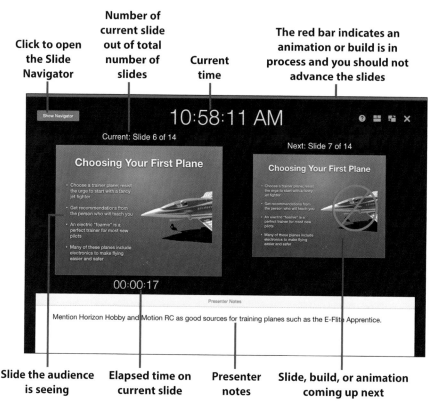

- Use the presenter display to get information about the presentation. This includes the slide the audience is currently seeing and the slide, build, or animation that is coming next. You also see the time and elapsed time. You can refer to any notes you've created for the slide in the Presenter Notes pane. You also see where you are in the presentation through the slide number information.

Enter a slide's number and click Go to show it

The green bar indicates the animations have finished and you are ready to advance to the next slide

Click the Help (?) button to see a list of keyboard shortcuts

Click to swap the presenter display with the slides

Browse the slides

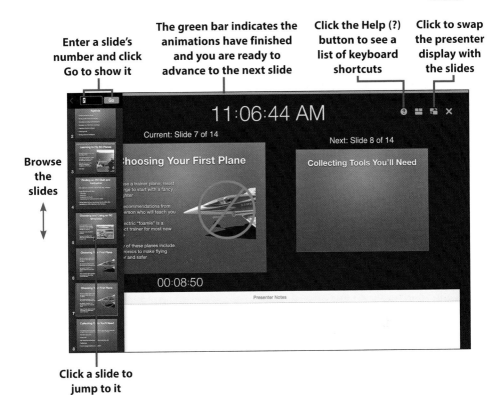

Click a slide to jump to it

- To jump to a specific slide, click Show Navigator. The Slide Navigator appears. You can browse up and down to see all the slides in the presentation. Click a slide to move to it and leave the Slide Navigator open, or double-click it to move to the slide and close the Slide Navigator. You can also move directly to a slide by entering its number in the box at the top of the screen and clicking Go.

- When the bar at the top of the screen turns green, you are ready to advance to the next slide or start the next animation or build (if it is configured to be triggered On click).

- To change the display on which the presenter display appears, click the Swap Display button. The slides and the presenter display change places.

- Keynote supports many keyboard shortcuts you can use to control a presentation. To see them, click the Help (?) button. You see a window that contains the shortcuts. Click its Close (x) button when you are done viewing the shortcuts.

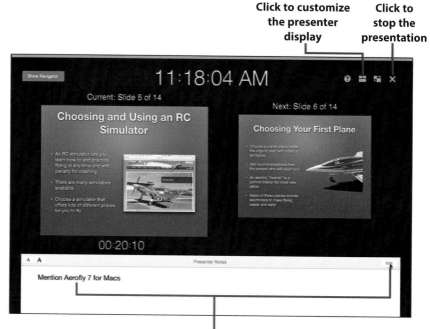

Change presenter notes on the presenter display

- Click the Customize Presenter Display button to make changes to the presenter display. The Customize Presenter Display dialog opens, and you can configure the presenter display to suit your preferences. (See Chapter 15 for details.)

- You can change the presenter notes from the presenter display screen. If a slide currently doesn't have notes, double-click in the Presenter Notes pane and type the notes. If it does have notes, click Edit and then change the notes as needed.

- To exit the presentation, click the Exit (x) button. Otherwise, the presentation stops automatically after you've shown the last slide (unless you disabled this through Keynote Preferences).

Presenters Are People, Too

If you run into technical or other problems during a presentation, try to keep a cool head, and don't get flustered. If you can just skim over the problem, such as a typo, with minimal disruption or it not being too obvious, do so. If you can't get past the problem immediately, it can be helpful to acknowledge the problem you are having to the audience, preferably in a humorous way. When you do this, the audience immediately relates to you as a person instead of just as a presenter, and the tension experienced by both you and the audience from the problem decreases greatly. In contrast, when you try to ignore a problem that is obvious to the audience, tension increases because the audience doesn't know if you realize there is a problem, which causes them stress. As the audience becomes stressed, you are likely to experience more stress, too, so everyone is worse off.

Use an iPhone as a Remote Control During a Presentation

Using a remote control to run a presentation can be useful because it enables you to move out from "behind" the computer and connect more directly to the audience. And if the computer is set up in an inconvenient location, such as the back of the room, using a remote control can enable you to be in a much more favorable place, such as at the front of the room so the audience can see you and the presentation at the same time.

You can use an iPhone as a remote control, which is handy because it is relatively small and easy to use as a remote. You can use an iPad as a remote control for Keynote, too, but its size may be unwieldy unless you are standing at a podium.

To use an iPhone (or iPad) as a remote control, you need to have the Keynote app installed on your iPhone or iPad (see "Use Pages, Numbers, and Keynote on an iPad or iPhone" in Chapter 17, "Publishing and Sharing Pages, Numbers, and Keynote Documents") and to set up the device to control Keynote. The Mac and the iPhone or iPad must both be using Wi-Fi and be on the same network. Then you can use the iPhone or iPad to control the presentation. Both of these actions are explained in the following sections.

Set Up an iPhone as a Remote Control

To prepare an iPhone for use as a Keynote remote control, do the following:

1. In Keynote on the Mac, open the Preferences dialog box.

2. Click the Remotes tab.

3. Check the Enable check box.

4. Open the Keynote app on the iPhone or iPad.

5. Tap the Remote button. You see the Welcome to Keynote Remote screen.

6. On the iPhone or iPad, tap Continue. In Keynote on the Mac, the device you configure should appear on the Remotes tab.

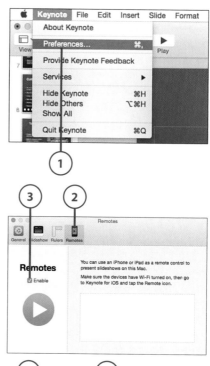

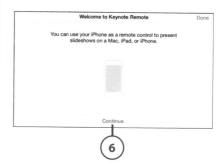

7. Click Link. The devices attempt to connect and you see a code displayed on the Mac and on the iPhone or iPad.

8. Compare the codes being displayed on each device.

9. If the codes match, click Confirm. The iPhone or iPad is ready to control presentations on the Mac.

10. On the Mac, close the Keynote Preferences dialog.

11. On the iPhone or iPad, tap Done.

Who Needs a Mac?

You can also present a Keynote presentation directly from an iPhone or iPad without a Mac. The information you need to do this is included in Chapter 17.

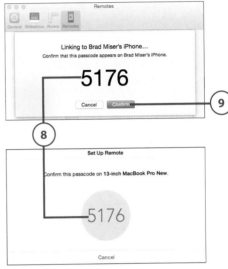

Control a Keynote Presentation Using an iPhone as a Remote Control

To use an iPhone to control a Keynote presentation, you can use the information in the following list:

1. On the Mac, open the presentation you want to show.

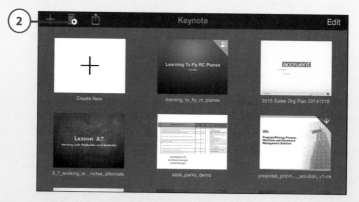

2. In Keynote on the iPhone or iPad, tap the Remote button.

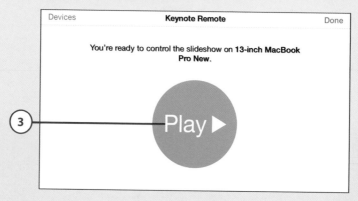

3. Tap Play. The presentation starts to play on the Mac.

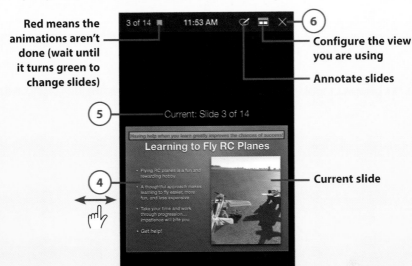

Red means the animations aren't done (wait until it turns green to change slides)

Configure the view you are using

Annotate slides

Current slide

4. Swipe to the left to advance the slide or to the right to move to the previous slide.

5. Use the other information and controls you see to control the presentation. These are similar to what you see on the presenter display on the Mac.

6. Tap Exit (x) to stop the presentation.

The Relationship Between Arrival Time and Technical Problems

In the course of delivering hundreds of presentations and software demonstrations, I'm convinced there is a relationship between the time I arrive at the presentation location for setup and the likelihood I'll experience technical problems. It seems that the earlier I get into a meeting room to set up for a presentation, the lower the chances are that I will have technical issues. (And, of course, there is also more time to solve problems before the presentation starts should they occur). And when you arrive early, it is likely you'll be there before the audience so you can focus on setting up without an audience watching you. This also means that the less time I have between when I arrive and when the presentation starts, the greater the chances are that I'll have technical issues. It's no fun trying to solve technical problems with an audience waiting for you to start the presentation. (Don't ask me how I know.) When you set up a presentation, find out when you can get access to the location to set up for your presentation. Setting up at least 30 minutes before the start of the presentation seems to be a good rule of thumb for me.

Protect the content of documents with a password

Share your documents with others via email or AirDrop

Export documents into a variety of formats, such as those used by other apps

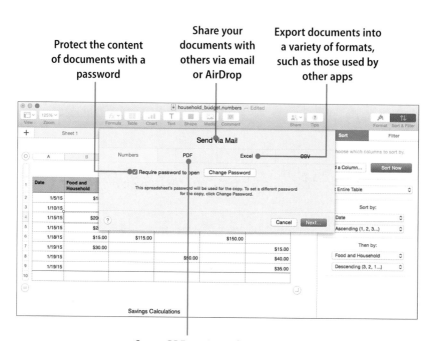

Create PDF versions of documents to make them compatible with any device

In this chapter, you learn how to do a number of useful tasks in Pages, Numbers, and Keynote. Topics include the following:

→ Use a Password to Protect Pages, Numbers, and Keynote Documents
→ Share Pages, Numbers, and Keynote Documents
→ Output Pages, Numbers, and Keynote Documents
→ Use Pages, Numbers, and Keynote on an iPad or iPhone

17

Publishing and Sharing Pages, Numbers, and Keynote Documents

Pages, Numbers, and Keynote enable you to share and output documents in a number of ways. You can share your documents by emailing them, using AirDrop, and so on. You can output documents by printing hard copies, creating Portable Document Format (PDF) versions, and exporting the content to a variety of other formats you can open in other applications.

All three apps have versions that run on iPhones and iPads, so you can share the documents you create on your Mac in the iOS versions running on those devices. For example, you might create a Keynote presentation on your Mac and make final touchups to it and deliver it using an iPad.

Before you share your documents, though, you might want to add a password to them so that they can't be opened without it.

Use a Password to Protect Pages, Numbers, and Keynote Documents

Adding a password to your documents is good practice when the content of those documents is sensitive. As an example, perhaps you've created unique content, and you don't want it to be available to just anyone. Or the content might not be ready for prime time yet, so you want to make sure you control who can see it.

If you don't want a document to be opened by "just anyone," it's a good idea to assign a password to it before using one of the techniques to share it that are explained in the section "Share Pages, Numbers, and Keynote Documents" later in this chapter.

Assign a Password to a Pages, Numbers, or Keynote Document

To protect a document with a password, take the following actions:

1. Choose File, Set Password.

2. Enter the password you want to create in the Password box.

3. Enter the password you created in the Verify box.

4. Create a password hint (this is optional) that can help people trying to open the document remember what the password is. Of course, your hint shouldn't be too obvious, or it defeats the whole purpose of adding a password to the document.

5. To have the password added to your keychain so you don't have to input it each time you open the document on your Mac, check the Remember this password in my keychain check box.

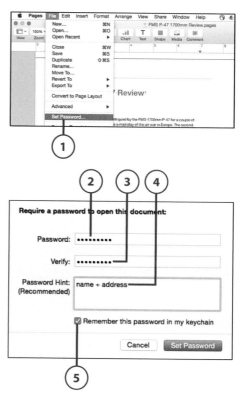

6. Click Set Password. The password is created and attached to the document. It is required to open the document from this point on. (If you saved the password to your keychain, you don't have to enter the password to open the document because it is applied automatically when you open the document on your Mac.)

Change or Remove a Password Assigned to a Pages, Numbers, or Keynote Document

To remove or change a document's password, perform the following steps:

1. Choose File, Change Password.

2. Enter the document's current password.

3. If you want to remove the password, click Remove Password. A password is no longer required to open the document. Skip the rest of these steps.

4. Enter the new password in the New Password and Verify boxes.

5. Create a password hint (this is optional) that can help people trying to open the document remember what the new password is.

6. To have the new password added to your keychain so you don't have to input it each time you open the document on your Mac, check the Remember this password in my keychain check box.

7. Click Change Password. The new password is applied to the document.

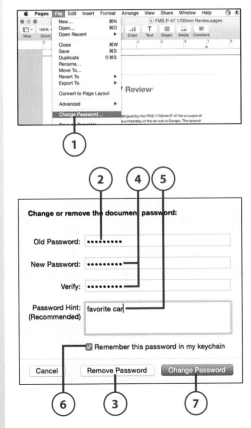

Share Pages, Numbers, and Keynote Documents

Pages, Numbers, and Keynote provide a consistent set of options for sharing documents by sending them to others using email, AirDrop, and Messages. Emailing documents is by far the most commonly used option and is convenient for the sender and receiver because you can send a document at any time, and the person to whom you send it can deal with it as she pleases. Using AirDrop is convenient when your Mac can communicate with other Macs or with iPhones/iPads because you can send documents immediately to the other devices, and the recipients don't need to bother with an email message.

Share with Messages

You can also share documents via the Messages app, although this isn't a common way to send documents to other people. Unless you have a specific reason to use Messages for this purpose, you should stick to email or AirDrop.

Use Email to Share Pages, Numbers, and Keynote Documents

Email is a great way to share documents. Here's how to do it:

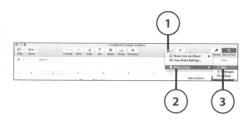

1. Click the Share button on the toolbar.

2. Choose Send a Copy.

3. Choose Mail.

4. Click the first tab, which is labeled with the name of the app you are using, to send the document in its current format. This requires that the recipient also have the same app or one that is capable of opening documents in the current app's native format.

Easier Sharing

If you aren't sure that the recipient has a compatible application on his device, you can use the PDF tab to create a PDF version to send. This has lots of benefits because PDF documents can be opened on any device, and they retain the document's formatting. The downside is that it is much harder to change the content of documents. If you are sending the document only to be read, using PDF is a great choice. You learn about using the PDF option in "Create PDF Versions of Pages, Numbers, and Keynote Documents," later in this chapter.

5. To require a password to open the document, ensure the Require password to open check box is checked; if the document already has a password, this is checked automatically. If the document doesn't currently have a password, check the check box and use the resulting Password, Verify, and Password Hint boxes to create one (these work as described in "Assign a Password to a Pages, Numbers, or Keynote Document," earlier in this chapter).

6. Click Next. A new email message is created in the Mail app and the document is attached to it.

7. Complete and send the email message. The recipient is able to download and use the document on his device.

Factors to Consider When Emailing Documents

If a document you email requires a password, you must communicate that password to the recipient (unless he knows it already). If you can provide a hint in the email messages that the recipient will understand, but no one else will, that's an easy way to communicate the password. Otherwise, use a different means to communicate the password, such as a text message or phone call so that the password and document aren't delivered in the same place.

Also, most email gateways limit the size of attachments to email messages. If the document is larger than allowed by the recipient's email gateway, your message will be rejected and you have to find another way to share the document (such as AirDrop). Typical email attachment size limitations are 5MB or 10MB, so if your document is larger than these sizes, it is unlikely you'll be able to email it successfully.

Use AirDrop to Share Pages, Numbers, and Keynote Documents

To use AirDrop to share documents, perform the following steps:

1. Click the Share button on the toolbar.

2. Choose Send a Copy.

3. Choose AirDrop.

4. Click the first tab, which is labeled with the name of the app you are using, to send the document in its current format. This requires that the recipient also has the same app or one that is capable of opening documents in the current app's native format.

5. To require a password to open the document, check the Require password to open check box; if the document already has a password, this is checked automatically. If the document doesn't currently have a password, check the check box and use the resulting Password, Verify, and Password Hint boxes to create one. (These work as described in "Assign a Password to a Pages, Numbers, or Keynote Document," earlier in this chapter.)

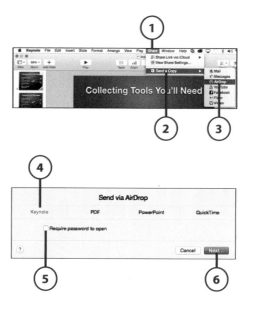

6. Click Next. Your Mac scans for possible AirDrop recipients and presents a list of them to you.

7. Click the person to whom you want to send the file. The file is sent to the recipient, and you see status information under his name. The recipient has the option to accept or reject the file, but you can complete your task before he makes a choice.

8. Click Done. The AirDrop dialog box closes, and the recipient has the file on his device, assuming he chose to accept it, of course.

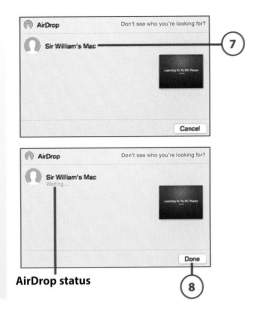

AirDrop status

Share in Real Time

Using AirDrop or Email to share documents is useful, but this method creates multiple versions of your documents. If you want to keep one master version of a document and have others access that common version instead of individual versions, share the document via iCloud. Sharing documents using iCloud also enables you to collaborate with others on documents in real time. The information you need to share documents using iCloud is provided in Chapter 6, "Collaborating with Others on Pages Documents."

Output Pages, Numbers, and Keynote Documents

There are several ways you can output documents from Pages, Numbers, and Keynote, including the following:

- **Printing.** Even in today's electronic world, you'll often want to provide hard copy versions of your documents to others. Pages, Numbers, and Keynote provide lots of options for printing your documents.

- **PDF.** Creating PDF versions of your documents is really useful because any device can open and read them through Adobe Acrobat Reader and many other applications. Also, creating a PDF version retains the formatting of documents so that they look the same no matter what device and software are used to read them.

- **Export.** When you want to use the content of a Pages, Numbers, or Keynote document in a different application, you can export that content into a variety of file formats.

Print Pages, Numbers, and Keynote Documents

To create a hard copy version of a document, do the following:

1. Choose File, Print.

2. Choose the printer you want to use.

3. Use the print preview to check the document to make sure it's ready for printing.

4. Choose the number of copies.

5. Choose the pages you want to print.

6. Click Print.

Details, Details

The options and settings you see in the Print dialog depend on the kind of printer you select. To see all the options selected for the printer you are using, click the Show Details button and configure the detailed options on the resulting dialog box.

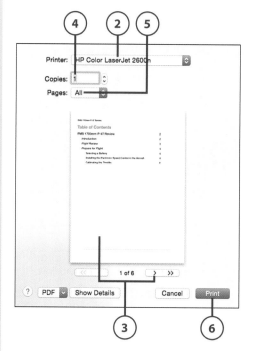

Create PDF Versions of Pages, Numbers, and Keynote Documents

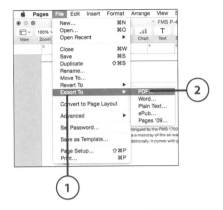

To create a PDF version of a document, follow these steps:

1. Choose File, Export To.

2. Click PDF.

3. Choose the image quality on the Image Quality menu. The higher quality you choose, the larger the resulting file is. If you are going to send the document to others, try the lowest quality setting first; then check the results to determine whether you need to use a higher quality setting.

4. To require a password to open the document, check the Require password to open check box; if the document already has a password, this is checked automatically. If the document doesn't currently have a password, check the check box and use the resulting Password, Verify, and Password Hint boxes to create one. (These work as described in "Assign a Password to a Pages, Numbers, or Keynote Document," earlier in this chapter.)

5. Click Next.

6. If necessary, edit the document's name.

7. Choose the location in which you want to save the document.

8. Click Export. The document is saved as a PDF in the location you specified.

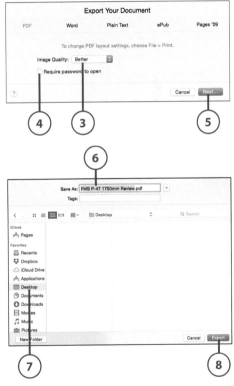

Save Time

It's really useful to email or AirDrop PDF versions of documents. You can combine creating a PDF version of a document with sending it to someone. Perform the steps in "Share Pages, Numbers, and Keynote Documents," except instead of performing step 4 in those tasks, click the PDF tab and use the settings you see to create the PDF version, which is then shared through the option you are using to share the document (such as Mail).

Export Pages, Numbers, and Keynote Documents in Other Formats

The following steps show you how to export information from a Pages, Number, and Keynote document into a different format:

1. Choose File, Export To.

2. Choose the type of file you want to create. The options you see depend on the app you are currently using. (For example, you see different file formats when you export a Pages document than you do when exporting a Numbers spreadsheet.)

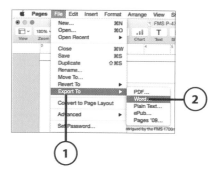

3. To require a password to open the document, check the Require password to open check box; if the document already has a password, this is checked automatically. If the document doesn't currently have a password, check the check box and use the resulting Password, Verify, and Password Hint boxes to create one. (These work as described in "Assign a Password to a Pages, Numbers, or Keynote Document.")

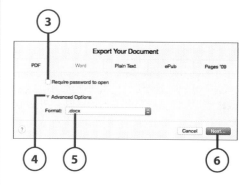

4. Click the disclosure triangle to expand any options you see.

5. Configure the options for the file type you selected in step 2. Each type has its own set of options.

6. Click Next.

7. If necessary, edit the document's name.

8. Choose the location in which you want to save the document.

9. Click Export. The document is saved in the format you selected in step 2 using the options you configured in steps 4 and 5 in the location you specified in step 8.

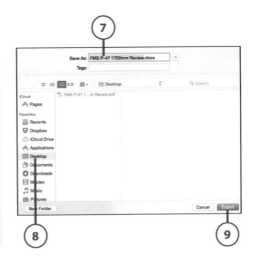

Use Pages, Numbers, and Keynote on an iPad or iPhone

One of the benefits of Pages, Numbers, and Keynote is that there are versions of each app that run on iPhones and iPads. These versions of the apps can work with the same documents as their Mac counterparts so you can easily share your documents among your devices.

Install and Configure

Of course, to use Pages, Numbers, and Keynote on an iPhone or iPad, you need to have those apps installed on the devices on which you want to run them. To download and install the apps, open the App Store app, search for the app you want to install, and then download it to your device. After you've done that, you'll want to configure the apps to work with your iCloud account so that you can access the documents stored on the cloud. To do this, open the Settings app; move to the Pages, Numbers, or Keynote Setting screen; and ensure that the Use iCloud switch is set to on (green).

This means you can work on the same documents on a Mac and an iPad, an iPad and an iPhone, an iPhone and Mac, well, you get the idea.

And There's Online, Too

On your iCloud website, you'll also find online versions of each app. This is great because you can use these apps to share and work on the documents stored on the cloud. This means that, in addition to a Mac or iPhone/iPad, you can work on your documents from any computer with a web browser and an Internet connection.

One of the most useful implications of this is that you can use an iPad or iPhone to deliver a Keynote presentation—no Mac required! Using one of these devices to deliver a presentation may be much better because you can more easily carry it around with you, and you don't need to set up in a particular place.

Besides this being a useful thing to be able to do, it also shows how you can access documents in any app on an iPhone and iPad so that even if you don't need to use this to make a presentation, you can use the information in this section to open different types of documents in the other apps.

Following this introduction are three tasks to get you up and running on an iPad or iPhone. The first task, "Use Pages, Numbers, and Keynote to Work on Documents on an iPad or iPhone," shows you how to access documents in any of the apps. The remaining two tasks show you the details of delivering a Keynote presentation using an iPad or iPhone. If you don't need to show a presentation like this, you can skip those tasks.

Before you get into using an iPad or iPhone to deliver a presentation, there are a few things you need to know. (If you aren't going to use Keynote to deliver presentations using an iPad or iPhone, skip to the task "Use Pages, Numbers, and Keynote to Work on Documents on an iPad or iPhone" now.)

To be able to transmit an iPhone's or iPad's video output to a display, you have the same options as for a Mac: use a cable or use AirPlay.

To use a cable, you need an adapter that goes between the iPhone's or iPad's Lightning port (current models) and the video input of the display you are using. The options are similar to those for a Mac, which are adapters for VGA, HDMI, or DVI.

However, with an iPhone or iPad, it is more likely you'll use AirPlay to wirelessly broadcast the video to a display. This has the same requirements as using AirPlay with a Mac: there is an Apple TV connected to the display you want to use, the iPhone or iPad can connect to the same network as the Apple TV, and the network supports AirPlay.

Because it's much more likely that you'll use AirPlay with an iPhone or iPad, in the last two tasks, you'll find the information you need to use this technique to present and control Keynotes from an iPhone or iPad.

Use Pages, Numbers, and Keynote to Work on Documents on an iPad or iPhone

To open a document in Pages, Numbers, or Keynote on an iPad or iPhone, do the following:

1. Open the app you want to use for the document you are working with. The Document Manager opens, and you see the documents stored on the cloud. (You must enable apps to use iCloud, as described in the earlier sidebar, for this to work as described here.)

2. Swipe around the screen to browse the available documents.

3. Tap the document with which you want to work.

4. Use the app's tools to work with the document. The tools available in the iPhone/iPad versions of the apps are somewhat different from those available in the Mac versions, but they are similar enough that you'll likely be able to use them without much difficulty.

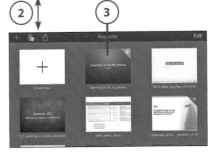

Set Up AirPlay on an iPhone or iPad

To prepare an iPhone or iPad to deliver a Keynote presentation using AirPlay, perform the following steps:

1. Swipe up from the bottom of the screen to open the Control Center.

2. Tap AirPlay.

3. Tap the Apple TV connected to the display on which you want to present.

4. Set the Mirroring switch to On (green).

5. Tap Done. The iPhone's display is sent to the Apple TV and appears on the display to which it is connected.

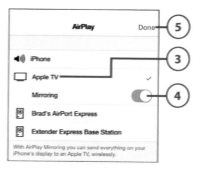

Run a Keynote Presentation from an iPhone or iPad

To run a presentation from an iPhone or iPad, use the following steps:

1. Open the presentation you want to deliver.

Tips Ahoy

When you first play a presentation, you see a screen with some handy tips on how to deliver a presentation in Keynote on an iPhone or iPad.

2. Tap the Play button. The presentation begins to play from the current slide. Like the Mac version, you see a presenter display on the iPhone or iPad while the audience only sees the slides.

3. Swipe to the left to advance the slide or to the right to move to the previous slide.

4. Use the other information and controls you see to control the presentation. These are similar to what you see on the presenter display on the Mac.

5. Tap the side of the screen to bring up the Slide Navigator.

6. Swipe up and down to browse the slides in the presentation.

7. Tap a slide to show it.

8. Tap Exit (x) to stop the presentation.

Annotate slides

Configure the presenter view you are using

Green means the animations are done and you can advance the slides at any time

Current slide

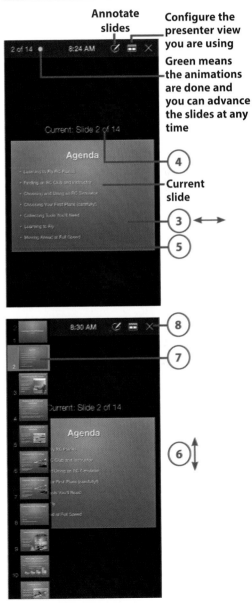

Index

T

REGISTER THIS PRODUCT
SAVE 35%*
ON YOUR NEXT PURCHASE!

How to Register Your Product

- Go to quepublishing.com/register
- Sign in or create an account
- Enter the 10- or 13-digit ISBN that appears on the back cover of your product

Benefits of Registering

- Ability to download product updates
- Access to bonus chapters and workshop files
- A 35% coupon to be used on your next purchase – valid for 30 days
  - To obtain your coupon, click on "Manage Codes" in the right column of your Account page
- Receive special offers on new editions and related Que products

Please note that the benefits for registering may vary by product. Benefits will be listed on your Account page under Registered Products.

We value and respect your privacy. Your email address will not be sold to any third party company.

* 35% discount code presented after product registration is valid on most print books, eBooks, and full-course videos sold on QuePublishing.com. Discount may not be combined with any other offer and is not redeemable for cash. Discount code expires after 30 days from the time of product registration. Offer subject to change.

quepublishing.com